TOMMY ATKINS

THE STORY OF THE ENGLISH SOLDIER

To those millions of Tommies
whose bones lie abroad,
in a thousand fields
I dedicate this monument

TOMMY ATKINS

THE STORY OF THE ENGLISH SOLDIER

JOHN LAFFIN

First published in 1966
This edition published in 2011

The History Press
The Mill, Brimscombe Port
Stroud, Gloucestershire, GL5 2QG
www.thehistorypress.co.uk

British Library Cataloguing in Publication Data.
A catalogue record for this book is available from the British Library.

ISBN 978 0 7524 6066 6

Typesetting and origination by The History Press
Printed in Great Britain by CPI Mackays, Chatham ME5 8TD

Contents

'Tommy Atkins'   vii

Three Centuries of Opinion   xi

1   The Paradox of Tommy Atkins   1

2   1642–1700 The New Model Army and its Influence   17

3   1701–42 Marlorough's Men   35

4   1743–70 Battles Glorious, Health Notorious   48

5   1771–1800 Very Active Service   60

6   1800–8 'These Are Defects but he is a
     Valuable Soldier'   73

7   1808–15 (1) Iron Men of the Peninsula   87

8   1808–15 (2) Heroes at Albuhera;
     Hoodlums at Badajoz   100

9   Punishment: 'Europe's Most Barbarous
     Martial Laws'   116

10   1815–59 (1) Some of Those Finest Hours   140

11   1815–59 (2) The *Sarah Sands*; The Crimea;
     The Mutiny   157

12	1860–1902 The Glorious Years	172
13	1900–18 (1) The Proud Professionals	194
14	1900–18 (2) Bloodbath for the Zealous Volunteers	210
15	1918–45 (1) The In-Between Years	223
16	1939–45 (2) Seven Actions of World War II	228
17	1945 Ubiquitous Mr Atkins	248
	Acknowledgements and Bibliography	252
	Index	256

'Tommy Atkins'

The origin of 'Tommy Atkins' as a sobriquet for the English soldier is still disputed. A widely-held belief is that the Duke of Wellington chose the name in 1843. But Lieutenant-General Sir William MacArthur, writing in the *Army Medical Services Magazine*, says that the War Office used the name 'Thomas Atkins' as a representative name in 1815. Specimen forms of the 'Soldier's Book', issued for both Cavalry and Infantry that year, bore against the space for the soldier's signature: 'Thomas Atkins, his X mark.' As education improved 'his X mark' was omitted.

However, the phrase 'Tommy Atkins' was in use before 1815. A letter sent from Jamaica in 1743, long before Wellington was born, referred to a mutiny among hired soldiery there and said: 'Except for those from N. America [mostly Irish Papists] ye Marines and Tommy Atkins behaved splendidly.'*

About the same time, incidentally, the English soldier was known as Thomas Lobster, because of his red coat. A reference to 'Thomas Lobster' and 'John Tar' is to be found in *The Craftsman*, 12 April, 1740.

Wellington's use of 'Thomas Atkins' is said to have been inspired by a battlefield incident in September 1794 when Wellington, then Arthur Wellesley, led the 33rd Foot, which formed part of General Abercromby's brigade, in action against the French at Boxtel in the Netherlands. French infantry pressed the brigade hard and their cavalry waited for the order to charge. Wellesley, in reserve with his battalion, moved his companies hinge-wise to allow the beaten battalions to pass through, then form line again. The 33rd fired three volleys, advanced with the bayonet

*Quoted in *Soldier* Magazine, April 1949.

and broke the French. After the action Wellesley noted among the wounded the right-hand man of the Grenadier Company, a fine, efficient soldier of 6ft 3in, a man of twenty years' service. Now he was dying of three wounds – a sabre-slash in the head, a bayonet thrust in the breast and a bullet through the lungs. He looked up at Wellesley and apparently thought that his young commander was concerned, for he said, 'It's all right, sir. It's all in the day's work.' And then he died.

The man's name was Private Thomas Atkins and his passing is said to have left such an impression upon Wellington that when he was Commander-in-Chief he remembered the name and used it as a specimen on a new set of soldiers' documents sent to him at Walmer Castle for approval. It makes a fine story, especially as the dying man's last words could well be a motto for the British Army. But, though repeated by many historians, the story does not appear to prove that Wellington was the first to use the name, but merely that he gave it more popular currency.*

Many other more fanciful stories exist. In 1900, Revd E.J. Hardy, an Army chaplain, gave what he described as a 'truer' derivation. At the time of the Indian Mutiny in 1857, when rebellion broke out at Lucknow, all Europeans fled to the Residency for protection. On their way the met a private of the 32nd Regiment (Duke of Cornwall's Light Infantry) on duty at an outpost. Many civilians urged the soldier to get away while he could, but he said he must remain at his post. And he died there. 'His name happened to be Thomas Atkins,' wrote Mr Hardy, 'and so, throughout the mutiny campaign, when a daring deed was done, the doer was said to be 'a regular Tommy Atkins'.'

Whatever the true origin of the name, it is peculiarly suitable, both in euphony and Englishness. For this reason I have used it throughout this book, even though it was certainly not in use during the earlier part of the period my account covers.

---

*About the time of the Crimean War (1845–5) *tommy* was the soldier's term for brown bread.

Significantly, no English officer has ever thought of himself as a 'Tommy Atkins', nor has the public mind ever associated the sobriquet with officers. This is in contrast to, say, the Australian officer who prefers to be called a 'Digger', in common with his men. The English are the only race to give their soldiers as a nickname a Christian and surname complete. The nearest approach is 'Jock', for the Scottish soldier.

Three Centuries of Opinion

Not everybody has found the English soldier and the British Army subjects for praise and even some of the most favourable comments have been spiked with forthright criticism. I have selected the following appraisals as much for their representative value as for what I consider to be their aptness. The object of this book is to show that there is some truth in all of them. Except for the first two, the opinions are listed in order of the periods of dates to which they refer. All the comments are noteworthy; the first two are specially so, because they express the opinions of men who are in some ways the most successful and famous of their respective races – Wellington and Rommel.

They are the scum of the earth and it is really wondeful that we should have made of them the fine fellows they are. With such an army we can go anywhere and do anything.

Wellington: referring to his own army in Spain, Portugal and France, 1808–14.

That day the Guards Brigade had evacuated Knightsbridge, after the area had been subjected all the morning to the combined fire of every piece of artillery we could bring to bear. This brigade was practically a living embodiment of the positive and negative qualities of the British soldier. An extraordinary bravery and toughness was combined with a rigid inability to move quickly.

Rommel, 'Papers', 13 June, 1942, four months before the Battle of El Alamein.

An English army of the 14th century, unlike its French counterpart, was the mirror of a nation, not a class. There now appeared for the first time upon the battlefields of the continent that steady British infantry, drawn from the humbler regions of society, which again and again has disconcerted the calculations of brilliant commanders.

Dr H.A.L. Fisher, 'History of Europe'.

Of the English I would say, they stand by one another, and are often seen to die together. They are spirited and have plenty of boldness . . . They are brave in fighting and full of resolution. They are the best of archers. Abroad, if things are going in favour of the enemy, they preserve good military descipline; and at all times are jovial yet quick in pride.

Robert Flud, 1617.

I must . . . do right to all the officers and men I had the honour to command. Next to the blessing of God, the good success of this campaign is owing to their extraordinary conduct.

Marlborough, speaking of the Battle of Blenheim, 1704.

The British value themselves too much, and think nothing can stand before them.

*Captain Blackader of the Cameronians, a Scottish Regiment,
after the Battle of Schellenburg, 1704.*

Have particular attention to that part of the line which will endure the first shock of the English troops.

Louis XIV to Villeroi in 1706.

I have seen what I never thought to be possible – a single line of infantry break through three lines of cavalry ranked in order of battle, and tumble them to ruin.

*Marquis de Contades, French commander at the Battle of
Minden, 1 August, 1759. (The saying is also attributed to
Marshal de Broglie.)*

All preconcerted arrangements were upset by the extraordinary attack of the British Infantry, a feat of gallantry and endurance that stands, so far as I know, absolutely without parallel.

Sir John Fortescue in 1929, writing of the Battle of Minden.

There are risks attached to the British service unknown to any other.

General Abercromby, 1800.

Well clothed, well fed and well lodged no man performs his duty more steadily and more efficiently than the Englishman, but as everything is new in war to persons who are born and bred in a country abounding with plenty . . . he is not always contented, not even subordinate to authority, when severely pressed by privations and hardships.

Dr Robert Jackson, Inspector-General of Army Hospitals, 'Formation, Discipline and Economy of Armies 1804' (last published, without change of views, 1845).

Notwithstanding the national propensity for war the English cannot be said to possess the character which is genuinely denominated military.

Ibid.

There is no beating these troops, in spite of their generals. I always thought they were bad soldiers; now I am sure of it. I had turned their right, pierced their centre and everywhere victory was mine, but they did not know how to run. (This is one of several versions – see p.106.)

Marshal Soult, after the Battle of Albuhera, 16 May, 1811.

Meanwhile the English, silent and impassive, with ordered arms, loomed like a long red wall; their aspect was imposing – it impressed novices not a little.

General (later Marshal) Bugeaud, of English troops in the Peninsula, 1812.

The British infantry is the best in the world; fortunately it is not numerous.

Ibid.

Nothing could stop that astonisihng infantry. . . .

Sir Charles Napier, referring to the Battle of Albuhera.

How beautifully those English fight! But they must give way.

Napoleon at Waterloo.

The British Army is what it is because it is officered by gentlemen . . . men who would scorn to do a dishonourable thing and who have something more at stake than a reputation for military smartness.

Wellington.

The barbarity of the English military code incited public horror [in Wellington's era].

Napier, 'History', Book XXI, Chapter 5.

The British army is an army of snobs but the universal snobbery produced here [at Waterloo] a maximum of good results.

Elie Halevy, 'A History of the English People in 1815'.

They came here in the morning, looked over the wall, walked over it, killed all the garrison, and retired for breakfast.

A Mahratta leader, circa 1803.

Once the British Army has agreed to do something, the thing is done.

Marshal Canrobert, circa 1855.

The helplessness of the British soldier, when left to himself, is proverbial.

J.H. Stocqueler, 'The British Soldier, 1857'.

The soldiers of other armies may bring knowledge and discipline into the field, and may comport themselves sternly and stubbornly from an enforced obedience. But have any of these men the moral force of the British soldier?

Ibid.

It is very difficult to make an Englishman at any time look like a soldier. He is fond of longish hair and uncut whiskers. . . . Hair is the glory of a woman but the shame of a man.

Colonel Sir Garnet Wolseley (later Field-Marshal Lord Wolseley).

It must be admitted that the distinguishing feature of the British soldier is intrepidity.

Thomas Gowing, Sergeant-Major, Royal Fusiliers, 'A Soldier's Experience,' 1617.

. . . the world has no stauncher fighting man than is the British soldier intrinsically.

Archibald Forbes, 'Barracks, Bivouacs, Battles', 1894.

If ever a people or a nation exemplified the phrase 'brave to a fault' it is the British. If they had been less brave, there would have been many fewer faults and more victories. Caution they have not; they just bunt ahead and take the consequences.

Captain Slocum, American military observer, 1902, in a report on the Boer War.

English soldiers are brought up with the idea that obedience is of more importance than initiative.

Colonel G.F.R. Henderson, a noted military writer, 'The Science of War', 1905.

The men of Badajos and Albuhera did far more than give the death-blow to the ambition of Napoleon; they set an imperishable example of unyielding fortitude, an example which was to influence the coming generations not only of their own islands, but of far distant continents, of Canada, of Australasia and South Africa.

Ibid.

Were it not that so many of my compatriots lacked that which is so largely characteristic of the British soldier – the quality of patriotism and the intense desire to uphold the traditions of his nationality – I would ask, what people in the world would have been able to conquer the Afrikanders?

General Ben Vijoen, 'My Reminiscences of the Anglo-Boer War', 1905.

. . . that sorely tried institution, the British Army.

Sir John Fortescue, 1910.

The Englishman still sits in Schwaben Redoubt.

Major-General von Soden, 1916. (The German general had been trying without success to get the Tommies out of the redoubt.)

One is entitled to doubt whether any other [army] would have demonstrated such dour bravery.

Leon Wolff, in 'In Flanders Fields', of the British in 1917.

They [British soldiers] love giving, they bear pain patiently. . . .

A British nurse in France, 1917.

There is no kinder creature than the average Tommy. He makes a friend of any stray animal. . . . When he's gone over the top . . . for the express purpose of doing in the Hun he makes a comrade of the Fritzie he captures. . . .

Coningsby Dawson, 'Glory of the Trenches'.

Though the little British Army that fought at Mons won glory enough to last the nation for all time, little more was said about it than if Mons had been a sham battle on Salisbury Plain.

Frederick William Wile (an American), 'Explaining the Britishers', 1918.

We had achieved great success, which we must not allow later events to make us forget. We had defeated the English [sic] Army.

Geneal Ludendorff, Memoirs, referring to the German offensive of March–April, 1918.

It is thought which unnerves the British, as it inspires the French.

Revd P.H. ('Tubby') Clayton, founder of Toc H, writing in 1919.

In our talks (1914–18) in the trenches, in the dugout, or on the fire-step, we often talked of the Tommy, and, as any genuine soldier will easily understand, we spoke of him very much more respectfully than was commonly the case with the newspapers of those days.

Lt Ernst Junger, 73rd Hanoverian Fusilier Regiment, and holder of the Pour le Mérite.

The Englishman never fights better than with his back to the wall. . . . There is not a country in the world where the dead are so quickly forgotten. . . . The element of pity is little known to the Englishman. . . . The English character is simple and hardly subtle.

General Huguet of France, writing in 1922.

The British Army will be remembered best not for its countless deeds of daring and invincible stubbornness in battle, but for its lenience in conquest and its gentleness in domination.

Sir John Fortescue, 'History of the British Army,' 1930.

The British soldier, supposed to represent physical force only, is a great moral force within and without the Empire.

Ibid.

And in every case the fighting spirit [of England], dogged determination and use of brutal means in conducting military operations have always remained the same.

Hitler, 'Mein Kampf'.

The British soldier must be driven to digging himself in the moment he occupies an area, and not to waste time in sightseeing, souvenir hunting and brewing tea.

G.O.C., 36th Division, in Arakan, 1944.

The British soldier . . . is at his best and has performed his most memorable feats when he has been faced with the greatest odds. Essentially his main characteristic is his discipline.

S.H.F. Johnston, 'British Soldier', 1944.

The British Army fought like lions.

A German comment on the men of Airborne Division who dropped on Arnhem, September 1944.

You are an ordinary soldier, but your culture is that of all the British, of all the Airborne Division. With death or imprisonment before your eyes you have . . . found that marvellously pure comradeship and simple strength of mind. . . .

Mrs Kate A. Ter Horst, a Dutch housewife, 'Cloud Over Arnhem'.

Once the British had got their teeth in, and had been in a position for twenty-four hours, it proved almost impossible to shift them. To counter attack the British (in 1944) always costs us very heavy losses.

General Blumentritt, Chief-of-Staff, West, then Corps and Army Commander.

Other armies have vaunted their might; we have gloried most when our soldiers have attained their victories as 'a thin red line'.

Lt Col Graham Seton Hutchison, 'The British Army', 1945.

The best ambassador for Britain is the British soldier.

Field-Marshal Lord Slim, 1947.

It was possible to destory a well-trained and disciplined British infantry battalion, but, as Albuhera proved, it was not possible to break one. And before it could be destroyed it could do an incredible amount of damage. The killing power of a British infantry battalion exceeded anything to be found on the battlefields of the early nineteenth century. The Germans found the same thing in 1914 and in 1944.

Sir Arthur Bryant, 'Illustrated London News', 20 May, 1950.

Everything we have and are is ours, and still exists, by grace and courage of the soldiers. They are the men of the century, because without them we should no longer be numbering its years – or numbering them only to curse the wretchedness of our survival in it.

Eric Linklater, 'A Year of Space', 1953.

I have read much military history. There arise in my mind the images of some of those warriors who have won immortal fame. . . . But above them all towers the homely but indomitable figure of the British soldier, the finest all-round fighting man the world has seen; who has won so many battles that he never doubts victory, who has suffered so many defeats and disasters on the way to victory that he is never greatly depressed by defeat; whose humorous endurance of time and chance lasts always to the end. The British soldier, too, has a quality of tolerance which extends even to the mistakes of his superiors.

Field-Marshal Lord Wavell, 1953.

The British soldier is one of the world's greatest humorists.

Field-Marshal Lord Wavell, 1953.

One

The Paradox of Tommy Atkins

The character and the psychology of the English soldier first interested me when, as a boy, I avidly read the colourful and heroic military adventures by G.A. Henty and Escott Lynn, among others. The heroes of their stories were always dashing young officers, but in the background were English soldiers, the raw materials with which the enterprising and daring officers brought off their *coups*. And raw the common soldier was. He seemed to be illiterate and inarticulate and he spoke English abominably. Dull in appearance – if the book illustrations could be believed – he had little intelligence but immense dog-like devotion to his officers and was cheerfully prepared to give his life for them. Though short on some things, he was long on fortitude and doggedness and he carried out orders with undeviating rigidity.

Not that he could very well do otherwise, since the orders rarely called for any show of initiative or enterprise. This was specially so when the troops were in square – that 'impenetrable' British square, which was, in fact, occasionally penetrated, as by the Dervishes at Abu Klea on 17 January 1885.

When I began to read military history I could see that many of the traits given to Tommy Atkins by the fiction writers were true. What struck me most forcibly was that Tommy Atkins, while undoubtedly brave, seemed to be bone-headed stupid. Time and again he marched into the most obvious traps; he would charge, horse and foot, into the teeth of fire from every kind of weapon, from breech-loading cannon to machine-guns. And, in his red coat, he was a fine target for the enemy.

It seemed to me nothing short of scandalous that the Charge of the Light Brigade should have been glorified while the Charge of the Heavy Brigade, on the same day, should have been almost unrecorded and forgotten. The first was a failure and the result of crass incompetence; the second was an astonishing success.

Another intriguing aspect of British military history as printed was that the names of private soldiers, or even of NCOs were very rarely mentioned in despatches or accounts of actions. The only exception was when an NCO or private won a Victoria Cross (after its institution in 1855), but often enough the decoration was awarded not for action against the enemy but for the rescue under fire of a comrade, or more usually of an officer. Many officers were given the decoration for the same act, which, though brave, would scarcely merit a minor award from 1914 onwards.

To all intents and purposes the British Army, in its 'glorious' years – say from 1700 to 1900 – consisted of officers and human machines, the former manipulating the latter.

After a lot of reading, and much talking with old soldiers, I saw English troops in action. I admired their steadiness, their ability to take things in their stride; I was appalled by their inability to act decisively and vigorously after they had lost their leaders. What I did not realize at the time was that their helplessness was often due to officers not having passed on information.

My reading had been extensive but not intensive. When I really got down to studying and analysing military history and to writing about it, many mysteries about Thomas Atkins began to resolve themselves – though 'mystery' is too strong a word to apply to such an uncomplicated being as the English soldier. The real mystery lay in how England could produce soldiers fit to fight, and usually to win, in so many hundreds of capaigns and battles. This was a mystery because the English, people and parliament, press and pulpit, made life as difficult as possible for the soldier, a state of affairs remedied only in quite recent times.

It would be impossible to exaggerate the difficulties under which Tommy Atkins has laboured for so many years, the savagery with which some of his officers treated him, the crass thoughtlessness with which the Government used him, the spite with which the general public abused him. Starved, poorly housed and woefully equipped, mercilessly worked, over-loaded and grossly underfed and underpaid, his health neglected, his private and personal needs ignored, Tommy Atkins has nevertheless done his duty and allowed his commanders to win their battles.

One of the most frequently told stories about the army is that a commander – he is variously cited as Marlborough, Clive, Wellington, Campbell and others – asked a soldier – here again you may insert what regiment you will – how he would like to be dressed if he had to fight again at Blenheim, Plassey, Waterloo or Lucknow. There is no variation in the answer. The soldier says, 'In my shirt sleeves, sir.' The story, though plaintive, must be apocryphal, for surely nobody ever deigned to ask Tommy Atkins what *he* would like to wear – or eat or how he would like to be accommodated or what he needed in the way of recreation. He was not considered to be entitled to likes or dislikes.

In his mammoth history of the Regular Army from the time of the Restoration to 1870 Sir John Fortescue wrote of English soldiers: The builders of this empire . . . were not worthy of such an army. Two centuries of persecution could not wear out its patience; two centuries of thankless toil could not abate its ardour; two centuries of conquest could not awake its insolence. Dutiful to its masters, merciful to its enemies, it clung steadfastly to its old simple ideals – obedience, service, sacrifice.

Crystallized here is the paradox of the English private soldier. How could he be so successful in so many countries and so many wars and campaigns and over such a long period and yet be so unappreciated in England? 'Unappreciated' is too mild a word. For many years he was reviled, mocked and detested. Even at the time when Kipling was glorifying Tommy Atkins the British public had little sympathy for him. At best he was a loyal but dull-witted oaf, at worst he was a repulsive fellow 'filled with beef, beer and lust'. Elderly ladies were apt to sack a maid caught in company with a redcoat, while a girl who married a serving soldier was generally regarded as having sunk about as low as possible. For many families it was a crowing disgrace to have a son who had 'gone for a soldier'. Even up to 1914 many a publican refused admission to men in uniform, as did theatre and music-hall managers. For decades *Punch* delighted in showing the soldier as a figure of fun or derision and the frequent good humour of its comment hardly softened the sting.

In 1945 Field-Marshal Wavell noted that for the first 250 years of his existence Tommy Atkins was treated with 'contempt, dislike and neglect'.

At varous times thoughtful people have asked why the English soldier fights well. In November 1898, *The Navy and Army Illustrated* went so far as to say that the British soldier 'has, as a rule, fought better than anybody else' and noted that the reason would be worth probing. The magazine editorial continued:

A reasoned answer might surprise some. The good old patriotic explanation that the 'Briton' is braver than other people has something in it, but not very much . . . Besides, they have run away a good deal from one another at home, and on occasion they have run away abroad.*

The real explanation of our uniform success, for really it all but amounts to that, lies in this, that no nation has enjoyed so fully the advantage of fighting with small and very highly-drilled corps.

If victories were ours, it is partly because an Englishman held the chief command (this was not the case at Minden) chiefly because the British troops present were 'the Old Guard' of the Army; in other words, the most drilled, the most carefully picked of all. The question why that should have been so is precisely what a good history of the British Army ought to explain.

---

* On the day before Talavera, 1809, for instance, two of Wellington's regiments fired into one another, panicked, and ran. Some French cavalry was very close, and if there had not also been an old and steady British regiment at hand, an ugly disaster might have followed.

English forces were certainly small or relatively small in the Middle Ages, at Crécy, at Poitiers, and at Agincourt, in Marlborough's wars, throughout the eighteenth century and in the Peninsula. The English were not commonly the majority even in the medieval battles. Gascons, who were monarchical subjects, and mercenary soldiers of all nations, swarmed in the armies of King Edward or King Henry. English-born soldiers were never more than about a fifth of any of Marlborough's armies. The proportion was 'greater in Wellington's armies; but even there the English were a minority, after deducting the German Legion, the Portuguese under English officers, and so forth.

A year later *Navy and Army Illustrated* was again seeking to explain Britain's martial prowess, this time with a back-handed compliment from 'a distinguished Frenchman'. Even if the magazine invented this Frenchman – why didn't they identify him? – the comments he made, or was supposed to have made, are interesting. *Navy and Army* commented that from his criticisms 'no truer explanation of Britain's military successes could be imagined'.

The British soldier is no better than any other, but he has won many battles by virtue of his insufferable conceit. Even when he has been handsomely beaten, this same has prevented him from acknowledging it and retiring from the field, as he ought to have done if he had played the game fairly. But what can you do with men who are so infatuated with conceit that every private soldier says to himself 'The British Army is the finest in the world, my regiment is the finest in the British Army, and I am the finest soldier in my regiment'? Clearly all argument, mental of physical, is lost on such people.

In fact, there is much truth in this. By all the customs and conventions of war English troops have been beaten on many occasions, but have refused to admit defeat and have either fought on to snatch incredible victory or have been wiped out in the trying.

As the 'distinguished Frenchman' implied, the regimental system has always been the backbone of English troops.

'A regiment is embodied tradition,' somebody wrote. 'It survives the changes and stress of fretting years.' More than that, because of the pride in which men held their regiment, it could survive the most savage blows of warfare. The well-being and honour of his regiment was the core of a good soldier's life – and I hope, making allowances for the modern soldier's wider range of interests, that this still applies.

It is rare indeed that an English regiment does not hold together. This indestructible cohesion – in Colonel Henderson's view the best of all the qualities that an armed body can possess – is based not merely on hereditary resolutions, but also on mutual confidence and respect. The men in the ranks have implicit and until recent times an almost childlike faith in their officers; the officers have a limitless belief in the staying power and discipline of their men.

For centuries only Tommy Atkins's endurance and courage kept him on his feet while actually in the throes of a serious illness – *esprit de corps* carried to extremes. Men have been known to march and fight while suffering from malaria, cholera, yellow fever, dysentery and typhoid – before the inevitable collapse. Field-Marshal Slim, commanding in Burma, found health 'his second great problem'.

In every campaign – as distinct from battles – in which a British force has taken part disease has claimed more victims than has the enemy. This applied even to World War II, despite the many advances in medicine, hygiene and surgery up to 1939.

Dr Johnson, who had shrewd ideas about most things, had some pertinent observations about the English soldier and pithily expressed some of his contradictions. He stated that 'the qualities which commonly make an army formidable are long habits of regularity, great exactness of discipline, and great confidence in the commander'. But he claimed that English soldiers were in no way regular, that their discipline was indifferent, that they had no reason to be confident in their commanders – yet they were, without doubt, 'the bravest soldiers in Europe'. The explanation lay, said the Doctor, in the independence of character of the Englishman, who called no man his master.

The Doctor was off target, for most Englishmen of his day and for long after were forced to call somebody master. I think that 'sturdiness of character' could be better substituted for 'independence of character'.

The class structure of British society has been perhaps the most important factor in determining the character of the British Army. Critics of the British Army and its system have alleged consistently that one of its main drawbacks is its lack of democratic flexibility. The charge is true enough, although those who refute the charge bring up the same few outstanding private-to-general examples. The point is, however, that it was no less democratic than many other armies and only at certain periods has it compared unfavourably with, say, the French.

It has always been difficult to overcome the initial disadvantages under which the Englishman, as a potential soldier, labours. Colonel G.F.R. Henderson expressed it clearly in 1905: 'Life in the British Islands, except perhaps on the moors and forests of the north was, and is, no preparation for war whatever.'

The great bulk of the population had no incipient or latent martial quality, unlike those countries which could draw on mountaineers, stockmen, bushmen, shikaris, tribesmen. The average English private had no instinctive feeling for weapons or even for horses as mounts. Something had to counterbalance these deficiencies and that something was pride of race and a certain predilection for good order – which is nothing more than good fellowship.

Henderson: 'It is certain that the British officer is what Britain makes him. His natural qualities, be they virtues or defects, are those of his race, and it is the country, not himself, which is primarily responsible for the development of the one and the correction of the other.'

This is the social structure at work. The officer came from a ruling class and was instinctively able to take command, even without previous military training. The men, being of a follower class – though by no means a debased or servile one – just as instinctively obeyed. The exceptions on both sides only prove the rule, and gave some force to the dictum that the army (and the navy) was a case of 'the worst led by the best'.

There can be no doubt about the class Emerson was writing of in 1850, when he gave his impression of the most striking characteristic of the English. 'In every efficient man there is at first a fine animal. In the English race it is of the best breed – a healthy, juicy, broad-chested creature, steeped in ale and good cheer and a little overloaded by his flesh.'

Sir John Fortescue, writing in 1950, said that the War of Dutch Independence had made the modern English soldier. 'It was, in fact, the school of the modern British Army,' he said, though I think this is too broad a statement. 'Moreover, there is with us a famous corps which dates its birth from those stirring times, and is, indeed, a standing memorial of the Army's prentice years.'

He was referring to the Buffs – Royal East Kent Regiment. On the outbreak of war between England and the Dutch in 1665, the descendants of the volunteers who had gone there in 1572 were still in Dutch service and were required to take the oath of allegiance to the Dutch Republic or be cashiered. Dismissal from the service meant ruin for the officers and misery for the men, but they refused the oath and were turned adrift. They made their way to England and were formed into the Holland Regiment and became third line regiment in seniority.

'So the Buffs remain the unique relic of British volunteers in the Low Countries,' wrote Fortescue. 'It has the longest pedigree of any corps in the service, and represents the original model of *that sorely tried institution*, the British Army.'

Yet, so sorely tried, English soldiers in their hundreds of thousands went all over the world to fight and suffer and often to die. Those who came after must have known what they were in for; they must have realized that when their army days were over – if they were lucky enough to live so long – they could make a living only by begging. Yet the army usually managed to find enough men, mostly volunteers, to fill its ranks. Despite their frequently gross maltreatment English soldiers were never bitter. They complained, as all soldiers will, but only rarely was their loyalty soured or their patience fretted. Their whole history is underscored by their steadiness and by their acceptance of whatever conditions happened to apply at any given time.

Occasionally, when trouble was in the offing or immediately after a victory, Tommy Atkins would be showered with verbal confetti; otherwise he would be reviled, as Kipling discerned.

> For it's Tommy this, an' Tommy that, and 'Chuck him out, the brute!'
> But it's 'Saviour of 'is country' when the guns begin to shoot.
>
> Then it's Tommy this, an 'Tommy that, an 'Tommy, 'ow's your soul?'
> But it's 'Thin red line of 'eroes' when the drums begin to roll.*

Wherever he was schooled and despite his soldierly qualities, Tommy Atkins lacks some of the traditional attributes of a warrior, as several commentators have observed. He finds it difficult to act the conqueror, in stark contrast to German, French, Japanese and American soldiers, among others. Even his most trenchant critics or his worst enemies could hardly accuse Tommy of arrogance or even of victorious pride. After a battle or war, he has remarkable ability to make himself at home and to get along with anybody. He has rarely varied from this, two infamous exceptions being the sacking of Badajoz and San Sebastian during the Peninsular War. Here he was guilty not merely of excesses but of foul crimes against a friendly population and though some writers pretend to find extenuating circumstances I can admit none. Still, that I

---

*The first two lines are from the fifth stanza, the second two from the third stanza of *Tommy*. Kipling's sentiments are similar to those expressed by Thomas Jordan (1612(?)–85):

> Our God and the soldier we alike adore
> When at the brink of ruin, not before.
> The danger past, both are alike required;
> God is forgotten, and our soldier slighted.

With minor amendments, the verse is said to have been cut by a soldier in a stone sentry box in Gibraltar.

can single out two instances during several centuries is some proof that excesses are rare. The ability with which Tommy normally makes friends with the local populace has often made soldiers of other nationalities envious.

The most frequent adverse criticism levelled against English soldiers is that they are over-disciplined – which is not their fault – and consequently that they are dull troops. Even Wavell, an enthusiastic Press agent for the English soldier, commented that British military training was stereotyped and unimaginative and believed that English troops in the field were apt to suffer through lack of guile and deception because of the simplicity of the English character.

Discipline as it affects the British Army is a touchy problem. I have myself been extremely critical in print about it, largely because I made the mistake of comparing Tommy Atkins with soldiers of other nations. Comparisons are fair and interesting, but conclusions are unwise and unfair because discipline must make allowances for national failings and strengths, for heredity and environment. So it is easy to say that Tommy Atkins has never been trained to think and then when he is in a position where he must think, he fails. The criticism needs much qualification. Wavell saw discipline merely as 'the soldierly spirit' but this is a soldierly understatement, since two types of discipline needs to be distinguished – that which produces good order and system in the military family and that which produces competent fighting men.

The question has always been: To what degree is a soldier to be drilled into instant non-thought obedience and how much is he to be encouraged to think for himself? But for many, many decades the Army had only one answer to the question: The soldier is not paid to think, merely to obey. For a long time this was a valid viewpoint, perhaps the only one. The common soldier was uneducated and had no idea *how* to think for himself. He was content to be led and regarded his officers, by virtue of their class alone, as demi-gods. Encouraging him to think for himself would have been fruitless. Even NCOs were merely mouthpieces for officers' orders. Their individual thinking went only so far as military drill. Again, there was no *need* for a private soldier to think, for the tactics and warfare of the times would have given him no opportunity to think. Those people who criticize soldiers of the sixteenth to nineteenth centuries as automatons forget that this is what they had to be. A military unit, to be effective, had to move as a unit, upright, in formation and in unison. Generally a commander won a battle by the cleverness with which he moved his various pieces chessboard-fashion about the battlefield to counter the moves made by the enemy commander.

His forces could not be badly damaged by musket fire beyond a range of 100 yards – this was the limit of accuracy – although there was the risk of having gaps blown in the ranks by cannon balls. On top of this the infantry had to stay in formation as a protection against cavalry. Once an infantry battalion broke formation every man was vulnerable to cavalry attack. Under these conditions all the soldier needed was absolute and instantaneous obedience and an implanted ability to operate his firearms. In fact, the soldier himself was a weapon operated by his officers or NCOs.

Many people thought, and some still think, that a soldier trained to automatic obedience is more dependable in a crisis and that to this end his training must be lengthy, thorough and detailed. This is why so much stress was placed on personal appearance, on spit and polish. Advocates of total obedience would say that if the soldier is taught to take orders promptly from his nearest superior he will never give way to uncertainty or panic. It was noticeable in World War I, under the appalling and demoralizing conditions of trench warfare, that men who had been trained to shave every day and keep their buttons (and their rifles) clean maintained their morale better than those who had not been so trained. Informality of dress, for instance, tends to express itself in informality of conduct, to inept performance of duty. But spit and polish should not be an end in itself and once a soldier has been thoroughly trained relaxation of controls is possible – the unshaven, unorthodox men of commando units and independent companies proves this.

There are obvious objections to total obedience. A soldier is no longer merely a redcoat in a shoulder-to-shoulder rank. It is no longer sufficient for him to know only how to operate his personal firearm. He must be given multiple skills – how to handle various weapons, how to use ground intelligently, how to camouflage himself, how to take hygiene precautions and many other things. By the very diversity of the abilities he is expected to possess he has inevitably been taught to think.

If you teach a man to think you make him restless, the diehards would have it. This risk must be taken. For the fact is that despite improvements Tommy Atkins is still not sufficiently encouraged to think for himself. Many Australian, New Zealand and Canadian frontline soldiers have been shocked by the spectacle of leaderless English troops huddled in groups not knowing what to do next. This has nothing to do with lack of courage; they simply have not been trained to use their heads.

It is significant that in the British Army officers, though, of course, vastly outnumbered by other ranks, win a greatly disproportionate number of awards for bravery or leadership. In the armies of the British Commonwealth the ratio is in proportion, with many more awards to other ranks. The conclusion is obvious, and again it has nothing to do with courage. Tommy Atkins has never lacked guts, but too often and for too long he has been considered pretty dumb. There have been many disgraceful instances of young officers, sent on patrol, keeping all orders and information to themselves. When killed or taken prisoner they leave the patrol helpless, with even the sergeant ignorant of the mission. Things have changed; subalterns are taught to take NCOs into their confidence. But old attitudes die hard and intellectually Tommy Atkins is still not trusted as much as he might be.

I have been unable to find any previous reference to the strange disparity between the number of officer and O/R escapees from POW camps. Again, O/R prisoners greatly exceeded officer captives, but many more officers got away, though they had no greater opportunity to do so. The point is provokingly significant. The men had not been taught to use their heads; left without officers they were helpless and resigned themselves to their fate.

Undiscerning critics can become really vocal about the 'class distinction' of separate messes for officers, sergeants and other ranks. But class distinction has nothing to do with this practice. Separation eliminates favouritism and enables each officer and sergeant to deal with his men more or less impersonally. Other ranks would object as strenuously as officers and sergeants to a common mess; they would be embarrassed, ill at ease and resentful of authority being present in off-duty hours.*

One other trait of the English soldier, rarely given enough importance in analytical study, is his sense of humour. It has always been extremely simple, often childishly so. Much of it would not raise even a faint smile with sophisticated people. But it has played a major part in giving Tommy Atkins his staying power and enabling him to retain his sanity under the great stresses of war.

The methodical Germans had noticed this. After the defeat of 1914–18 they considered at length the matter of morale[†] and came to the conclusion that much of the English soldier's steadiness was due to his sense of humour. They planned to instil such a sense of humour into German soldiers – though they should have known that a national trait of character cannot be transplanted. In a manual about sense of humour the Germans published one of Bruce Bairnsfather's famous drawings of 'Old Bill', sitting in a wrecked building with a great shell-hole in the wall. A rookie asks, 'What made that hole?' 'Mice,' replied 'Old Bill'. The Germans added a footnote: 'It was not mice; it was a shell'.

Writing in 1938, Ian Hay noted that 'the soldier of today undoubtedly suffers from a definite inferiority complex – which is not altogether surprising or creditable to those directly responsible for it. The present generation have been so sedulously inoculated . . . with the belief that war is a crime

* The Revd P.B. ('Tubby') Clayton, founder of Toc H (see footnote p. 226), speaking of a lieutenant who died of a wound, said 'It was he who discovered to me the fact to hard for the civilian mind to grasp – that in the very fixity of the gulf between each grade (sic) of command lay the scope for an intimacy and mutual understanding impossible otherwise.'

† Discussed at length in the author's *Jackboot: The Story of the German Soldier.*

– even a righteous war of defence against wanton aggression –
and that all who participate therein are either hired assassins
or helpless dupes, that today it is difficult for a soldier to
perform his highly altruistic duties with any sort of satisfaction
or comfort of mind.'

To some extent this attitude still applies. The anti-
militarists, the anti-bomb agitators, the anti-colonists
have become shrilly hysterical. Some newspapers and
magazines make it clear that they regard soldiering as a dirty
occupation and some minor political parties use propaganda
cleverly designed to make a would-be soldier think that
in uniform he would be nothing more than a licensed
murderer. It remains difficult for a soldier to carry out his
duties with peace of mind.

You may regard a soldier as a hero or a butcher, for there is
no profession on which it is so difficult to take a dispassionate
point of view. This is because few people are able to
discriminate between soldiers and war. Consequently, when
in other books I have found virtues and qualities in soldiers
I have been accused of glorigying war. This is not so. I am
concerned only in seeing that the soldier has his due – that
all soldiers have their due. It is wrong to think that soldiers
lust for war, and in any case it is not possible for soldiers to
bring war about – the politicians do that. Soldiers are merely
instruments of policy. It is quite possible to see glory in
soldiers' actions without glorifying war. This is my position.

There is glory enough in the campaigns and battles of
Tommy Atkins – glory unique in quality and character, unique
in quantity. Much of the spirit of British service abroad is
contained in an old song, wrongly believed to be of World War
I vintage. Usually titled 'Here's To the Last Who Dies', it was
written probably in the early part of the nineteenth century.*

---

*One correspondent to *Navy and Army Illustrated*, 1 October 1898,
attributed it to a Captain Darling, who died of cholera in India.
Another said that he, with other students, sang it at Heidelberg
University in 1860. The magazine believed that it was written and
sung by a party of British officers dying of the plague in a West Indian
island.

We meet 'neath the sounding rafters,
And the walls around are bare;
As they echo to our laughter
'Twould not seem that the dead were there.
So stand to your glasses steady,
'Tis all we have left to prize,
Quaff a cup to the dead already,
And one to the next who dies.

Who dreads to the dead returning,
Who shrinks from that sable shore
Where the high and haughty yearning
Of the souls will be no more?
So stand to your glasses steady, etc.

Cut off from the land that bore us,
Betrayed by the land we find,
When the brightest have gone before us,
And the dullest remain behind.
So stand to your glasses steady, etc.

There's a mist on the glass congealing,
'Tis the hurricane's fiery breath,
And 'tis thus that the warmth of feeling
Turns ice in the grasp of death.
So stand to your glasses steady, etc.

There is many a head that is aching,
There is many a cheek that is sunk,
There is many a heart that is breaking
Must burn with the wine we have drunk.
So stand to your glasses steady, etc.

There is not time for repentance,
'Tis folly to yield to despair,
When a shudder may finish a sentence,
Or death put an end to a prayer.
So stand to your glasses steady, etc.

TOMMY ATKINS

Time was when we frowned on others,
We thought we were wiser then;
But now let us all be brothers,
For we never may meet again.
So stand to your glasses steady, etc.

But a truce to this mourful story
For death is a distant friend;
So here's to a life of glory,
And a laurel to crown each end.
So stand to your glasses steady, etc.

A life of glory – with a laurel to crown each end.

Two

1642–1700
The New Model Army and its Influence

In some ways, it could be said that the history of the English soldier began at Crécy, 1346, Poitiers, 1356, and Agincourt, 1415. An English soldierly spirit and tradition was born on these battlefields, but few people were aware of the birth, despite Shakespeare's efforts to establish it, as in the rousing passages of *Henry V*. Some other memorable battles, such as that of Zutphen 1586 – where Sir Philip Sidney died of his wounds – could be chosen as a starting point, but they would be artificial, for England had no regular, standing army at these times. The Wars of the Roses, 1455–87, had resulted in such a deep-rooted dislike for the professional soldier that for 150 years England was left without an army – at a time when military organization on the Continent was becoming a science.

My analysis must begin with the New Model Army of the Civil War of 1642–9. Some historians may quarrel with this starting point on the ground that the oldest English regiment, the Coldstream Guards, can, as a unit, trace its history as far back as 1650. But the Puritan soldier of Cromwell's time is the link between soldiers of earlier periods and later times. In him many traits of the English soldier were founded and established. In any case, the New Model Army was the most original military organization ever set up in Britain and no account of the English soldier can afford to ignore it. With the

New Model Army came the first genuine idea for a disciplined, methodical, trained standing army.

When civil war broke out no standing army existed and both king and parliament resorted to the usual system of raising a fighting force. The 'trained bands' – the constitutional troops – were untrained and poorly armed and quite undisciplined. After a few initial displays of courage the trained bands became useless. Cornishmen mutinied and refused to march in Devon; Yorkshiremen refused to march south. Trained bands of Gloucestershire were described as 'effeminate in courage and incapable of discipline'. Those from Hertford and Essex were 'mutinous and uncommandable'.

The King commissioned leading men to raise regiments and the young nobility rallied to his standard. In the end he had far too many regiments and colonels. By August 1643 Parliament, unable to secure enough volunteers, pressed men into service and in 1644 the King followed suit. And still indiscipline was rife on both sides.

The army was far from popular with the public. Early in 1645, the Committee of Both Kingdoms – the Parliamentary governing body – wrote to a colonel in the west of England to censure him for 'the very great complaints of the intolerable carriage of the troops'. They were guilty of all kinds of indiscipline and violence – robbery, arson, spoiling, drunkenness, abusive behaviour and all kinds of debaucheries.

The common people of England suffered almost as much as the inhabitants of any country racked by war – and from both sides. The heavy exactions of the Scots in Cumberland and Westmorland for month after month reduced the inhabitants to despair. In Northumberland and Durham the charges on the farmers were so heavy that the landlord had little or nothing. On each side at this time the soldiers lived mostly by plunder. They carried off cattle and cut down crops, sequestered rents and assessed fines. They kept up a multitude of small forts and garrisons as a shelter to flying bands who despoiled the country, parts of which were rife with squalor and brutality.

To the observant, it was clear that before long extreme measures would be needed if either side was to achieve decisive victory. In Parliament, Sir William Waller said, 'Till you have an army of your own, that you may command, it is impossible to do anything of importance.' The crisis brought forth Oliver Cromwell, who pleaded with Parliament to 'put the army into a new method'. The result of his efforts was the Self-Denying Ordinance of December 1644, which created a proper command for the armies. The New Model Army came into being, though its seed had been present in Cromwell's own troop. As early as May 1643 a newsletter journalist had recorded: 'As for Colonel Cromwell, he hath two thousand brave men, well disciplined; and no man swears but pays his twelvepence; if he be drunk he is set in the stocks or worse. . . .'

A letter Cromwell wrote to a friend on 11 September 1643 reveals the key to his system of discipline. 'I have a lovely company; you would respect them, did you know them. They are no Anabaptists, they are honest, sober Christians; *they expect to be used as men!*'*

The New Model Army, significantly, was of lesser stength numerically than the 'old' army, for worthless men were weeded out. The army consisted of 14,400 infantry, 6,600 cavalry and 1,000 dragoons. The whole body was given thorough drill and discipline at Royal Windsor and the effect was apparent the moment the Parliamentarians met the enemy, although a cavalier described them as 'a collection of raw, inexperienced, pressed soldiers'. It has often been assumed that because the New Model Army accomplished so much its members must have been volunteers. In fact, Parliament had to compel men to enlist for it seemed England did not have 20,000 men of militant conscience, willing for the cause to leave shop and farm, wife and home, to submit themselves to iron discipline and face all the perils of very active service.

The artillery, up till now neglected, was reorganized and the army was given a powerful train, eventually brought up to 56 guns, some of 6 in or 7 in calibre, plus some 12 in bomb-throwing mortars. At this time, too, the red coat, earlier adopted by Cromwell for some troops, became general,

* Author's italics.

19

to remain so until 1914, although each regiment had for its facings the private colours of its colonel.*

The Parliamentary soldiers were paid regularly, an astounding thing for those times. The New Army soldiers earned about as much as they would have done as ploughmen or carters. They carried knapsacks but no water bottles and each man had portion of a tent. Their staple rations were bread and cheese, considered adequate, honest food. Oddly enough, this new army had no field hospitals and wounded men had to rely on what help their comrades could give them or on their help to get them to some sympathetic housewife near the battlefield.

The establishment included a Judge Advocate General and a Provost Marshal General under whom was a squad of mounted police. Up to sixty lashes – then called 'stripes' – could be inflicted, but flogging was comparatively unnecessary in this army of Bible soldiers. As we shall see, Cromwell's successors were not so moderate – and they used a cat-o'-nine-tails, while a staff or rod was used in the New Model Army.

At this point it is instructive to look at parts of the Soldier's Catechism composed in 1644 for the Parliament's Army. It was 'Written for the Incouragment and Instruction of all that have taken up Armes in this Cause of God and his People; especially the common souldiers,' and is presented here in the spelling of the period.

Q. What profession are you?
A. I am a Christian and a souldier.
Q. Is it lawfull for Christians to be souldiers.
A. Yea doubtlesse; we have Arguments enough to warrant it.
    1. God calls himself a man of war, and Lord of Hosts.
    2. Abraham had a Regiment of 318 Trained men.
    3. David was employed in fighting the Lords battles.

* An early 'uniform' had a piquant touch. When engaged on a forlorn hope at night the men would hang out their shirt-tails, so that their comrades could distinguish them from the rear. A night attack came to be known as a *camisado* – from the Spanish word for shirt.

4. The Holy Ghost makes honourable mention of Davids worthies.
5. God himself taught David to fight.
6. The noble gift of valour is given for this purpose.

Q. What are the principall things required in a Souldier?
A. 1. That he be religious and godly.
   2. That he be courageous and valiant.
   3. That he be skilfull in the Militarie Profession.

Q. How do you prove that our souldiers should be religious?
A. 1. By Scripture: Deut. 23.9 Luke 3.14.
   2. Besides there be many Reasons to confirme it.
   1. Because they lie so open to death.
   2. They stand in continuall need of God's assistance.
   3. They fight for Religion and Reformation.
   4. God hath rais'd them up to execute justice.
   5. Men may be as religious in this profession as in any other.
   6. We read of brave souldiers that have been very religious.
   7. A well ordered Camp is a Schoole of Virtue wherein is taught, 1. Preparation to death, 2. Continence, 3. Vigilance, 4. Obedience, 5. Hardnesse, 6. Temperance, 7. Humilitie, 8. Devotion, etc.

Q. Who do chiefly offend against this rule?
A. 1. Such souldiers as give themselves to whoring and uncleannesse.
   2. Such as use to swear, and blaspheme the name of God.*
   3. Such a fellow that swinish sin of drunkennesse.
   4. Such as plunder and steale whatsoever they come near.

Q. Are not these things tolerable in souldiers?
A. No more in them than other men; the Scripture saith generally to all men whatsoever:

---

* In 1655 a 'Foot Souldier' named Robert Hull was convicted at court-martial of 'unlawful oathes and execrations'. He was sentenced to three days in gaol on bread and water, then 'to stand upon a joynt stool, with a cleft stick upon his tongue during the space of half an hour.' Then he was dismissed from the Army.

1. That whoremongers and adulterers God will judge, Heb. 13.5.
2. That the Lord will not hold him guiltlesse that taketh his Name in vaine.
3. That drunkards shall not inherit the Kingdome of God. 1. Cor. 6.9, 10.
4. That he that doth wrong, shall receive for the wrong he hath done, and there is no respect of persons. Col. 3. ult.

Q. What is the reason then there be so many lewd and wicked men in the Parliament's Army?

A. 1. Because Commanders in Chief are not more carefull in choosing godly officers.
2. Because honest religious men are not more forward to put themselves in this service of God and his Church.
3. Because Order and Discipline is not more strictly executed by Superiours.
4. Because Officers in Towns and Counties aim to presse the scumme and refuse of men, and so by easing themselves pesture our Armies with base conditioned people.

Q. Is it well done if some of your Souldiers (which seem to be religious) do break down Crosses and Images where they meet with any?

A. 1. I confesse that nothing ought to be done in a tumultuous manner.
2. But seeing God hath put the Sword of Reformation into the Souldiers hand, I think it is not amisse that they should cancell and demolish those Monuments of Superstition and Idolatry, especially seeing the Magistrate and the Minister that should have done it formerly, neglected it.

Similarly the Catechism's answers found justification for 'tearing and burning' the Book of Common Prayer, because 'it belongs to the Parliament Souldiers, upon the matter, to remove all scandalous things they meet with, having covenanted and ingaged themselves in the work of Reformation.'

Q. What do you say concerning valour and courage?
A. I say, it is a most noble and heroicall virtue, that makes some men differ from others, as much as all men differ from beasts.

I say it is impossible for any to be a good souldier without it. An Army of Harts led by a Lion, is better than an Army of Lions led by a Hart.

I say, that one valiant man in the Army, is better than a thousand cowards.

I say, that a coward degenerates from man, being of a base and ignoble nature.

1. God took speciall care that all faint-hearted cowards should be cashiered out of his Armies. Deut. 20.8.
2. Cowards ever do more hurt than good, being like an X before an L.
3. And for the moste part cowards miscarrie sooner than those that are courageous.

The Catechism lists ten 'chiefe Arguments' to make a souldier couragious in the Parliaments Service, including the assurance 'that not a haire can fall from our heads without the providence and permission of God', and that 'the great reward of honour here, and glory hereafter, that shall be given to every one that is valiant for the Lord'.

Q. What are the principall enemies to courage and valour?
A. 1. Want of experience; fresh-water souldiers are commonly faint-hearted souldiers; whereas they that have been used to the Warres are usually of undaunted spirits.
2. Want of metall: some mens spirits are naturally so low and base, that they will never prove good souldiers. As it is with cocks so it is with men. . . .
3. Want of Faith. . . .
4. Want of Innocency and a good conscience. . . .
5. Want of wisdome and consideration: for surely if men would seriously consider the evills of cowardice and the excellency of valour, it would make them abhorre the one and be ambitious of the other.

Q. Is there any great need of skill and cunning in this profession?

A. 1. Yea doubtlesse: for David doth thankfully acknowledge the Lords goodness in teaching his hands to warre, and his fingers to fight, Psal., 144.1.

2. Great wisdome, policie, and experience is required in Commanders. And no less skill and dexterity in common souldiers; they must know how to handle their Armes, how to keep ranks etc.

3. Certainly a few well-trained Souldiers are better than a multitude of raw, unexperienced men.

Q. What should be done to make souldiers skillfull in their art?

A. 1. Officers should be very diligent on teaching and exercising their men.

2. Common souldiers should make it their business to learn and get what cunning they can.

3. Every souldier should seeke to God by prayer, that he would instruct and teach them: for it is the blessing of God that makes men profit in any profession.

4. Both Commanders, Officers and common Souldiers may advantage themselves by reading and observing what hath been written by eminent Souldiers, of this Art.

Q. How ought commanders and officers to carry themselves towards their souldiers?

A. 1. Religiously ... lovingly ... discreetly ... justly. ...

Q. How should inferior Souldiers demeane themselves towards their Commanders and Officers?

A. 1. They must acknowledge and honour them as Superiours and account them as men set over them by the providence of God and wisdome of the State.

2. They must be exactly obedient to their command evern for conscience sake. Ro. 13.5. Of all men Souldiers are most strictly tied to obedience, the want whereof may prove of very dangerous consequences.

Q. What is your opinion of those Souldiers that run away from their Colours?

A. 1. Such are, by Martiall Law, to suffer death, and surely, they deserve it. ...

Nay it is a foule wickednesse, being offensive to God and man, Psal. 78.9.

Q. How ought souldiers to be incouraged and rewarded?

A. 1. They ought to be highly honoured, especially such as have been couragious and faithfull in their Countreyes Service.

2. They ought to be well maintained, with sufficient allowance, while they are abroad in imployment; for no man goeth on warfare at his own charges.

3. They that have received any hurt or losse by the warres, ought to be liberally provided for, and comfortably maintained all their dayes, by them that sent them forth.

Q. What Arguments have you to prove that such honour and respect should bee done to our souldiers?

A. 3. They shew themselves men of public spirits, and true lovers of their Countrey.

4. They shew themselves valiant and couragious, which are very high deserving qualities.

5. No men undergoe such hardship and hazards as the souldier doth.

Despite all that was done to establish the army, and notwithstanding the exalted language of the Soldier's Catechism – 'None deserve better than they [soldiers] either of Church, Commonwealth or Posterity' – the army and the English soldier suffered eclipse. The soldier did not get what he deserved for the army sank into a morass of incompetence and vicious abuse.

Nevertheless, Tommy Atkins had been born. That he was the product of the bloody union of civil war is in no way shameful or derogatory. One might say that the coming together of Parliamentary and Royalist troops resulted in the best qualities of both being distilled into the offspring. If this seems too poetic, I can only say that it seems this way to me. Perhaps the most piquant aspect of the New Model was that it was, after all, a revolutionary force. To think that a revolutionary army should provide the basis for the British military service is ironic indeed.

When Cromwell died in 1658 England was left without a parliament strong enough to rule and with a military force that began to squabble now that Cromwell's iron hand had gone. In May 1660 Charles II arrived in London, where troops of the New Model Army cheered him, though Lord Macaulay suggests that the cheers spoke for the soldiers' discipline rather than for their enthusiasm for a monarchy. By stages the army was disbanded and the soldiers were given the privilege of entering trades without having to serve an apprenticeship. It was probably the last real privilege discharged soldiers were given for two centuries. But before the army was completely disbanded some religious fanatics caused an insurrection in London and it was clear that a small force at least must be maintained to safeguard the King. Colonel John Russell was to raise a regiment of Guards, the Earl of Oxford a regiment of cavalry (1st Life Guards) and Lord Gerard a troop of horse guards. In addition, The Duke of York's troop of Guards, then in Holland, were recalled, to become the 2nd Life Guards. All of these, except for Lord Oxford's regiment, consisted of Royalist gentlemen. But one regiment of New Model infantry was intact, Lord Monk's regiment of Foot Guards. Monk, a competent and greatly respected leader, had earlier assembled his men at Coldstream near Berwick and marched them to London. At a parade on Tower Hill his troops laid down their arms as soldiers of the Commonwealth and took them up again as The Coldstream Guards.* Thus was the Regular Standing Army born.

One minor but interesting change that followed the institution of a regular army was that surgeons became regimental officers, buying their commissions or obtaining them through influence. Some drew pay as combatant officers as well as surgeon's pay, a practice which was long tolerated because a surgeon's prospects of promotion were few. The regimental surgeon ran his own hospital and

---

* In 1675 Charles ordered that the First Guards (later the Grenadier Guards) would take precedence as the first regiment and that the Coldstream Guards would be the second.

supplied his own medicines, towards which the troops contributed from their pay.[†]

Britain now owned Tangier and Bombay – dowry presents from Charles's queen, Catherine of Braganza – and these places required garrisons. The small professional army of English and Scottish troops was soon reinforced by Irish and Welsh soldiers. This was the beginning of the British Army and the end of the English Army.

The bright prospects of this new force soon faded. At the time of the Restoration a man was proud to be seen as a soldier. A decade later his profession was something to hide. Even a Life Guardsman showed no pride in his uniform. The reasons for the soldier's eclipse were compelling. The Puritans had been too strict and now violent reaction set in against the previous rigidity. The army meant authority so the public took out their feelings in hatred for the army. This disrespect and reaction adversely influenced the troops. The moral fervour of the great days of the New Model Army soon dissolved and with it came a devil-may-care what-the-hell approach to all morality. Men showed no restraint at all. When they were billeted in private houses they helped themselves to their hapless host's womenfolk, his wines and his wares. Any civilian who protested was savagely threatened and if threats did not keep him quiet he was mercilessly beaten. Drunkenness, which was to become for centuries the British Army's greatest problem, was already evident.[*] On top of all this, army administration was more corrupt than at any time before or since.

No ordinary man could see any reason for the existence of

---

† In Henry V's army, physicians ranked after shoemakers and tailors, but before washerwomen. A sick man might be given a strong dose concocted by boiling two live newborn puppies in oil of lilies and adding earthworms purified in white wines.

* A century earlier, Camden, in his *Annals* (1561) noted: 'The English who hitherto had, of all Northern nations, shown themselves the least addicted to immoderate drinking, first learned in their wars in the Netherlands to swallow a large quantity of intoxicating liquor, and to destroy their own health by drinking that of others.' In 1617 Robert Flud had written 'Many [English soldiers] are given to drunkenness like the Germans.'

an army. Not that he bothered to try to find a reason; he was
still too resentful of the indignity of military rule. Even so, he
was apt to say, 'Why do we need an army? There'll never be a
war in England – the ships'll keep out any enemy.'

An interesting innovation at this time – 1678 – was the
formation of a grenadier company in each regiment formed
of picked men of good build and stamina. They were armed
with hand grenades and axes to break down palisades. Rather
later – probably in 1740 – their work was described and their
prowess celebrated in 'The British Grenadier', one of the
earliest of Tommy Atkins's songs and one of the longest lived.

Some talk of Alexander, and some of Hercules,
Of Hector and Lysander, and such great names as these;
But of all the world's great heroes, there's none that can
    compare,
With a tow, row, row, row, row, row, to the British
    Grenadier.

Where'er we are commanded to storm the palisades,
Our leaders march with fuses and we with hand
    grenades,
We throw them from the glacis, about the enemies' ears,
Sing tow, row, row, row, row, row, – the British
    Grenadiers.

And when the siege is over, we to the town repair,
The townsmen cry, Hurrah, boys, here comes a Grenadier;
Here come the Grenadiers, my boys, who know no doubts
    or fears,
Then sing tow, row, row, row, row, row, – the British
    Grenadiers.

Then let us fill a bumper, and drink a health to those
Who carry caps and pouches, and wear the louped
    clothes;
May they and their comrades live happy all their years,
With a tow, row, row, row, row, row, – the British
    Grenadiers.

But while some military progress was made, few people were interested in the fate of old soldiers. One of the few was the King's playmate, Nell Gwynne. It is said that she induced Charles II to found the Royal Hospital at Kilmainham, Dublin and, in 1681, the Royal Hospital at Chelsea. These were pleasant gestures, but they could not cope with the problem of the thousands of soldiers crippled or ruined in health for army service. Eventually the Chelsea authorities paid small pensions to discharged soldiers. But from where did this money come? Naturally, from the pay of the man who could least afford it – Tommy Atkins. For a century a halfpenny a week was deducted from his pay so that a pension of up to 6*d* a day could be paid to certain old soldiers. This was as hard as it was mean, but perhaps in retrospect it had one redeeming feature. One could say that the soldiers were looking after their own.

In 1685 the King's 'Bounty to Soldiers' for the loss of an eye or a limb, or the total loss of the use of a limb was one year's pay – £12 2*s* 8*d* – with 'other wounds in proportion'.

Recruiting became a major problem – and was to remain one for many years. With hindsight it is easy to see that all the State had to do was to give the soldiers adequate and regular pay to make soldiering attractive as a career. But the whole history of the British soldier has been marked and marred by the meanness with which he has been treated. In the mid-seventeenth century many aspects of a military life were unenviable. The normal term of engagement was for life. The only exceptions were for volunteers who existed by 'beat of drum' for a shorter term and in time of war.

The State did not itself directly operate the recruiting system. This was the task of the colonels of regiments, who were, in fact, known as the 'owners' of their regiments. The colonels would depute company captains to recruit men. The company captain and his NCO recruiters practised every form of deception from white lies to blackmail to induce men to join the colours. The first bait was the bounty the recruit received on being attested. This money caused trouble for two centuries. Another inducement was a promise, vaguely but excitingly worded, of the prize money and loot to be obtained as a soldier. And many a poor dupe enlisted because a recruiting sergeant recognized in him the makings of a fine corporal or sergeant and hinted as speedy promotion to these dizzy heights.

If words were inadequate the recruiters could fairly easily get a prospect drunk, slip the King's (or Queen's) Shilling into his pocket and have his name or mark on the dotted line before he sobered sufficiently to know what he had done. If drink could not do the trick the stand-over tactics might.

Astonishing things happened. In 1693 the Tooley scandal was exposed when Mr Tooley, a recruiting agent of unorthodox methods, kidnapped a servant working for a member of the House of Commons. It came to light that Tooley was doing very well obtaining sailors and soldiers and that many army officers were on to a good thing with Mr Tooley. In those days a company captain was not specially upset if a man deserted. He would not report the man as missing and would continue to draw his pay, which went into the captain's own pocket. But occasionally an inspection was held and then paper strength and actual strength had to agree. This was where Tooley came in – for a fee he could provide a stand-in at short notice. In his private cells in Holborn Tooley had, at any time, several men duly attested and waiting 'posting' to a regiment to cover up for some officer.

The army increased in unpopularity year by year throughout the reign of Charles II until he died in 1685, then through that of James II until he fled from England in 1688 to make way for William of Orange, William III of England.

During William's reign wars were becoming longer and a soldier's trade more difficult and complicated. Few men relished it except the officers – but many of these evaded all training and were absent from their regiments for months at a time. For all his hardship and misery the foot soldier received 8d a day after the Restoration. One of the most extraordinary facts of the British Army is that *no increase in pay occurred for 123 years!* The soldier had only a brief glimpse of his 8d, for 6d was paid to the company captain for 'subsistence' and the other 2d was kept by the regiment for 'off reckonings'. The captain gave 4d of his 6d to the innkeeper or other perosn on whom the man was billeted; the other 2d covered many things, such as the soldier's laundry. The regiment's 2d share of the man's pay was balanced against issue of clothing or other items. The soldier himself might finish the week with a few pence for himself.

The State actively encouraged corruption. For instance, it introduced the 'faggot' or 'Warrant-men' system. A faggot was a non-existent man carried on the strength of a company. Each colonel or company officer was entitled to a certain number of 'faggots' for whom he could draw pay and allowances to offset any unforeseen expenses. Every company commander was permitted a faggot for burial expenses for deceased soldiers. To overcome the inevitable abuse of the system a twice-yearly muster parade was later held. In single file, every man in every regiment marched before the 'Muster Master', whose duty it was to see that the Government had its pound of soldier. This practice continued until late in the nineteenth century.

There were no barracks at this time and during William's reign the outcry against soldiers being billeted on private people was so great that the practice was abandoned. Soldiers were either kept in cheap disreputable inns or in royal castles or in defence works, many of which were unsuitable for housing men.

In 1688 occurred the battle of Killiecrankie, interesting for this study because it led to an improvement in weapons. General Mackay, the English leader against the rebellious Scots, realized from bitter experience that the plug bayonet which fitted into the muzzle of the soldier's musket was a handicap and introduced into his regiments a new type of bayonet from France. This could be screwed on to the outside of the muzzle, so that a soldier could fire his musket with bayonet fixed. However, not until 1693 did all British infantry have this socket bayonet.

According to an 'Accompt of the English Army as it was 1st April, 1689', the country's military strength consisted of:

Three troops of Guards with three troops of
    Grenadiers to them, making together   768 men
One troops of Scotts [sic] Guards consisting of   118 men
Ten Regts. of Horse in 66 troops, each troop of 50,
    making together   3,300 men

Four Regts. of Dragoons in 26 troops, whereof 20
   have 60 men and the other six 49 each, making
   together   1,494 men
Two Regts. of Foot Guards in 45 Companies of 80
   each, making together   3,600 men
Twenty-six Regts. of Foot, whereof one has 26
   Companies of 60 each, another has 14 Companies
   of 79 each, and the remaining 24 Regts. have
   13 Companies of 60 each, making together   21,386 men
Four Independent Companies of 50 men each   200 men
So that the above particulars, which are all computed
without reckoning the officers, make up 4,186 horse, 1,494
dragoons, and 25,186 foot; in all, 30,866 men.

The whole unhappy state of this army was exposed in
the same year when William sent an expedition to Ireland
to fight ex-King James. Some deplorable armies have left
British shores over the centuries, but probably never one
so hopelessly unsoldierly and incompetent as this one.
Officers knew nothing of leading and were so despicable
that Headquarters had to publish an order threatening with
cashierment any officer who refused to pay his troops.
Nobody knew anything about a soldier's trade. The men were
ordered to build shelter huts for themselves, but ignorant
and lazy and without leadership they did nothing, and when
cold weather struck many died from pneumonia. Sickness
proved nearly fatal to the expedition. A chaplain named
Story wrote that English troops marched boldly up to the
ground from which they had recently been driven. This was
'only natural for Englishmen,' he said. 'It is observable that
they are commonly fiercer and bolder after being repulsed
than before; and what blunts the courage of all other nations
commonly whets theirs – I mean the killing of their fellow
soldiers before their faces.'

With comments like this one can see the spirit of Crécy and
Agincourt trying to find new expression.

An order of 1690 noted that 'Bravery, Integrity, Generosity
and Humanity are inseparable. Cowardice, Cruelty,
Treachery, and Avarice, Vanity, Pride, Folly, and Ignorance,

beget each other.' Bravery and Integrity were evident when William took his troops to the Low Countries and blooded them against the French at Steenkirk and Neerwinden in 1692. The English soldier in this campaign could not claim a victory but was perhaps all the more impressive for this, for his courage in adversity brought respect from his enemies.

In 1695 William and his English troops were more fortunate, when they attacked and captured Namur, one of the most strongly fortified towns in Belgium. As a result of this victory the army gained its first battle honour won on the Continent of Europe, though not all the men who helped to win it could be called enthusiastic volunteers. In 1696 all insolvent debtors were compulsorily enlisted as punishment.

By 1697, when both sides had fought themselves to a standstill, the English soldier had established a reputation for courage and steadiness. And somehow he had managed to rise above the many frustrations and troubles that bedevilled him. During William III's reign whipping became more severe. Sterne, in *Tristram Shandy*, describes a grenadier whipped to the point where he begged to be shot to be put out of his agony. He had supposedly been found in possession of stolen ducats.

The soldier's frustration and troubles were also evident at home after a war when, thrown out of his regiment, the ex-soldier could only beg or steal. Several ballads illustrate his plight, but few better than *The Maunding Soldier, or the Fruit of War is Beggary*. It was written during the Protectorate, but the situation it described applied right up to the end of the following century.

> Good worship, cast your eyes
> Upon a soldier's miseries:
> Let not my leane cheeks, I pray
> Your bounty from a soldier stay,
> But like a noble friend,
> Some silver lend,
> And Jove will pay you in the end.
> I pray your worship think on me,
> That am what I seeme to be,

No rooking rascall, nor no cheat,
But a soldier in every way compleat:
I have wounds to show
That prove it so. . . .

But so did Shakespeare's Pistol have 'wounds', and he was typical of the fake military beggars who made it harder for honest old soldiers to beg for their living.

At this time, with the century nearings its end, Tommy Atkins needed a leader worthy of him, somebody to bring out his best qualities and to establish him once and for all as a fighting man worthy of his foes.

Writing from Flanders to his uncle in Yorkshire, Molyneaux Bunny said, in part, 'For I must deal plainely with you I am very wearry of a souldier our pay is very small we have much to do to live. I have not had one letter from my brother Edmund since I come in to Flanders he hath bien very unkind to me. . . .'*

Many men were 'very wearry of a souldier' and most felt neglected by the people at home. They were due for a period of better treatment.

*From an original letter in the author's possession.

Three

1702–42
Marlborough's Men

The man who brought to fulfilment the English soldier's promise of competence was John Churchill, second* son of a Winston Churchill of Mintern in Dorset. In 1702, at the age of 52, Churchill – he was soon to become the Duke of Marlborough – was appointed by the new monarch, Queen Anne, as Captain-General of the English forces at home and abroad.

Marlborough's experience included two years under the French commander, Turenne, the greatest leader of his time. Biographers and historians have written millions of words about Marlborough but few have given enough attention to his ability to bring out the best in the common soldier. He assumed effective command of 12,000 British common soldiers at Nimuegen† in June 1702, as well as 48,000 Allied troops.

Wellington would have seen little difference between these men and his own; he would have recognized them at once as 'the scum of the earth'. But a fascinating scum, with which Marlborough performed great deeds in the following ten years.

Recruitment of men for the army was akin to an art at this time. Among other steps taken under the Mutiny Act of 1702 all convicted felons who enlisted were given a pardon. In 1703 another act saw to the enlistment of 'all such able-bodied

---

* According to most recrods. (Some say the third son.)
† Now Nijmegen.

men as had not any lawful calling or visible means for their maintenance and livelihood'. Parish officers were induced to help in recruitment because for each pauper enlisted the parish was paid a pound.

In 1704 George Farquhar wrote his *The Recruiting Officer*, memorable for its scenes in which appear the competent and cunning Sergeant Kite and his scheming and unprincipled superior, Captain Plume. The play is valuable evidence because Farquhar himself had been a soldier and a recruiting officer. Kite is shown, as the play opens, recruiting by beat of drum in Shrewsbury market place. Out for at least twenty recruits, he delivers his spiel.

'If any gentlemen, soldiers or others have a mind to serve Her Majesty, and pull down the French king; if any prentices have severe masters, any children have undutiful parents; if any servants have too little wages, or any husband too much wife, let them repair to the noble Sergeant Kite, at the sign of the Raven in this good town of Shrewsbury, and they shall receive present relief and entertainment. Gentlemen, I don't beat my drum here to ensnare or inveigle any man; for you must know, gentlemen, that I am a man of honour! Besides, I don't beat up for common soldiers: No, I list only grenadiers – *grenadiers*, gentlemen!'

Discoursing at length, flattering, cajoling, wheedling, Kite invites his audience to his quarters where 'there is a tub of humming ale'.

'This is the Queen's drink,' he says. 'She's a generous queen and she loves her subjects – I hope, gentlemen, you won't refuse the Queen's health?' He makes it sound like treason to do so and, of course, the men follow him and his drummer. His bag is five – the strong man of Kent, the king of the gipsies, a Scotch pedlar, a scoundrel attorney and a Welsh parson. Captain Plume rejects the attorney. 'I will have nobody in my company that can write: a fellow that can write can draw petitions. Discharge him this minute.'

Kite goes on another expedition, trying this time to trap yokel farmhands because they make good soldiers. He brings in two of them – drunk; but not too drunk to join in the ballad, '*Over the Hills and Over the Main*'.

> Over the hills and over the main,
> To Flanders, Portugal and Spain,
> The Queen commands and we'll obey
> Over the hills and far away.

Perhaps the most significant lines were:

> Our 'prentice Tom may now refuse
> To wipe his scoundrelly master's shoes,
> For now he's free to sing and play –
> Over the hills and far away.

The sentiments appealed to simple country boys but some found that their new military masters were rather more scroundrelly than the civil masters and that there wasn't much singing and playing in Flanders, Portugal and Spain.

The play shows many more of the recruiters' wiles and exaggerates none. Kite would promise a butcher that he would become an army surgeon-general; he turns fortune-teller to inveigle a man into accepting the Queen's shilling; he persuades the town magistrates to hand over alleged defaulters to him and to the army.

Blackader (then a lieutenant), sent on a recruiting mission to Glasgow in 1705 found himself unsuited to recruiting. He wrote: 'Sobriety . . . is a bar to success. The greatest rakes are the best recruiters. I cannot ramble and rove and drink and tell stories, and wheedle and insinuate, if my life were at stake.'

During Queen Anne's time, nevertheless, many men were genuine volunteers, for the duration of a war or for three years. These were the men who craved adventure and excitement, loot and rape. A few, a very few, were soldiers by instinct, or patriots. All these types of men – yokels, criminals, drunkards, adventurers – were the raw clay from which armies were fashioned. And what superb armies.

Marlborough was a great maker of soldiers, but even he could not reform his men. They were hopelessly addicted to drinking, black-foul language, looting and fighting. Officers were as bad as the men in most respects. Nearly everybody drank heavily because there was so little else to do and boredom was rife. They swore because foul language comes easily to men's lips in an army. The language of most armies has always been filthy and blasphemous, but in the late seventeenth and early eighteenth centuries it must have been outstandingly depraved, especially if we believe Colonel Blackader. He wrote, 'Marching all day in the middle of an English army (Blackader was Scottish) I need say no more to give a notion of what a hell on earth it is.' On another occasion: 'My mind chafed and vexed the whole day with villainy and abominations of all sorts, both against the laws of God and man. Cursing, swearing, drunkenness, robbing, thieving, mutiny, etc. . . . some officers rather encouraged the villains.' But Blackader was a notorious Puritan so his comments would tend to be extravagant.

One expression – I do not know its origin – became a classic – 'The army went to Flanders and swore horribly.'

Blackader preferred to march with German troops. 'They are not such old, profane sinners and do not swear so much; and when they do, it does not make my flesh creep, or sound in my ears with the hellish ringing echo that English oaths do.'

Robbery and looting was as much part of army life as swearing. The troops 'foraged' far and wide – sometimes too wide for safety and were caught by enemy patrols or set on and beaten or killed by angry peasants. If a civilian made a formal complaint to authority and a soldier robber was identified he was punished severely. In extenuation, the soldier of Marlborough's first years of command was poorly fed. He could, if he had the money, buy other provisions from the sutlers – the civilian traders who accompanied armies for centuries. When he was worked, marched and fought hard the soldier became hungry, so it is not really surprising that he was sometimes desperately empty and would go to any lengths to find food.

At the sack of a town, too, soldiers would go to any length. Sometimes (as we shall see later) they committed gross atrocities.

Strictly, according to codified and recognized rules, a fortress could be sacked after it had had its wall breached and had refused a request to surrender. A surrendered fortress could not legally be sacked, nor could an open town. However there are many instances on record of troops looting a captured town or village and the occupants seemed to accept this as inevitable. As troops progressed through a town they would load themselves with loot, much of it useless, and then smash or burn everything in reach. After the mid-seventeenth century, all states had made efforts to rid war of the excesses which had characterized the Thirty Years War, but it took a long time for these efforts to be fruitful.

Soldiers did not keep their booty for long. Behind every army in those days followed hundreds of pedlars and dealers. They would descend like vultures on to a battlefield – once the fighting was over – and snatch up anything that could be sold. They stripped the dying and helpless as brutally as they stripped the dead. Within hours of a fight or of the capture of a town the first soldiers with their loot would be offering it to the pedlars. They had no idea of value and would sell a priceless necklace for a bottle of wine, or a valuable fur for twopence. Unholy dealing went on continually and the only ones who scored were the dealers, some of whom were wealthy enough to employ bodyguards.

Sir William Temple conceded that, 'It is the known and general character of the English nation to be more fearless of death and dangers than any others.' But he confessed that Englishmen also disliked labour or hardships even when it was a matter of 'making the provision of such food and clothes as they find or esteem necessary for sustenance of their lives, or for the health and strength and vigour of their bodies. This appears among all our troops that serve abroad, as indeed their only weak side; which makes the care of the belly the most necessary piece of conduct in the commander of an English army, who will never fail of fighting well, if they are well fed.'

Stocqueler wrote: 'So loose and irregular was the whole conduct of the soldiery, that the poet's* stinging lines were fearfully applicable to the great mass, and unfortunately continued so for many years subsequently.'

* Stocqueler did not identify him – Author.

To swear, to game, to drink, to show at home,
By lewdness, idleness, and Sabbath breach,
The great proficiency he made abroad;
T' astonish and to grieve his gazing friends,
To break some maiden's and her mother's heart:
To be a pest where he was useful once,
Are his sole aim, and all his glory now!

Swearing and blasphemy reached such foulness that the punishment was introduced of borning the tongue with a hot iron.

Marlborough listed hundreds of rules, regulations and prohibitions for his army. For instance, 'All men who are found gathering peas or beans, or under the pretence of rooting, to be hanged as Maroders [sic] without Trial.'

Other points:

'When the soldiers go to market, a sergeant to go with them who is to be answerable for their behaviour in the towns and villages.

All the men to be acquainted that whoever is taken fishing Ponds, draining them, or cutting the Dykes, shall suffer death.

Soldiers who take their Arms out of Bell-tents after Retreat to suffer death; and the Officers of Quarter Guards to be answerable.

No Avenues to be cut down on Pain of Death.

When Regiments send out to cut Wood, an Officer of a Regiment to go with the men, and be answerable for Disorders committed.

Any Soldier taken out of Camp, without a Pass in writing from his commanding Officer, or without a non-commissioned Officer with him, will be hanged.'

Not only the men, but officers, even Commanding Officers, were liable to punishment. 'One Waggon is to be allowed to each Regiment, for the Sick unable to march, to go in rear of the Regiment. No Women, Children or Baggage to be suffered to go in it; commanding Officers who suffer it, will be put in Arrest.'

Many other offences were liable to 'severe punishment or most severe punishment or the utmost punishment'. Not that all the regulations concerned offences. It is no exaggeration to say that Marlborough and his staff foresaw every possible contingency and evolved an order to cover it.

But Marlborough was no mere martinet. He was the first British commander to realize that an organized medical service could save manpower. Up to this time a common soldier was as expendable as his boots and what medical service existed was little more than an organization for clearing wounded and dead men from the battlefield. A soldier who became ill on the march was left in a village if there was no transport for him – and that was nearly always.

Marlborough apparently attracted young doctors and surgeons into his service, for they were keen and humane. They even set up hospitals of sorts in defended garrison towns abroad. For ambulances they used unsprung carts and river barges. Perhaps even more importantly, Marlborough's MOs brought in a system of camp hygiene and sanitation.

Marlborough went to great lengths to keep his men fit and contented on the march. He increased their rations, paid them all in advance so that they could buy extra food. Marlborough's progress from Holland to the Danube in 1704 was one of the British Army's first great marches. On the six weeks' march through the Rhineland the army averaged ten miles a day, a good steady pace. The speed of the march completely surprised the French and led to the victory at Blenheim.

The troops found shoes, bridges and hospitals – three of the most important things in a soldier's active service life – waiting for them wherever they were needed. The night's stop was always known in advance and all the men had to do on arrival was to pitch their tents, boil their kettles and lie down to rest. Captain Robert Parker, who took part in the march, wrote: 'Surely never was such a march carried on with more order and regularity, and with less fatigue to man and horse.' It was not surprising that the troops affectionately called Marlborough 'Corporal John'.

Not that all Marlborough's officers emulated him in his consideration for his troops, and sometimes their harshness brought retribution. At one siege, probably at Lille, after an attack on some outworks the grenadiers of the 15th Regiment had to retire, possibly because of the springing of a mine, or the superiority of the enemy's fire. In this retreat the lieutenant of these grenadiers, notorious for his ill-treatment of them, was wounded, and fell. The grenadiers passed him by, ignoring his pleas for help. At last he grabbed hold of a pair of shoes tied to the waistbelt of one grenadier. The grenadier took out a knife, cut the string, and left the shoes with him, saying, 'There! There is a new pair of shoes for you, to carry you to Hell.'

At the Battle of Blenheim, 1704, the same regiment was one of the few that attacked the strongly defended village. The Major, rather apprehensive, addressed the regiment, confessed he had been guilty of poorly treating the men and begged to fall by the hands of the French, and not by theirs. He promised, if he survived, that he would become a reformed character. A grenadier is said to have replied, 'March on, Sir; the enemy is before you, and we have something else to do than to think of *you* now.'

After the victory the Major faced about to the regiment, and took off his hat to give a huzza. He had just got out the words, 'Gentlemen, the day is our own,' when a musket-ball hit him in the forehead, and killed him instantly. 'Whether this ball came by accident or design, was never yet discovered, though more believed the latter than the former,' said an anonymous historian of the incident.

Warfare of the time was a strange business by modern standards. Armies, brigades, battalions and platoons were moved about the field like so many chess pieces and usually the commanding general had a place of vantage from which he could observe the movements of his enemy and then deploy his own troops accordingly.

Nearly always a battle depended on two things – in the beginning upon the coldly clever brain of the general and at the end upon the dogged discipline of the private soldier. Almost inevitably any battle would develop into a close-quarter hand-fight between opposing infantry regiments or with an infantry regiment withstanding an enemy cavalry charge.

Battles had to be fought at close quarters because muskets had an accurate range of less than one hundred yards; there was no point in firing at greater range. Many times infantry advanced to within twenty yards before firing. And since reloading, by skilled troops, took about twenty seconds, every shot had to count. The men stood steady in their lines, perhaps for hours, while enemy cannon balls tore through the ranks. This was a tough test of discipline, both imposed and personal. On the restricted front of battle, from a few hundred yards to, rarely, three or five miles, bodies would lie in heaps about the troops still standing.

There was a good reason for these rigid tactics. If infantry were caught out of formation, the hovering cavalry would pounce and cut them to ribbons. The only real infantry defence against cavalry was steadiness. As men fell, so the survivors closed their ranks, always presenting that shoulder-to-shoulder wall of resistance.

By tact and discipline, Marlborough made the soldiers do all that he required of them. When being thanked by the House of Lords in acknowledgement of his victory at Blenheim, Marlborough took the remarkable step of paying a tribute to the bravery of his men.

In the address by the Lords there occurred this passage: The honour of these glorious victories, great as they are, under the immediate blessing of Almighty God, is chiefly, if not alone, owing to your grace's conduct and valour.'

To this Marlborough replied: 'I am extremely sensible of the great honour your lordships are pleased to do me; but I must beg on this occasion to do right to all the officers and men I had the honour to command. Next to the blessing of God, the good success of this campaign is owing to their extraordinary conduct.'

The troops' 'extraordinary conduct' was about the only factor Marlborough could depend upon during his campaigns. He met only obstruction, procrastination and faint hearts among his Dutch allies, he had strong and bitter enemies at home, the German princes were hesitant, dilatory and incompetent and the weather was often against him.

As at Blenheim, the steadiness of his troops was largely responsible for Marlborough's victories at the Schellenberg, at Ramillies, 1706, Oudenarde, 1709; Malplaquet, 1709 and the forcing of the *Ne Plus Ultra* Lines in 1711. The French so called these defensive lines, which stretched from Montreuil on the Canche River to Namur at the confluence of the Sambre and Meuse, because they were intended to be Marlborough's '*ne plus ultra*' – so far and no farther.

But Marlborough's genius and Marlborough's men between them broke these proud foritifications. The details are irrelevant to this study, but by 4 p.m. on 5 August – after a march of forty miles in about nineteen hours – the infantry crossed the Scarpe River and penetrated into the French lines. It was Marlborough's greatest exploit.

It seems surprising that the commanders who came after Marlborough did not realize that his troops marched and fought for him with unique devotion because he had gained their trust and respect through humane treatment and not through fear.

During Marlborough's time the soldier won a new respect from his countrymen. Trevelyan wrote, 'Marlborough's victories helped to make England proud of her soldiers, yet the treatment of Marlborough himself in the last years of Anne shows how little, even then, the country cared for a Redcoat or was dazzled by the glory of war.'

The country cared so little for the Redcoats that it still treated them abominably. The maladministration, thoughtlessness and callousness seem incredible. For instance, it was about this time that troops were more frequently sent abroad to garrison the growing number of possessions Britain was acquiring. The 38th Regiment (South Staffordshire) was sent to the West Indies in 1707 and left there – abandoned would be a better word – for sixty years, the longest period of unbroken service by any British regiment. This was nothing more than transporation for life for soldiers sent to the station. No attempt was made to provide suitable food or clothing or medical attention. In tropical stations men died in thousands from disease; in North America they froze to death because they had no winter clothing. And to add insult to injury the army imposed foreign service as punishment for court-martial offences.

George I, who succeeded Anne in 1714, was ignorant of the English language and character – he was the Elector of Hanover – but he managed to bring in some improvements for the army, including a uniform system of drill and regular inspections by generals. The steel ramrod for muskets had by now been introduced, too. This was an essential development, for when the old wooden ramrod became wet and swollen it could not be used and musket and soldier were out of action.

But, obtusely, regiments which had distinguished themselves in the War of the Spanish Succession were disbanded. As a result of the Rebellion of 1715 twenty-one regiments had to be raised in a hurry and some of them continued into modern times – the 9th and 12th (Lancers) and the 10th, 11th, 13th and 14th (Hussars).*

In the early part of the Hanoverian rule discipline was woefully lax and officers were no better than their men. Some officers kidnapped a leading citizen of Trowbridge, forcibly made him dead drunk and then enlisted him. Disputes, brawls and desertion were commonplace.

In 1727 George II became monarch – and an affliction to the army. As a young man George II had been a gallant soldier – he had fought under Marlborough at Oudenarde – but he had an obsession for pretty uniforms. He thought they helped recruiting, which they probably did, and that they added to a soldier's martial qualities – which they did not. The old practical long stockings were replaced by tight white thigh-high gaiters called spatterdashes; soldiers had to wear their hair in a pigtail and were ordered to powder it; grenadiers had to wear side whiskers.

That same year, 1727, Lieutenant-Colonel Humphrey Bland, of His Majesty's Own Regiment of Horse, published a book on military discipline in which he gave officers some profound advice which should have been more frequently followed. 'It being a general remark that the private soldiers when they are to go upon action, form their notions of the danger from the outward appearance of the officers, and according

* Though 'Hussars' and 'Lancers' are nineteenth-century descriptions in the British Army.

to their looks apprehend the undertaking to be more or less difficult (for when they perceive their officers dejected or thoughtful, they are apt to conclude the affair desperate); in order therefore to dissipate their fears, and fortify their courage, the officers should assume a serene and cheerful air; and in delivering their orders, and in their common discourse with the men, they should address themselves in an affable and affectionate manner.'

Between 1720 and 1738 England developed and prospered but the army was, as usual, neglected, and numbered only about 18,000 men – apart from those in Ireland. The one big development was the establishment of the Royal Regiment of Artillery in 1722. Four companies had been ordered in 1716 by Marlborough, but only two had been raised. These first regular gunners began a great tradition.

The years 1739–41 saw one of those disgraceful debacles which have punctuated British military history. As always, the chief sufferers were the common British soldiers. In 1739 the Prime Minister, Walpole, had to give way to public opinion and gone to war with Spain over the loss of an ear, owned by an English smuggler, Captain Jenkins. Walpole sent an expedition to fight the Spaniards in the West Indies and Central America. This force consisted of eight battalions, mostly of raw recruits, but with the West Yorks and the South Wales Borderers to give them spine. Four other battalions were raised in the American colonies. By the beginning of 1741 nearly 2,000 men had died of yellow fever – 'Yellow Jack' to the troops.

The survivors were used to lay siege to Cartagena, Colombia, with General Wentworth, weak, hesitant and petty, commanding the land forces. Wentworth and Admiral Vernon, the naval commander, quarrelled frequently and the whole operation was a shameful shambles. The men were fed with 'putrid beef, rusty pork and bread swimming with maggots'. We have the word of Assistant Surgeon Tobias Smollett for it.

More than a quarter of the troops were killed or wounded and the survivors had great difficulty reaching their ships. Fever broke out afresh on the ships and then in the camps in Jamaica. As fast as reinforcements arrived they, too, went down with sickness. There was an idiotic attempt to seize the Isthmus of Darien, but of course it failed; there were too few fit men left to fight. In the end 90 per cent of the British force died. It is not surprising that this unhappy episode is usually omitted from history books.

Four

1743–70
Battles Glorious, Health Notorious

In June 1743 English soldiers gave further proof of their worth on a battlefield – this time at Dettingen, under the personal leadership of George II, the last British monarch to command his troops in a pitched battle. Aged sixteen years but adjutant of his regiment, James Wolfe ended his first campaign at Dettingen. His fifteen-year-old brother also fought here. 'I sometimes thought I had lost poor Ned when I saw legs and heads beat off close to him,' Wolfe wrote.

A more humble English soldier on the field that day was Trooper Tom Brown of Kirkleatham, Yorkshire, who served in Bland's Dragoons, the 3rd King's Own Hussars. The English dragoons had a fierce fight against nine French squadrons and at its height Brown saw one of the regiment's three standards, already slashed and shot, fall from the hands of the badly wounded cornet who carried it. Brown quickly dismounted to retrieve it, but had three fingers sabred off his bridle hand. His horse bolted and took Brown through the enemy lines. Mastering the horse, the trooper made his way back and saw a French soldier with the standard. He attacked and killed the man, gripped the standard pole between his knee and the saddle and, sword flashing, cut his way to safety. He had seven wounds, some in the face, and three shots had gone through his hat. An inaccurate story says he was knighted in the field by George II.

The grim courage shown by Trooper Brown at Dettingen

was emulated by whole battalions at Fontenoy in 1745, when the Duke of Cumberland – popular with his men though detested by historians – commanded the British forces. When his Dutch and Austrian allies could make no progress against the French, under the redoubtable Marshal Saxe, Cumberland trusted in the fire-power and Marlborough-bred discipline of his British infantry and advanced. His seventeen battalions, supported by some Hanoverians, paraded steadily through heavy artillery cross-fire. Fifty yards from the French defences – which Saxe believed too strong to be attacked – they received the first French fire.

Then the British fired – their volley* sounding like one great shot – and the French first line simply was no longer there. Further volley fire – the hallmark of British troops of the period – settled five other French battalions and Tommy Atkins marched into the enemy positions. But with their allies inactive, the British could not hold these positions in the face of Saxe's reserves. As controlled and ordered as in the advance, the British battalions withdrew, giving the French their first victory over British troops since the time of Joan of Arc, over three centuries before, though it was only technically a French victory as the British were driven off by Irish regiments in French service. More than 6,000 British and Hanoverian soldiers were killed or wounded, but the French lost as many, and possibly more.

One of the most interesting incidents of the battle concerned Private Thomas Stevenson of Ligonier's Horse, later the 7th Dragoons. Stevenson had his horse shot from under him shortly after the battle commenced on 11 May and did not rejoin his regiment until late the next day. His comrades were so proud of being styled a 'Ligonier' that, believing him to have run away, they drove Stevenson out of the lines. Stevenson demanded a court-martial before which

---

* Or 'general discharge'. Strictly speaking the volley was a *feu de joie* and it was always fired with the ranks at half distance without bayonets and with the muzzle elevated. A general discharge was always fired with fixed bayonets and levelled arms, that is, at the enemy.

he produced a lieutenant of the Royal Welsh Fusiliers, who highly commended the soldier for his voluntary service and gallantry in the ranks of the Fusiliers. Stevenson was not only restored to his troop with honour, but Cumberland granted him a lieutenancy in the Royal Welsh.

But no amount of gallantry could prevent stoppages of pay. In 1747 this order was published: 'The Commander in chief being convinced that the weekly Stoppages in the marching regiments of Foot, are of great benefit to the Men, by enabling them to be provided with good Shoes, Gaiters, Linen and other Necessaries, and to serve as a Fund for making good the too frequent Waste of Ammunition, and Loss of Arms and Accoutrements through Idleness and Neglect, it is the Commander in Chief's Orders, that the Foot Guards be put under the same Regulation of Stoppages.' The stoppage was 6*d* for a private, 7*d* for a drummer, and 9*d* for a corporal and 1*s* for a sergeant.

Illness was still a great problem. At the end of the campaign of 1743 about 3,000 men were left in the general hospitals, and in 1747, before going into winter quarters the returns of the sick amounted to 4,000.

The British Army was now entering upon a long period of extensive and intensive active service, but I can deal only with those actions which further an analysis of the soldier rather than those which merely show British military activity. It is interesting to note in passing that only in 1751 did the custom of calling regiments by the names of their colonels end officially.*

R.J.T. Hills says of the British Army of the mid-eighteenth century, 'In spite of fire-discipline and downright gallantry, it was a stiff-backed, futile army.' How stiff-backed and how futile was shown in June 1755 when General Braddock set

* For many years only two regiments have had titles which include the names of commoners. These are the Green Howards named after Colonel the Hon. Charles Howard (they were originally so designated to distinguish them from the 3rd Buffs commanded by another officer named Howard) and the Duke of Wellington's Regiment, the 33rd West Riding Regiment.

out with his two regiments – the 44th and 48th – and 600 irregulars on a march to Fort Duquesne. About nine miles from it he was ambushed by Indians led by French officers. The result was disastrous. The men, in their scarlet uniforms and white spatterdashes, marching in columns, were the sort of target an ambush force dreams of. Helpless because they could not even see their enemies, some of the English troops broke for cover and fired from behind trees. This appalled Braddock and his officers; they considered skulking behind trees both undisciplined and unsoldierly. So they drove the Tommies back into column, where, of course, they were butchered. It was only poetic justice that Braddock himself was shot, to die in the retreat of the survivors. The whole episode was glaring proof that neither leaders nor the system under which they operated were worthy of the troops they used.

But even Brigadier James Wolfe was critical of the troops. Writing to his father on the failure of the Rochfort Expedition, he said: 'These disappointments, I hope, won't affect their courage; nothing, I think, can hurt their discipline – it is at its worst. They shall drink, and swear, plunder and massacre with any troops in Europe, the Cossacks and Calmucks themselves not excepted; with this difference, that they have not quite so violent an appetite for blood and bonfires.'

In a letter to Lord George Sackville, dated 5 February, 1758, he wrote:

The condition of the troops that compose this garrison (Portsmouth) – (or rather vagabonds that stroll about in dirty red clothes from one gin shop to another) excels belief. There is not the least shadow of discipline, care, or attention. Disorderly soldiers of different regiments are collected here; some from the ships, others from the hospital, some waiting to embark – dirty, drunken, insolent rascals, improved by the hellish nature of the place, where every kind of corruption, immorality, and looseness is carried to excess; it is a sink of the lowest and most abominable of vices. Your Lordship could not do better than to get the Company of Artillery moved out of this infernal den, where troops ought never to be quartered.

Wolfe could not say anything bad enough of Britain's premier naval port. To his mother he had written about the same time: 'The necessity of living in the midst of the diabolical citizens of Portsmouth is a real and unavoidable calamity. It is a doubt to me if there is such another collection of demons upon the whole earth. Vice, however, wears so ugly a garb, that it disgusts rather than tempts.'

Nevertheless, English troops fought well for Wolfe at Quebec the following year when he won the Battle of the Plains of Abraham. The spirit of the troops was high enough, as illustrated by a song composed by Sergeant Ned Botwood of the 47th.

Come, each death doing dog who dares venture his neck,
Come, follow the hero that goes to Quebec:
And ye that love fighting shall soon have enough:
Wolfe commands us, my boys: we shall give them hot stuff.

Wolfe, a major-general at 32, a veteran of seven campaigns, was killed in the action. A prize was offered for the best ode written on his death. Among others sent in was one which commenced:

He marched without dread or fears
At the head of his bold grenadiers;
And what was most remarkable, nay very particular,
He climbed up rocks which were perpendicular!

One of Tommy Atkins's most impressive victories – *the* most impressive in some ways – was that of the Battle of Minden, north-west Germany, on 1 August 1759. Here he performed a feat of arms never before equalled and certainly never since surpassed. He broke in succession three lines of French cavalry, repulsed heavy counter-attacks by columns of French infantry and at the end of a bloody battle routed the enemy.

About 170 years later Sir John Fortescue wrote: 'All preconcerted arrangements were upset by the extraordinary attack of the British Infantry, a feat of gallantry and endurance that stands, so far as I know, absolutely without parallel.'

The infantry regiments which won this immortal fame were the 12th (later the Suffolk Regiment and now embodied in the 1st East Anglian Regiment); the 20th (now the Lancashire Fusiliers); 23rd Royal Welsh Fusiliers (now the Royal Welch Fusiliers); 25th (now the King's Own Scottish Borderers); 37th (now the Royal Hampshire Regiment) and 51st (now the King's Own Yorkshire Light Infantry).

Two batteries of the Royal Artillery, then known as Foy's and Macbean's, also played a big part in the victory, but the 'Brown Bess' musket in Tommy Atkins's hands did most of the damage.

The six foot-regiments had been sent to Germany in 1758 to reinforce the Army of Prince Ferdinand of Brunswick, an ally of Britain. Earlier that year the Prince had driven the French from Hanover and Hesse, but by the end of July 1759, the enemy had again advanced into Germany. Marshal Contades had established his 60,000 men around the town of Minden with his right flank on the river Weser and his left on a marsh.

Ferdinand approached Minden in the hope of bringing the French to battle. On 1 August Contades had on the field about 51,000 troops and 162 guns, Ferdinand about 41,000 and 170 guns. At midnight the French columns marched out of their camp and two hours later Ferdinand put his troops on the road.

On their way the British troops halted near a rose garden and picked roses with which they adorned their hats.*

Ferdinand placed Captain Foy's battery of guns at Hahlen and while at the Hahlen windmill he saw the division which included the British Infantry, deploying and ordered it to advance, *when the time came*, with drums beating. Fortescue says that this order was apparently misunderstood for 'the leading brigade shook itself up and began to advance forthwith . . .' towards the French cavalry.

The forward line of these troops comprised the 12th, 37th and 23rd Regiments, under Brigadier Waldegrave; the second line comprised the 20th , 51st and 25th Regiments, under Brigadier Kingsley, with three Hanoverian battalions in support.

---

* Since then all the regiments, except the Royal Welch Fusiliers, have worn roses on their headdresses on Minden Day every year.

While the second line was deploying the drums began to roll and the first line, in perfect order, advanced on the French Horse. The second line then moved off, completing its deployment on the move. And so the nine battalions marched steadily forward into a cross-fire which tore gaps in their ranks, and approached the French horsemen, astonished to see infantry attacking unbroken cavalry.

Delighted at the opportunity to ride down exposed infantry a dozen squadrons charged the scarlet-coloured line. Waldegrave's brigade halted and stood firm. When the horsemen were within ten yards the troops poured in a volley which staggered the squadrons and sent them back in confusion. Then the British resumed their steady advance.

Lord George Sackville was ordered to bring his cavalry into action to exploit the French reverse, but he advanced his squadrons a little way and halted. He ignored a second message, asking why he had not come up.

A second line of cavalry charged the advancing battalions and massed infantry and thirty-two guns from the French left began to enfilade the Redcoats. Momentarily, the British and Hanoverians wavered, then steadied to meet the galloping cavalry. A single shattering volley blasted them off the field, then the British turned on the French infantry, who were beaten back with heavy casualties.

Again Sackville was ordered up, again he declined to attack. For the third time French horsemen thundered down. This time they broke through the first line, but were destroyed by the second.

Ferdinand's left wing now attacked and the German cavalry routed the French Infantry opposing them. As the French army retreated rapidly, the batteries commanded by Foy and Macbean harassed them. His army demoralized, Contades retired to Cassel. Later he paid the British Infantry the remarkable tribute quoted at the beginning of this book.

Allied losses at Minden were 2,600 killed and wounded, of whom 1,400 were British. Of the six British Infantry regiments, originally 4,434 strong, 78 officers and 1,252 other ranks were casualties. Heaviest losses were in the 12th Regiment (302) and the 20th Regiment (322).

Prince Ferdinand said of the British infantry: 'Notwithstanding the loss they sustained before they could get up to the enemy; notwithstanding the repeated attacks of the enemy's cavalry; notwithstanding a fire of musketry well kept up by the enemy's infantry; notwithstanding their being exposed in front and flank, such was the unshaken firmness of these troops that nothing could stop them; and the whole body of French cavalry was routed.'

Lord George Sackville, who had not only betrayed the infantry but had also not given his cavalry a chance to shine, was sent home and court-martialled. He was pronounced 'unfit to serve the King in any military capacity whatsoever', but the oddest things have happened to the British Army, and Sackville was one of them: he turned up again as Secretary of State for War and in this capacity mismanged the American Colonies campaign for the next reign.

In the middle of July the following year it was the cavalry's turn to perform spectacularly, with Eliott's Light Horse – the 15th Light Dragoons – capturing the limelight. One of the youngest English soldiers ever to go to war fought with this regiment. He was Cornet John Floyd, who was commissioned at the age of 12. He joined his regiment a month before it sailed for Germany. His father, Captain John Floyd of the 1st Dragoon Guards, had fought at Minden in 1759 and had died from wounds received in the battle. Captain Floyd entrusted his son to the Earl of Pembroke and it was through the earl's patronage that he was granted a commission.

Eliott's Light Horse was a remarkable regiment. With more troops needed, the War Office had asked Colonel George Eliott to raise a light regiment of dragoons. At that time there was unemployment in the tailoring trade and a number of clothiers had come to London to present a petition to parliament about their grievances. Nearly all of these men found their way into Eliott's regiment.

On a July morning as the regiment faced the French at Emsdorff Major Erskine ordered every man to place an oak twig in his helmet. 'Remember the English oak,' he said. 'The English oak and all its qualities.'

Then the regiment charged – young John Floyd with them.

They pierced the French lines at least three times, chased some units fifteen miles and compelled their surrender – one of the most outstanding feats in cavalry history. John Floyd's horse was shot from under him and he lay on the ground about to be sabred by a French dragoon when he was rescued by Captain Ainslie. After the fight John was presented with a French sabre in memory of his first battle.*

At Dettingen, Fontenoy and Minden the army had proved itself and for once the public responded. The traditional, unreasoning hatred for a standing army began to dim. The public openly showed a little more sympathy for the discharged soldier – but only a little. Beggary was still the sole means of survival for old soldiers, apart from those supported by Chelsea Hospital. Some of them became professional war raconteurs, telling their stories in taverns for an ale or a meal. Battle stories went down very well in country villages, where nobody could read and where people spent all their lives in a square mile of countryside.

The army's own better spirit stirred. One sign of this was the change in the nomenclature of regiments, which until now had been known by the name of their respective commanders. Now numerical titles were adopted and the numbers appeared on the men's buttons. This was a step towards pride of regiment.

A better type of officer appeared, because the more useless officers had disappeared during the harsh war years, but punishment was still brutal. Despite it or because of it the troops remained steady in battle and able to endure the extreme hardships of active service.

In 1760 'an old officer' published *Cautions and Advices to Officers of the Army* and said emphatically: '*Never beat your soldiers*: it is unmanly. To see as I too often have done, a brave, honest old soldier, battered and banged at the caprice and whim of an arrogant officer, is really shocking

---

* Floyd had a brilliant career in India and played an outstanding part in the fight against the notorious Tippoo Sahib. In a battle against Tippoo a musket ball penetrated his cheek and lodged in the back of his neck; it remained there until Floyd's death. He became a general in 1812, a baronet in 1816.

to humanity: and I never saw such scenes, but it brought to my remembrance the saying of a general, who seeing a young officer, perhaps the day after his joining his regiment, threshing an *old soldier*, very probably for no other cause but to shew his authority, or to look big in the sight of those who came to see him mount his first guard, called out to him, 'That is well done, Sir, beat the dog; thresh him: for you know he *dare not* strike again.'

One compensation – though an uncertain one – was the chance of prize money, though so far as Tommy Atkins was concerned it could amount to little. During the Seven Years War a payment-for-trophies system operated for a time. After Havana was capured from the Spaniards in 1762 the troops collected arms, ammunition, stores, merchandise and treasure and the proceeds were divided thus:

Commander-in-Chief	£122,697
Second-in-Command	£24,539
Major-Generals	£6,816
Brigadier-Generals	£1,947
Field Officers	£564 14*s* 1*d*
Captains	£126 4*s* 7½*d*
Lieutenants	£116 3*s* 0½*d*
Sergeants	£8 18*s* 8*d*
Corporals	£6 16*s* 6*d*
Privates	£4 1*s* 8¼*d*

But money was little use in the West Indies where health and hygiene had not appreciably improved. When the 31st Regiment was stationed at Pensacola in 1765 the regiment suffered so severely from yellow fever that sufficient men could not be found to carry their comrades to the grave. The men who attended funerals as mourners in the morning were often themselves buried in the evening. At one period, only one corporal and six privates could be mustered as fit for duty.*

* When the regiment returned to Gravesend in July 1797 its strength was only eighty-five NCOs and men.

However, in 1768 Sir John Pringle, Physician to Her Majesty, did his bit when he published his *Observations on Diseases of the Army.* Had this book of sound common sense been used as a guide it might well have resulted in better hygiene in barracks and camps and in the consequent saving of life, but Sir John was treated like all pioneers of progress in the British Army – he was read and ignored. Two centuries later some of his comments make interesting reading.

The mildness of our winters, and the little duty of our troops in time of peace, make exposition to cold less frequent at home. But in war, it is to be remembered what a change a soldier undergoes, from warm beds and the landlord's fireside in England, to cold barracks, scanty fuel and sharp winters in the Netherlands: and all this without any addition of clothes.

We are to observe that no orders will be able to restrain soldiers from eating and drinking what they like, if they have money to purchase it. Therefore a fundamental rule, and indeed almost the only needful, is to oblige men to eat in messes. . . . A soldier, in time of war, by the smallness of his pay is secured against excess in eating, the most common error in diet.

For inflammation of the eyes, prevalent in his day, Sir John advocated bleeding and blistering.

Blisters are usefully applied behind the ears, especially if they are to be continued for two or three days, and if the sores are afterwards kept running. . . . But what I have observed to be sometimes more efficacious is bleeding by leeches; when two or more are applied to the lower part of the orbit, or near the external angle of the eye, and the wounds allowed to ooze till they stop of themselves. Therefore in all greater inflammations, after bleeding in the arm or jugular, I have used this method, and repeated it more than once if required.

For inflammation as well as other troubles Sir John also advocated a 'brisk purge'. However, for all the medical ignorance of his era Sir John was in advance of his time. He pressed for better tents, more efficient sanitary arrangements, more hygiene, improved hospitals and more attention to personal cleanliness, among other things. He was quite frank:

> The *lues Venerea* and the itch are infections of a different kind. The first, not being more incident to soldiers than to other men, I shall pass over. But the latter, being so frequent in camp, barracks and hospitals, may be reckoned one of the military diseases.

Five

1771–1800
Very Active Service

There was always somebody trying to make the soldier's life even more difficult than it was. Among the chief tormentors were the officers who evolved the various parts of uniform which not only adorned the soldier but at times harassed him to distraction. There has rarely been a period in British Army history in which the majority of the men have been satisfied with their uniform. Surely not a single man could have approved the stock, the powdered hair and queue and the white breeches and gaiters. The stock, a high leather collar, was nothing more than an instrument of torture, for it cut into the neck and chin and prevented the soldier from bending his head. In hot weather it was abominably uncomfortable and in wet weather it successfully channelled water into the soldier's clothing.*

Tommy Atkins probably felt as plagued by his uniform as by the itch. What with one thing and another he needed two hours to prepare for parade. But he had gained ground on one point: the white breeches and gaiters had not lasted long and in 1767 they became black, which did not need so much bother to keep clean. Discomfort was acute. As Quartermaster

* This wretched thing survived until after the Crimean War. The Guards may have had something to do with its unlamented demise: At Varna in 1854 they appeared on the Queen's Birthday Parade without stocks, to the astonishment, distress and anger of the die-hards.

Anton wrote, everything was '. . . made so tight and braced up so firm that we almost stood like automata of wood, mechanically arranged for some exhibition on a large scale. To stoop was more than our small clothes were worth; buttons flying, knees bursting, back parts rending, and then the long heavy groan when we stood up, just like an old corpulent gouty man after stooping to lift his fallen crutch.'

The queue led to one regiment being called the 'Hard and Tights'.[†] The 'hard' and 'tight' referred to the colonel's instruction about the setting of the queue. It was said that he wished to make it impossible for a man to close his eyes when on guard. It was certainly true that there were times when nearly every soldier could not close his eyes because of the tightness of his queue. Still, some men – perhaps in other regiments – did go to sleep. Anton revealed that, 'It was no uncommon circumstance, when on the guard bench and asleep, to have rats and mice scrambling about our heads, eating the filthy stuff with which our hair was debaubed.'

Regulations prescribed a certain length and thickness for the queue, once the recruit had had time to grow it – sometimes twelve months. In some regiments a sergeant, under an officer's eye, would apply a gauge to check the dimensions. The best an offender could hope for would be an order to remove himself from parade to redress his hair while the worst would be a flogging. The powdering and arrangement of his hair and queue gave the soldier endless trouble before it was abolished in 1804, though the order was not fully implemented until 1814.[*]

And in this impossible outfit the men were not only expected to march and fight, but actually did march and fight. Truly their worst enemies were often not the French but their own superiors.

Uniforms and queues notwithstanding, the real trouble throughout the century was the soldier's meagre pay, for the men acutely resented the injustice of the various charges made

---

† I am unable to identify the regiment.
* Further details of the torture of the queue are given in the following chapter.

against it. Until 1771 5 per cent of a man's annual pay was deducted as a fee to the paymaster-general; a ½d a week went to the regimental surgeon and another ½d to the regimental agent. Dragoons had to pay a ½d a week to the riding master.

Careless critics of the British Army have often said that British arms fell to a low standard during the American War of Independence, but only in some ways is this correct. The commonly held idea that the Redcoats stupidly advanced shoulder to shoulder through forest to be picked off at will by concealed American sharpshooters – as Braddock had forced them to do in 1755 – is quite wrong. The case of the 17th Foot (later the Leicestershire Regiment) proves it wrong. In December 1776 George Washington was active near Princeton, where under cover of winter, darkness and Christmas festivities, he captured the 900 Hessian mercenaries who formed the British outpost line. Lord Cornwallis marched to take Trenton and sent to Princeton for reinforcements. But Washington was clever. Leaving his camp fires burning, he moved north to attack the British depot at Princeton. This was when he came into contact with the 17th, commanded by Lieutenant-Colonel Charles Mawhood, marching to help Cornwallis. The regiment's strength was 224 and they were outnumbered about twenty to one.

The American General Mercer, with, among other units, the Virginia Regiment, took up a defensive position in an orchard. The 17th attacked at once, disregarded the American fire, gave a British volley and followed it up with the bayonet. The Virginians broke and ran and the English troops followed them through the orchard, from the edge of which they saw the long column of Washington's main force. Washington got his men into battle order as the 17th fired volley after disciplined volley, causing great confusion. Washington knew that his men might break so he rode into the fight himself to steady the wavering line. When American artillery came up the small force of Englishmen were under fire from both flanks and front, and soon they were encircled. Major Staubenzee, now in command, decided to cut his way out to the rear. All but one officer and seventy men got clear – and most of these were wounded.

The Americans regarded the Battle of Princeton as a victory, with some justification. But the 17th did not regard it as a defeat, as they showed some years later in a recruiting poster, part of which read:

> 17th or Leicestershire Regiment
> The Heroes of Prince-town
> Who, alone, upon a former occasion fought a WHOLE ARMY, being at that time and since that period mostly compleated by GALLANT LEICESTERSHIRE MEN . . . no doubt but that the 17th or Leicestershire Regiment will again . . . defeat the enemies of our Good King and Old England.

The 15th Foot, the East Yorkshire Regiment, earned a nickname – The Snappers – during the American War of Independence. In 1776 this regiment was one of the first sent to North American to reinforce the garrison, and they took part in the Battle of Brandywine, where the Americans were so heavily defeated that a British force commanded by Lord Cornwallis was able to capture Philadelphia. During the fight the 15th's ammunition ran short while they were in heavy timber, with large numbers of enemy advancing. Told of the predicament, the CO said, 'Then snap, and be damned!'

In short, the regiment's best shots took all the ball ammunition, while everybody else 'snapped' – fired small blank charges of powder. As they fired they ran from tree to tree. The ruse – such initiative was rare in those days – held the enemy until British reinforcements came up.

The privations and discomforts which soldiers had to endure were legion. Their daily pay during the American War was about 6¾*d* and they had to obtain their 'necessaries' through the Quartermaster and Sergeant, at an extortionate rate and of inferior quality.

When the men were billeted in most cases they were put in garrets with an unglazed window, or in damp, foul cellars. There was a regiment in which, when stationed at Perth in Scotland, the men were under stoppages that left them with only 3*d* a day. Their breakfast was a half-penny roll and a half-penny worth of Suffolk cheese.

Hunger compelled the men to commit petty thefts which were frequently followed by severe punishments. Penny's *Traditions of Perth*, says it was not uncommon to see 'six or even ten of these unfortunate wretches suffer from 100 to 500 lashes each'. A soldier, who had a wife and four children, stole a few potatoes from a field. He was tried, and sentenced to receive 500 lashes. Seven men were brought out for punishment the same evening and several of them were tied up before this man. Some 'cried out terribly, which greatly roused the feelings of the multitude'. When it came to the soldier's turn, he bore the first part of his punishment stoically, then his cries were loud and piercing. His wife set down her baby, rushed into the square, and grabbed the hand of the drummer carrying out the flogging. She was seized and dragged away screaming. 'This was the signal for the washerwomen, who, backed by the multitude, broke through the line, and liberated the prisoner. Most of the officers escaped unhurt; not so the Adjutant, for he was laid on his belly, in which position he was held by some scores of vigorous hands, till he got a handsome flogging on the bare posteriors, in the presence of thousands, inflicted with an energy that would remain imprinted on his memory till the day of his death.'*

At this time, 1777, Chelsea Hospital could accommodate relatively few of the men entitled to its 'charity', so there were many 'out-pensioners', as they were called, who lived in their home towns or villages. Each out-pensioner was paid £7 12*s* 6*d* a year and this was a great assistance to recruiting. It was considered, Charles Grose said,† 'particularly in the North as a comfortable provision for old age, which every man might obtain by twenty years' faithful service. But an injudicious piece of economy put in practice about 1777, has taken away much of its attraction; this was a general call on all out-pensions whatsoever, without any exception to want of limbs, or extreme old age.'

* Penny's *Traditions of Perth*.
† In his *Military Antiquities*, 1801.

64

These men were ordered to assemble as the chief towns of their respective counties for possible re-induction into the army. Many of them came thirty and even forty miles from their homes and had to go so deeply into debt to do it that they became beggars the remainder of their lives. Those who could not walk, or had no legs, came in carts, wheelbarrows and donkeys, begging through every village they passed. At their rendezvous they were given neither money nor rations nor quarters. 'They were literally dying for want in the streets,' Grose said. 'After being examined by field officers appointed for that purpose, a very few were found in any way fit for service, and indeed most of those (who were found fit) were discharged by the commanding officers of the regiments to which they were sent. The remainder were dismissed to get home as they could, without subsistence, exhibiting such a picture of military misery as cannot be described, but which gave a wound to recruiting that will not soon be healed. . . .'

This sort of treatment to old soldiers certainly did not exactly encourage men to join the Army and in 1779 yet another recruiting act was passed. This one authorized the enlisting of vagabonds, thieves and many other undesirables, including cripples. Pushed into regiments near London, these men answered roll call for only a few weeks before they nearly all deserted. This was due not so much to their own dislike of army life, as of the dislike of the steadier, professional soldier for *them*. The unwanted recruits were virtually forced to desert. Often they could choose between starvation and desertion. In Ireland during the 1780s one-sixth of the army was made up of deserters; special depots were set up to receive arrested deserters, who were sent in companies to foreign stations. The 60th Royal American Regiment, later the King's Royal Rifle Corps, was formed almost wholly from deserters and foreigners, mostly Germans. Yet the regiment prospered. Fortescue wrote: 'Nothing is more remarkable than the splendid record of this regiment in the field, at a time when few soldiers entered it untainted by crime.'

Elsewhere at this time other English soldiers were seeing some very active service – and none more hectic than on

Gibraltar, which the Spaniards were besieging. Samuel Ancell of the 58th Regiment who served throughout the siege, 1779–83, wrote to his brother:

I cannot, dear Brother, omit penning an entertaining conversation I had with a soldier in Irish Town yesterday. I met Jack Careless in the street, singing with uncommon glee (notwithstanding the enemy were firing with prodigious warmth), part of the old song,

> 'A soldier's life, is a merry life,
> 'From care and trouble Free.'

He ran to me with eagerness, and presenting his bottle cry'd, 'D—m me, if I don't like fighting: I'd like to be ever tanning the Dons: – Plenty of good liquor for carrying away – never was the price so cheap – fine stuff – enough to make a miser quit his gold.' 'Why, Jack,' says I, 'what have you been about?' With an arch grin, he replied, 'That would puzzle a Heathen philosopher, or yearly almanack-maker, to unriddle. I scarce know myself. I have been constantly on foot and watch, half-starved, and without money, facing a parcel of pitiful Spaniards. I have been fighting, wheeling, marching, and counter-marching; sometimes with a firelock, then a handspike, and now my bottle' (brandishing it in the air). 'I am so pleased with the melody of great guns, that I consider myself as a Roman General, gloriously fighting for my country's honour and liberty.' A shell that instant burst, a piece of which knocked the bottle out of his hand; with the greatest composure he replied (having first graced it with an oath), 'This is not any loss, I have found a whole cask of good luck,' and brought me to view his treasure. 'But, Jack,' says I, 'are you not thankful to God, for your preservation?' 'How do you mean?' he answered. 'Fine talking of God with a soldier, whose trade and occupation is cutting throats. Divinity and slaughter sound very well together, they jangle like a crack'd bell in the hand of a noisy crier: Our King is answerable to God for us. I fight for him. My religion consists of a firelock, open touch-hole, good flint, well rammed charge, and seventy rounds of powder and ball. This is my military creed. Come, comrade, drink success to the British Arms.'

India was another trouble spot of the period. One of England's most vicious enemies was Tippoo Sahib, son of Hyder Ali. In 1780 Hyder Ali's troops ambushed a small British force and butchered most of them on the spot, but kept alive fifty officers. Some were taken out that night and cut to pieces; seventeen others were poisoned. The CO, Colonel Bailey, knowing that his food was poisoned starved himself for several days, then in agony ate the food and died in even greater agony. Several officers were allowed to live, but were kept in chains for several years.

Just before the day of retribution, nineteen years later, Tippoo had twelve prisoners of the 33rd Regiment murdered – by strangling. Other English soldiers had nails driven into their skulls. Tippoo died in the British assault on his capital, Seringapatam. When his body was found it was buried – *with full military honours.* It really is no puzzle that other nations should be bewildered by English behaviour.

One of the most reliable witnesses we have for the life of a soldier at this time is Cobbett, who enlisted as a private in 1784 and years later won a seat in Parliament. Complaining of the impossibility of living on 'a miserable sixpence a day', Cobbett wrote: 'Judge of the quantity of food to sustain life in a lad of 16, and to enable him to exercise with a musket [it probably weighed nearly 11 lb] six to eight hours a day. . . . I have seen them [his comrades] lay in their berths, many and many a time, actually crying on account of hunger. The whole week's food was not a bit too much for one day.'

Before he could think about buying food, the soldier had to pay for washing, mending, soap, flour for hair-powder, shoes, stockings, shirts, stocks and gaiters, pipe-clay and much else.

Cobbett had a genuine appreciation of soldiers. 'I like soldiers, as a class in life, better than any other description of men. Their conversation is more pleasing to me; they have generally seen more than other men; they have less of vulgar prejudice about them. Amongst soldiers, less than amongst any other description of men, have I observed the vices of lying and hypocrisy.'

In the year in which Cobbett joined the West Norfolk Regiment the Lord George Gordon riots in London showed that police duties – to which Tommy Atkins was liable – could be almost as dangerous as active service abroad. At home the troops were expected to maintain law and order and this, naturally enough, did not endear them to the general public. However, no other suitable force was available for keeping the peace. At times thousands of men were kept busy – and incidentally kept away from their army training – chasing or trying to trap smugglers. The revenue officers were quite unable to cope with smuggling, so cavalry and infantry detachments were scattered along the coasts. When troops were used to put down industrial unrest and riots their position became more unenviable. To the more militant among the populace soldiers were no longer protectors but oppressors.

The daily life of the soldier began to change in 1792 when barracks were ordered. This move had met with great resistance. In 1786 when Pitt had urged the building of complex military works, including barracks, as a defence measure against the French threat, the outcry was shrill and instantaneous. Pitt's opponents said such a move was not financially justified; it would mean increasing the standing army (the old hatred coming out again); it would lead to financial restrictions being imposed on the navy 'the great foundation of our strength, our glory and of our characteristic superiority over the rest of Europe'. In short, most people could see little glory in the army. But as an invasion appeared to become imminent the tune changed and barracks were built.

In 1792, too, there was a slight improvement with the granting of 1½d a day 'bread allowance.'

In the war-crowded years towards the end of the eighteenth century British troops were again in the Low Countries for the Netherlands campaign of 1793–5. Two brigades of infantry were sent hurriedly to Flanders, under the Duke of York, favourite son of George III. The troops fought a fine action at Lincelles, a small detachment beating a much larger French force. After this battle sergeants received one guinea prize money and privates 1s 9d. But this magnificent bounty did not make up for the lack of food, clothing and equipment, or for the incompetent leadership. After suffering 10,000 casualties, mostly from sickness and neglect, the Duke of York had to retreat. He retreated in later campaigns, too, inspiring the song:

> The Grand old Duke of York,
> He had ten thousand men,
> He marched them up to the top of the hill
> And he marched them down again.

The French troops fought to the tune of *Ça Ira*, a chant of liberty and as popular as the *Marseillaise*. Their drums sent the call all over the battlefield and the ragged Revolutionary troops were inspired by it. At a fierce engagement at Famars, when the French were winning, the colonel of the 14th, Welbore Ellis, was also inspired. 'Come on, boys!' he shouted, 'We'll beat them to their own damned tune! Drummers, strike up *Ça Ira*.' And as their drummers and fifers struck up the 14th attacked, Famars was captured and Valenciennes fell. Later the 14th – they became the West Yorkshire Regiment in 1881 – habitually marched past to their captured tune.

Sir Henry Bunbury has said that British military power was so weak in 1793 that its condition would be difficult to comprehend. He uses phrases like 'loose discipline . . . licentious violence . . . drunk and disorderly'.

In 1794 conditions were not much better, but British cavalry, supported by Austrian horsemen, fought three brilliant actions – at Villars-en-Cauchies, Beaumont and Villars. It may have been because of these actions that a definite rate was soon after fixed for trophies – £20 for a field gun, £10 for a pair of colours, £10 a tumbril, £12 a horse.

Major-General Craig explosively summed up the state of the army abroad that year in a letter to the War Office. 'That we are the most undisciplined, the most ignorant, the worst-provided army that ever took the field is . . . certain. But we are not to blame for it. . . . There is not a young man in the army that cares one farthing whether his commanding officer, his brigadier or the commander-in-chief himself approves of his conduct or not. His position depends not on their smiles or frowns – his friends can give him a thousand pounds and in a fortnight he becomes a captain. Out of the 15 regiments of cavalry and 26 of infantry which we have here 21 are literally commanded by boys or idiots – I have had the curiosity to count them over. . . . We have no discipline, we don't know how to post a picquet or instruct a sentinel in his duty, and as to moving, God forbid that we should attempt it within three miles of an enemy! . . . Plundering is beyond everything that I believe ever disgraced an army. . . .'

In contrast is the testimony of the Marquis of Anglesey (Lord Uxbridge) who noted that, 'Whenever danger was to be apprehended, and difficulties encountered, the 28th Regiment (Gloucestershires) was sure to be called upon. Whatever its difficulties, however it was harassed or distressed, the 28th always turned out stronger than any other corps. Hospitals were their aversion. Their home was their battalion, and they were never happy away from it. It was commonly said by commanding officers, that you might as well kill a man in the field as send him to a general hospital; he was at least lost to the battalion for the campaign. Not so the Twenty-eighth. These poor ragged fellows (for they had lost their clothing) whatever had been their casualties, were always crawling back to their home, their battalion. You saw them in small groups, deserting, as it were, from the hospital, helping each other along, half naked indeed, but always bringing with them their arms, and in high order. The locks were clean, the bayonet sharp.'

The 1793–5 Campaign was not entirely wasted. The young lieutenant-colonel of the 33rd Regiment did so well during the disastrous retreat that he was chosen to command the rearguard. His name was Arthur Wellesley, then aged 24, whom we shall meet again later in Iberia, where he became the Duke of Wellington.

The army was serving and fighting in many parts of the world. As the Netherlands Campaign was ending the 15th Regiment (East Yorkshires) was sent to the West Indies to help fight a negro insurrection. One hundred and two wives accompanied or followed their husbands. When the regiment returned hom a few years later only seven wives came back. Yellow Jack had killed the rest.

But some observers noted an improvement. That year Thomas Reide – in his *Military Discipline* – was able to note that 'a very great alteration has taken place within these last four or five years in the discipline of the British Army, which is now entirely modelled on that of the Prussian, as established by Frederick the Great . . . Major General David Dundas . . . compiled a set of movements and manoeuvres, principally from the writings of Prussian technicians, which he published in 1788. . . .'

But Prussian-type discipline was not enough and standards were still so low in 1799 that when Sir Ralph Abercromby took an expedtion to Flanders he left behind two regiments as they were 'unfit to appear in the presence of an enemy'. Ill-trained, worse led, half the force became casualties, mainly from sickness.

It was not surprising that the reputation of the English soldier sank very low in Europe and something remarkable was needed to restore it. Fortunately Abercromby rebuilt pride and confidence, during his Egyptian campaign in 1801, though he himself was mortally wounded. Too little is known about Abercromby, a fine soldier's soldier.

Tommy Atkins was paid a little more now, for in 1797 his daily pay had gone up to 1s and the Government undertook to pay any extra expense in cost of living. The undertaking was worthless – that 1s a day remained static for 94 years. Men certainly did not enlist in the expectation of living well on their pay. What brought many into the army was the bounty or signing-up fee. Usually it was four or five guineas, but as much as 14 guineas was paid to a dragoon recruit. The bounty was relatively good money, but few soldiers kept it intact or held it long enough to send it home to mother. All old soldiers – and a man could be an 'old' soldier in his twenties – saw a bounty as community property, to be borrowed from or boozed away until it vanished. While a recruit had any of his bounty left he also had many friends, including the sergeants who generally had a party evening at the new recruit's expense. There were 'friends' to clean his shoes and brush his clothes but when the money went he was abused as if he were at fault in not being able to make it go further.

The eighteenth century had been a hectic one for Tommy Atkins but despite some brilliant moments he reached the end of it without a high reputation as a soldier and without much hope for the future as far as his own life was concerned. He had shown on the Continent, in America, in the West Indies and in India that he could take punishment of one kind and another. He now suffered most from inept leadership at all levels. But two men were soon to be at work to put heart into common soldiers and a better system into the army. Tommy Atkins did not know it, but he did have some friends in high places.

Six

1800–8
'These Are Defects but he is a Valuable Soldier'

The two men who did most in this era to reform certain weaknesses in the British Army and to make better use of their human raw material were the Duke of York and Geneal Sir John Moore.

The Duke is best remembered for his deplorable generalship, when he should be noted for his great administrative ability. As commander-in-chief he was responsible for better accommodation, food, pay and dress. Moore was one of the most level-headed, intelligent and far-sighted generals who ever served Britain.

The Duke's contributions are not so spectacular as those of Moore, but they are none the less important. He could see that the Army was in poor state and he put his finger unerringly on the basic weakness – lack of discipline and training of the officers. At this time officers took leave practically whenever they felt like it – and for almost as long as they liked. The Duke forced all officers to apply for leave and to follow procedure in other respects as well. He brought in confidential reports on officers. This step was considered offensive and insulting. He made a point of meeting many officers and saw to it that they could approach him without difficulty. He put a stop to officers buying themselves into field rank before they had had some experience. No officer could become a major until he had served six years. The Duke took the revolutionary step of founding the Corps of Waggoners – the very first regular transport system in the British Army. And to sum up quickly, he started a Chaplain-General's Department, the Adjutant-General's and Military Secretary's Department and initiated an Intelligence branch.

Pitt's barracks had been increasing all this time and it is not the Duke's fault that the whole business was mismanaged. True enough, by 1805, no fewer than 203 barracks with a total accommodation capacity of 17,000 cavalry and 146,000 infantry existed, but nobody had asked any private soldier what he expected of a barracks and the rash of barracks-building was notable for the remarkable scandals it caused.

Dragoons were accommodated eight to a room, the infantry twelve to a room – fixed figures although the size of rooms varied considerably. Regulations were blind-stupid. For instance, twelve infantrymen were permitted from ¾ lb to 1½ lb of candles a week, while eight dragoons were given 1½ lb to 2½ lb, depending on the size of the room. One roller-towel per week was considered adequate for the twelve infantrymen or the eight dragoons. Many men slept two to a bed, a practice, which, despite its shortcomings, was at least warmer than sleeping alone; the blanket allowance was two per man. Each room was allotted two large bowls, a beer-can and two tin mugs – again for twelve infantrymen or eight dragoons. Each man was given a small bowl and spoon. A small bowl was adequate, since there was never enough food to fill a large one.

Conditions, nevertheless, were better than on Gibraltar, where many barrck rooms were crowded with sixty or more men. As 'G.B.' wrote: 'This greatly destroys social comfort, for one or two individuals can molest all the rest so that select retired conversion cannot be enjoyed. Any thing of that kind is always ready to be interrupted by the vicious and ignorant, who scoff and gibe at what they do not understand. Among so many men, too, there will always be found some who take a malicious pleasure in making their neighbours unhappy. This, along with other things, induces those who have a little money, to spend the evening in the wine house with their more select companions. Different sorts of vermin are very plenty in the barracks; and it is the common excuse for drinking, that they cannot get a sound sleep unless they be half drunk.'*

In 1801 the Experimental Corps of Riflemen had been formed to test the Baker rifle. The unit prospered and in the following year the Corps, now numbered the 95th,[†] with the 43rd and 52nd Light Infantry, was built into a brigade. Sir John Moore took command of this brigade at Shorncliffe. The scope and influence of his work can be seen by Fortescue's opinion: 'No man, not Cromwell, not Marlborough, not Wellington, has set so strong a mark for good upon the British Army as John Moore.'

Moore was a firm but humane leader and among other things he managed to lessen the severity of discipline and confounded his critics by, at the same time, improving efficiency. Moore was ruthless with inefficient officers and weeded them out. He selected his regimental commanders for their qualities as professional soldiers, for Moore himself was a dedicated professional with little tolerance for those who saw an army rank merely as a social status.

Moore wanted soldiers able to move fast and with much more initiative and independence than was the case with men of ordinary regiments of the Line. For his Light Infantry regiments Moore demanded 'more powerful and active soldiers, fitted for complex duties'. They had to be sharpshooters, their manoeuvring had to show 'celerity and expertness' and they had to have all the order and cohesion of a 'firm battalion'. For the age Moore demanded what was virtually impossible – but his energy and spirit achieved it.

Moore took great pains to make the soldier understand what he was doing – and, just as important, to interest him in what he was doing. He achieved his first object by intelligent training and the second by kindly and considerate treatment.

---

* *Narrative of a Private Soldier in one of His Majesty's Regiments of Foot.*
† The 95th Rifles, the fifth corps to bear the number, is the only regular regiment of infantry never to have worn the red coat. Its soldiers wore a green jacket from the unit's inception. The other four 95th regiments all wore the red coat.

Moore believed that even a small formation could be trained to act efficiently. Flouting the traditional belief that a battalion was the only workable-in-action unit, Moore gave company commanders much more authority and trust. Of course, this applied only to his Light Division; many decades had to pass before his system came to be generally used, but such is army conservation. His methods, much criticized by conventional officers, would soon be vindicated in battle.

Wellington was at this time (1803) in India, also learning lessons. One of them was the value of swift marching. His force was forty miles from Poona when he heard that Indian mutineers intended to set fire to the city on the approach of British troops. Although his men had already marched twenty miles under a broiling sun that day, the Duke set out that night with a small force of 400 troopers and a battalion of Infantry and reached the city undetected the following afternoon. Poona was saved. After the Battle of Assaye that year the Duke marched his men for sixty miles across rough country and in intense heat in thirty hours, including a ten-hour halt.

In 1804 the *Britannic Magazine* published 'The Soldier's Alphabet', a piece of doggerel verse revealing in its lines. It seems to have been fairly popular at the time.

A stands for ATTENTION, the first word he knows,
And B stands for BULLET, to tickle his foes,
C stands for a CHARGE, which the Frenchman all dread;
And D stands for DISCHARGE, which soon lays them dead.
Next, E brings EASE, at which sometimes he stands;
and F bids to FIGHT, when our enemy lands.
G stands for GENERAL, GRAPESHOT, and GUN,
Which together combin'd must make Buonaparte run.
Then H begins HONOUR, to soldiers full dear;
And J stands for JUSTICE, which next they revere.
But K bids them KILL, for their country and King,
For whose health each true Briton doth joyfully sing.
L is LOVE, which the soldier will ofentimes feel
And M bids him MERCY, when conqu'ror, to deal.
N stands for a NATION, of Englishmen free;
And O for an OUTPOST – but ours is the sea.

The P stands for PICKET, and for PIONEER;
And Q shews our enemies QUAKING with fear.
Next R stands for REGIMENT and ROLL of the drums;
And S for SALUTE when the general comes.
So T both for TOUCH-HOLE and TRIGGER may stand:
And V for the brave VOLUNTEER of this land.
Then W whispers that WAR will soon cease;
And X, Y and Z will rejoice at the peace.

'S' might with more justice have stood for SICKNESS rather than SALUTE. On 13 March 1804 – about the time the Alphabet appeared – a grenadier company of the 19th Regiment (the Green Howards) marched from Colombo to Cattadinia, a small post in the interior of Ceylon – three officers and seventy-five men, all strong and healthy and aged between eighteen and twenty-three. By the end of the month one officer and two privates were alive; all the others were dead from disease. (Yet the 19th survived, as a regiment, for twenty-four long years in Ceylon.)

That same year Robert Jackson, M.D., Inspector-General of Army Hospitals, published a much more searching and critical account of Britain, its population and its soldiers. Forty-one years later he published another edition of his book, significantly without finding it necessary to make amendments to his views, some of which are interesting and provocative especially as he is describing the men who fought with Moore and Wellington.

He saw England as 'the gathering place of adventurers and the asylum of the destitute . . . and the people who dwell in it a mixture of all the nations of Europe.'

He tried hard to sketch what he called 'the national military character', by an analysis of the ordinary English civilian – which seems to me a valid approach. Jackson found the English peasant 'bold and confident, open and blunt, apparently sincere, sometimes generous, often rude, boisterous and overbearing, rarely gracious and courteous to strangers . . . little disposed to form personal attachment from pure love . . . arrogant when he possesses money, abject when he is without it . . . proud of his nation, contemptuous of others. He is rude, but not cruel or vindictive and he rarely ill-treats an enemy after the chance of war, or any other chance, has brought him within his power.'

This is a remarkably fair and balanced judgement, on which Jackson expounds as he follows the peasant into the army as a recruit 'with a balance of advantages'. The new soldier, Jackson says, is

. . . well made with strong, thick and browny arms. The trunk is particularly ponderous and the balance of power is conspicuously in the upper extremities. . . .* As a labourer he does not endure toil, or bear hardship or privation with the same cheerfulness as the peasants of many other countries. . . .

The artizan is of less physical force than the labourer, usually of inferior size, of a less florid complexion, a less comely and pleasing aspect, more alert in movement, more dexterous in manual operation, and as such more easily trained to military evolution.

There are differences; but . . . steady courage, actual force, and promptitude in applying force to the proper point of attack, belong to all. These properties are military properties; and it cannot be denied that the part of the army, which is recruited in England, stands on fair ground in this respect with its other parts – on advantageous ground with the military materials of most nations.

Military service does not bring distinction in England as it does in many parts of Europe; and, as the profession of arms is not here held in the first estimation, the better class of the peasantry do not leave the plough or the shuttle for the sword; consequently the recruits of infantry regiments are not on a level with the mass of the nation. They are often drawn from the refuse of manufacturing towns; for instance, from destitute workmen, who enrol themselves in the army through necessity or want of bread, not in love of arms.

---

* A recruit's minimum height has varied greatly. When Jackson was writing it was 5ft 7in, in 1813, 5ft 3in and in 1900, 5ft 4in.

Manufacturers are often dissipated[†] and effeminate, inferior in good qualities to the common standard of the country; the military character of the British nation is not therefore fairly judged as estimated by the qualities of recruits who may be drawn from the refuse of its population.

The ranks are thus filled with men; they are not filled with soldiers, for we do not admit those to be soldiers who have no higher motive to induce them to assume the soldier's garb than a pecuniary bribe, as instigation of vanity, or a necessity arising from want of bread; and, as the mass of English recruits consists of such, its military character is not what it might be, that is, not on a level with the bulk of the nation.

It must still be allowed that the English officer and the English soldier uniformly maintain a national character in the conflicts of war. They display a cool and deliberate courage in battle, decision in difficulty and exertion in danger, equalled by few and surpassed by none. This is true in itself; but it may be added at the same time, that the spirit of enthusiasm, which stimulates to the enterprise of hazardous acts, is not, as things now stand, a prominent feature of the English Army. . . .

The English soldier is not impetuous to the same extent as the soldiers of some countries; but he is courageous and determined as any, and he has this advantage, that he ordinarily retains command of himself, so that if he does not succeed in his purpose he retires from it, defeated, not routed. He performs his duties with correctness; but he performs them as duties which are not to exceed a certain limit; there is in fact something like discretion – a bargain with himself in all his acts. He is capable of attachment, not susceptible of enthusiastic devotion. . . .

---

† Such as those whom Thomas Jackson enlisted in 1803, in a regiment he called 'The King's Own, Stafford'. He marched with 300 volunteers from Windsor to Winchester. '. . . Every man drunk every day, every night; all command was lost; such a sight, perhaps, was never seen; three hundred soldiers, mostly mad drunk. They would march how they liked, and when they liked, and here and there stop and fight a battle on the road.' *The Eventful Life of Thomas Jackson*, Birmingham, 1847.

He expects to find a reason for his attachment connected with something that applies to himself. He thus, even as a soldier, retains the base of the national character, namely, a spirit of independence, that is, a power to dispose of himself according to his own way of thinking – and necessarily connected with his real or supposed advantage.

Military enthusiasm does not, as already observed, rise high in the English army. The expression of ardour beyond literal duty is ridiculed rather than encouraged by superiors; and, if not encouraged by approbation, or stimulated by reward, it is not likely to exist; for few objects come under the eye of the peasant in early life which have a tendency to inspire romantic sentiments of chivalry. The labourer performs his labour on a given condition, and after a regular routine. He works for hire, and has little interest in the work which he performs. . . . The phantom of military glory has no artificial food; and, if the love of gain, or casual necessity, did not operate on the peasant class, it is reasonable to believe that English volunteers for military service would actually be few in number. The return of a soldier to his native home, though covered with what are called honourable wounds gained in glorious battles, did not make an impression on vulgar opinion, so as to incite the youth of the neighbourhood to volunteer military service. It was thus little to be expected that the English peasant should be of a direct military caste.

It is notwithstanding true that he possesses qualities which give him advantages in war, and which contribute materially to beget coolness, self-command, and resolution in action, which the peasant of few nations possesses in an equal degree. An Englishman is accustomed from early youth to enter the lists of combat without what may be called personal enmity. He contends until he is overpowered; he gives in when he discovers his inferiority – and he does so without the sensation of shame and confusion which is manifested by his northern neighbour [the Scots] under similar discomfiture. This practice in trial of strength, without passion or enmity, is almost peculiar to the people of England; and to this, perhaps, may be ascribed that good sense and self-command which gives up a contest in the more serious conflicts of war, without feeling or manifesting such vexation and despair as create confusion and lead to total rout.

The English soldier has thus a cool and determined courage, either natural, or artificially acquired by habit; and, possessing this quality, he possesses a valuable property for the practice of common warfare. In point of intelligence, he is inferior to many, and, though powerful in actual force, he is not, as already said, hardy in bodily constitution. He is accustomed to full living at his home; and, as he expects a certain condition of things to be present in war as well as in peace, he does not submit to privation without murmur; nor does he endure toil, even when inevitable as a part of his duty, with cheerfulness. These are defects; but, with these defects, he is a valuable soldier, he is honest and manly in sentiment, cool in action, and firm in courage. On these qualities dependence may be placed; and though they are not all the qualities which a soldier ought to possess, they are of great value to generals who conduct extensive military operations.'

As we shall see, these qualities were of great value indeed to a number of generals conducting both extensive and intensive military operations.

It is now necessary to retreat a little in time – to the year 1795 when John Shipp joined the army. Shipp is important to any study of the British soldier, mainly because he left some memoirs of his chequered career. This began one winter's day when young Master Shipp, an orphan, was working in a farm field. A parish officer came up to him and said, 'Shipp, I have frequently heard of, and observed your great wish to go for a soldier.' If this was so, the officer said, the parish would rig him out decently and he would take him to Colchester. In these early days of the French Revolutionary Wars recruits were difficult to come by.

Three regiments, the 22nd 34th, and 65th, were almost skeletons from disease mortality in the West Indies and they were ordered to be completed to 1,000 rank and file by enlisting boys of from 10 to 16 years of age. This measure was taken partly as a recruiting experiment, partly to relieve parishes of the burden of supporting pauper boys. The regiments concerned were called 'Boy Regiments'. It was believed that by sending these battalions to the Cape of Good Hope they would become acclimatized and better able to stand service in India than recruits sent direct from England. Though the bulk of the rank and file consisted of these boys there was a backbone of trained soldiers. The boys were drilled, armed and treated like adult soldiers.

'My little heart was in my mouth,' Shipp wrote of his enlistment. 'I repeated the parish officer's words "Willing to go!" and eagerly assured him of the rapture with which I accepted his offer. The affair was soon concluded so down went my shovel, and off I marched, whistling, "See, the Conquering Hero Comes".' The conquering hero was only ten years old.

He felt very unheroic his first morning in barracks, despite his red jacket, red waistcoat, red pantaloons and red forage cap. He was very tall for his age, but the clothes were much too large and his sleeves were two or three inches over his fingers. His head was shaved nearly bald, too, except for a small patch behind, from which he would have to grow his queue. Shipp was mercilessly subjected to banter and abuse and before long another boy tried to tweak his nose. Shipp, quivering with anger, told him that if he touched him he would knock him down. This brought all the boys around, shouting 'Well done, Johnny Raw!'; Well done, old leather-breeches!' and 'That's right, Johnny Wapstraw!'

When Shipp did not strike the first blow his tormentor called him a coward. This was too much; Shipp hit him and the two fought hard for six rounds, after which the other boy gave in. Shipp later wrote the best account of the operation of having his hair tied for the first time.

A large piece of candle-grease was applied, first to the sides of my head, then to the hind long hair. After this, the same kind of operation was performed with nasty stinking soap – sometimes the man who was dressing me applying his knuckles instead of the soap, to the delight of the surrounding boys, who were bursting their sides with laughter to see the tears rolling down my cheeks. When this operation was over I had to go through one of a more serious nature. A large pad, or bag filled with sand, was poked into the back of my head, round which the hair was gathered tight, and the whole tied around with a leather thong. When I was dressed for parade I could scarcely get my eyelids to perform their office; the skin of my eyes and face was drawn so tight by the plug . . . that I could not possibly shut my eyes. And to this an enormous high stock [collar] was poked under my chin, so that I felt as stiff as if I had swallowed a ramrod. Shortly after I was thus equipped dinner was served, but my poor jaws refused to act on the offensive, and when I made an attempt to eat, my pad went up and down like a sledge hammer.

When only 15 Shipp was tried by regimental court-martial for desertion and sentenced to 999 lashes, but this brutal punishment was cancelled by his humane CO Not all boys were so fortunate. He was one of the stormers of the capture of Deig, India, in December 1804 and as a sergeant he led the forlorn-hope storming column in three out of the four desperate but unsuccessful attacks on Bhurtpore in January–February 1805.

Late he wrote:

A strong fortress is about to be stormed. An officer or an NCO steps forward as a candidate to lead 12 volunteers to lead the column of the attack . . . to stand the torment of shot, shell, rocket, explosion and hoist Old England's banner on the highest pinnacle of glory.

All eyes are upon you. If you escape, attribute the cause to Him alone who could shield you from such dangers. It is a post of honour, a station that places upon your brow laurels that never fade. But, believe me, the situation with all its honours is not enviable. There is, however, when performing this service, an heroic ardour, a nobleness of soul that carries and impels you to complete the noble task. And when your duty is done you have but an imperfect recollection of the perils you have encountered, the dangers you have escaped.

Where one escapes, hundreds fall. When I led the three forlorn hopes at Bhurtpore all were killed save myself and one other man.

Shipp was unusually lucky. Not only did he survive he was also commissioned and was presented with two camels, a horse and a tent. It would have seemed a generous reward to him.

He sold his commission in 1808, but found the call of the army too strong and re-enlisted. Again he rose from the ranks to win a commission. This double-commissioning by the time Shipp was thirty was an achievement unique in the annals of the British Army.

In Shipp's day the best recruits were employed on the Continent, and the gaols were often combed to find men for India, especially for those in the Honourable East India Company's service. 'In India the troops experienced little kindness or cordiality at the hands of their officers: they were treated as a caste of inferior character. The 'European pariah' was the designation they consequently obtained from the observant Hindoos.'* From the hour of their arrival in India, nobody gave a damn about the soldiers' health or morals. For three days after the arrival of a regiment, or a batch of recruits, they had permission to run riot in the bazaars, and they made full use of the licence. Wild scenes of drunkenness, often accompanied by violence to the natives, were frequent. The authorities considered that a blow-out was a necessary indulgence after the five or six months of confinement to which the troops had been subjected on the voyage to India.

'In the three days' terrible saturnalia the seeds of mortal diseases were laid, and numbers of the men only emerged from the debauch to be conveyed to the hospitals of the garrison, whence they were rarely removed alive.'†

Such debaucheries were not, as a rule, permitted in Europe but they did, on occasions, mar the good name of Tommy

* Stocqueler.
† Stocqueler.

Atkins. In 1806 he added laurels to his name and vindicated Sir John Moore's methods in the process when he won a battle at Maida, in southern Italy. Heavily outnumbered by French columns, the little British force formed double line, stood steady and by controlled fire followed by a bayonet charge routed the French in what Colonel de Watteville calls 'that scintillating little victory'.

The triumph at Maida, minor though it was, pointed the way towards Tommy's battle discipline in Iberia, where Britain became involved in war in 1808. In some ways the soldiers who fought in Spain and Portugal were the most interesting and successful that Britain ever sent abroad, so it is enlightening to read W.H. Fitchett's picture of the Tommy of the Peninsula as 'stocky in body, stubborn in temper, untaught and primitive in nature. With no apparent education, his horizon was limited but his endurance was limitless. Laden like a donkey, with shoddy ill-fitting boots and half-filled stomach he toiled on with dogged courage until his brain reeled. His vices, like his virtues, were primitive.' Colonel Colborne, who commanded the 52nd – one of the finest units – believed that even at the end of the war every regiment had from 50 to 100 bad characters that no discipline or punishment could improve. This, he said, was due to a hopelessly bad recruiting system.

In the winter of that first year on the Peninsula British soldiers experienced the misery of a cold retreat through difficult country. Circumstances obliged Moore to pull back to Corunna in north-west Spain. He realized that only by rapid marching could he save his troops from dying of hunger and cold in the mountains of Galicia. But the troops resented having to retreat and at such a pace and this, coupled with poor discipline in some units, compounded the hardships. The French killed or took many stragglers and only a fine rearguard action handled by a tough officer, Robert Craufurd, prevented the French from swamping the British rear. On 11 January the starving, ragged army reached Corunna.

Rifleman Harris was convinced that many casualties could have been avoided but for 'the infernal load we carried on our backs. The weight I myself toiled under was tremendous, and I often wonder at the strength I possessed at this period, which enabled me to endure it; for, indeed, I am convinced that many of our infantry sank and died under the weight of their knapsacks alone. For my own part, I marched under a weight sufficient to impede the free motions of a donkey; for besides my well-fitted kit, there was the greatcoat rolled on its top, my blanket and camp kettle, my haversack, stuffed full of leather for repairing the men's shoes, together with a hammer and other tools (the lapstone I took the liberty of flinging to the devil), ship-biscuit and beef for three days. I also carried my canteen filled with water, my hatchet and rifle, and eighty rounds of ball cartridge in my pouch.'

Moore was mortally wounded at Corunna. Also wounded was Samuel Evans, a private in the grenadier company of the 2nd Foot. Taken to England, he died on 30 January in the military hospital at Plymouth. A post mortem disclosed that Evans had been shot through the heart, but had survived sixteen days. His heart was for many years preserved in the hospital. We shall see other examples of astonishing staying power.

Not that all soldiers were prepared to endure, soldier on no matter what. Sir Charles Napier tells of a soldier of the 28th Regiment who, in that first year on the Peninsula, taught his comrades to produce artificial ophthalmia by holding their eyelids open while another man scraped some lime from the barrack ceiling into their eyes.

Wellington (still Wellesley) was about to take chief command in the Peninsula, but he was deprived of 40,000 men who should have been serving in the Peninsula by the imbecile Walcheren Expedition of 1809. The object of the expedition was to attack Antwerp, but for eight weeks the troops were kept on unhealthy Walcheren Island in Zeeland. The military commander, Lord Chatham, and the naval commander, Sir Richard Strachan, were a dull, hesitant, incompetent pair. While they dithered 7,000 men died; another 14,000 had their health permanently ruined and many thousands more were ill, mostly from malaria. Only 217 were killed in action. While dying the men were given no attention and little to eat. Sick men were expendable. Truly Tommy Atkins's leaders have sinned against him wickedly.

Seven

1808–15(1)
Iron Men of the Peninsula

The object of any army in the field is to kill the enemy and win battles. Wellington's men in the Peninsula did both effectively, but before we study any specific battle it is more important to know what these men were like, how they lived from day to day, how they were fed, what they endured. They endured much.

An interesting subject for debate would be 'Did Wellington succeed in the Peninsula because of his soldiers or despite them?' He himself seems to have believed that he triumphed despite 'the scum' he had the misfortune to lead.

Years later, he told a Royal Commission set up to inquire into flogging, 'They [English soldiers] are the scum of the earth. . . . [They] are fellows who have enlisted for drink. . . . I have no idea of any great effect being produced on British soldiers by anything but the fear of immediate corporal punishment.'

In view of the Iron Duke's assessment of his men it is all the more interesting to see what they did for him in the Peninsular War and at Waterloo. He did little for them; he even opposed, many years later, the idea that the survivors o fthe Peninsular War be given campaign medals. Naturally, he himself had medals.

Writing a dispatch to Lord Castlereagh, Secretary of State for War, on 17 June 1809, two months after he had arrived in Lisbon, Wellington said, 'It is impossible to describe to you the irregularities and outrages committed by the troops . . . there is not an outrage of any description which has not been committed on a people who have received us as friends by soldiers who never yet for one moment suffered the slightest want or the smallest privation. . . . We are an excellent army on parade, an excellent one to fight, but we are worse than an enemy in a country.' And a few months later, 'I really believe that more plunder and outrage have been committed by this army than by any other that was ever in the field.'

The plundering urge of the British private was not restricted to his enemies or to friendly civilians, as Rifleman Harris revealed. Serving with the Rifles was an officer named, so Harris thought, Cardo, 'a great beau and although rather effeminate . . . a most gallant officer.' Cardo was killed in action in the Pyrenees and a rifleman, named Orr, saw on his finger a ring well known in the regiment to be worth 150 guineas. The ring was so tightly in place that it could not be wrenched loose, so Orr cut off the finger at the joint. After the battle Orr offered the ring for sale among the officers, who were incensed and had him court-martialled. He received 500 lashes on the spot.

A biographer of Wellington, Godfrey Davies, would have us believe that Wellington 'did his best to see that the men were not unnecessarily fatigued or tried beyond their strength'. But the British soldier at this period was often fatigued and tried byond his strength, sometimes necessarily so, war being what it is. For the first four years on the Peninsula they had no tents! The First Battalion the 52nd Regiment lost 2,750 men between 1806 and 1816, out of a strength of about 10,000. And this was a seasoned, well-led unit.

In a dispatch to his brother on 8 August 1809, Wellington wrote, 'A starving army is actually worse than none. The soldiers lose their discipline and their spirit. . . . The officers are discontented and are almost as bad as the men; and with the army which a fortnight ago beat double their numbers [at Talavera*] I should now hesitate to meet a French corps of half their strength.'

---

* The Rifle Brigade marched fifty-two miles in twenty-four hours to take part in the Battle of Talavera.

Generally, one gets the strong impression that Wellington was not popular with the common soldier; certainly he did not court popularity and he was incapable of grand gesture, of being 'one of the boys'. But then this applied to any senior English officer. Costello (*Adventures of a Soldier*) shows that Wellington could, however, be human. Costello, wounded, was lying packed in a cart with other wounded when Wellington rode up. He sent an aide to bring other carts and bread and wine.

Despite all that was said against the common soldiers many references show that when billeted in occupied houses they behaved themselves and, as always, made pets of the children. The unknown author of *Journal of a Soldier* taught the children of a Spanish family to read. Others, hungry though they often were, would give food to their Spanish hosts. Behaviour like this makes the savage sacking of San Sebastian and Badajoz (discussed later) all the more vicious.

There was much to be said in mitigation of the soldier's offences or supposed offences and Joseph Donaldson (*The Eventful Life of a Soldier*) was one who said it.

The soldier . . . was one of the veriest slaves existing, obliged to rise two or three hours before day to commence his cleaning operations. His hair required to be soaped, floured, and frizzed, or tortured into some uncouth shape which gave him acute pain, and robbed him of all power of moving his head unless he brought his body round with it. He had his musket to burnish, his cap and cartridge box to polish with heel-ball, and his white breeches to pipe-clay, so that it generally required three or four hours hard labour to prepare him for parade; and when he turned out, he was like something made of glass, which the slightest accident might derange or break into pieces. He was then subjected to a rigid inspection, in which, if a single hair stood out of its place, extra guard, drill, or some other punishment, awaited him. When to this was added the supercilious tyrannical demeanour of his superiors, who seemed to look upon him as a brute animal who had neither soul nor feeling, and who caned or flogged him without mercy for the slightest offence, we cannot wonder that he became the debased being, in body and mind, which they already considered him, or that he possessed the common vices of a slave – fawning servility, duplicity, and want of all self-respect; to add to this, what was his reward when worn out and unfit for further service? – a pittance insufficient to support nature, or a pass to beg.

Donaldson painted a disagreeable portrait of men and officers. 'Blackguardism was fashionable, and even the youngest were led into scenes of low debauchery and drunkenness, by men advanced in years. Many of the officers, who, at least, ought to have been men of superior talents and education, seemed to be little better, if we were allowed to judge from the abominable oaths and scurrility which they used to those under their command, and the vexatious and overbearing tyranny of their conduct. . . .'

The brutality of some commanding officers was exemplified by Lieutenant-Colonel Royall, CO of the 61st. One incident in which he was concerned is sufficient. He had had Sergeant Andrew Pearson tried for some alleged offence, but the court-martial not only aquitted the sergeant but praised him. Royall read the verdict to the assembled regiment, then tore it to pieces and ground it into the dirt. He ordered the drum major to cut off all Pearson's badges and reduced him to the ranks.

'Now sir,' he said, 'I will let you and your friends know that I command this regiment. I will . . . make a public example of you at the first opportunity.' Treatment like this led to desertion, but later, according to Pearson's autobiography, the entire 61st Regiment signed a petition and had it presented to the Duke of York, who dismissed Royall. An arrant personal coward, Royall, when action was imminent, had the regimental surgeon 'recommend' that he retire to the rear because of 'ill health'.

The adjutant of another regiment, following his CO's lead, habitually roused out exhausted men at all hours of the night and would knock down the last man to reach his post. One soldier objected to this treatment, so the adjutant had him tied between two guns and left him there unattended for several days and nights.

Rifleman Harris went to some trouble in his *Recollections* to emphasize that relationships between men and officers were often amicable. 'Officers are commented upon and closely observed. The men are very proud of those who are brave in the field, and kind and considerate to the soldiers under them. An act of kindness done by an officer has often during the battle been the cause of his life being saved. I know from experience, that in our army the men like best to be officered by gentlemen, men whose education has rendered them more kind in manners than your coarse officer, sprung from obscure origin, and whose style is brutal and overbearing.'

Pay was often weeks or months in arrears. This was serious enough for many young officers; it was calamitous for private soldiers. They then had nothing to eat except their rations which were, in the Peninsula, a pound of meat, a pound of bread or biscuit (the term of the day for twice-baked bread) a pint of wine or a third of a pint of whisky. Rations often arrived just as the order was given to continue the march. The food was merely a hacked-off lump of meat, still bloody from the field butchery, together with hard biscuits. In a man's haversack the two often became worked into a mash, which must have been horrible to eat.

The meat could only be stewed and it was often tough; even Judge Advocate General Larpent wrote that it was like shoe-leather. It must be remembered, though, that most of the men ate as well as they would have done at home, and in some cases better.

The commissary department was for a long time inefficient and in its ranks were many rogues, guilty of peculation, misappropriation and criminal negligence. As in every war or campaign the men at the front received the poorest rations; everybody *en route* helped himself to what passed through his hands. Under Wellington's direct influence and with the honest and able efforts of the Commissary General, Robert Kennedy, matters did improve.

Besides their weapons, the marching infantry of the early nineteenth century carried their house on their back. In a man's knapsack were two pairs of shoes and an extra pair of soles and heels, spare socks and shirt, a greatcoat or blanket.

Strapped to the knapsack was a tin camp-kettle – one between six men and carried in turn. In the haversack, worn at the hip, were a clasp knife, fork, spoon, tin mug and other personal gear, and three days' ration in his pack; he had a tendancy to eat what he had and starve until the next issue. Even the Portuguese were trusted with six days' rations, while the French carried fifteen days' supply, though admittedly this was largely because they had no proper transport system.

The water bottle was filled and there were a hatchet, bayonet, musket and eighty rounds of ammunition. The total weight was appalling and, what was worse, it was awkwardly placed.

Water was always a problem; it was not chlorinated and nearly always men drank it unboiled, sometimes with frightful results.

At times not more than one biscuit was served out each day; we have the word of Costello of the 95th Regiment for this. So it was not surprising that groups of men rooted around the fields with their swords in the hope of finding potatoes or something else edible. The best prospect was to surprise the French; then the enemy usually abandoned some of his provisions.

A favourite topic of debate among soldiers was which was the worst soldiering season – winter or summer? Was it better to fry or freeze? Actually, their opinions were adjustable according to what they were suffering at the time of the discussion.

Amenities were non-existent; there was not even a tobacco ration. A private soldier was not supposed to need amenities – although officers usually dined well in comfortable quarters. Some of them needed a dozen horses to carry their gear, which on occasions included dressing-tables and easy chairs.

Home leave was practically unknown. Many a soldier served overseas from shortly after his enlistment until his retirement; an unbroken spell of ten years abroad was commonplace. If a married man was lucky he could take his wife with him on service – but as only five or six wives per company were allowed he had to be very lucky indeed. What these women endured and suffered cannot be imagined.

These incredible women were tough and loyal, despite their faults. Most of the wives tried to have a mug of tea ready for their men before they set off on a march. Then they would try to get ahead of the column so that they could have tea ready for the men when they came in. Many of them had donkeys and could move faster than the infantry, with whom they often became entangled. One irate provost marshal ordered the women to stay in the rear or he would shoot their donkeys. He carried out his threat when they persisted, but somehow – by getting more donkeys or finding a cart – the women were ahead next day.

The strength and endurance of some of the soldiers' wives would seem unbelievable were it not vouched for by reliable sources. On one occasion Dan Skiddy of the Rifle Brigade collapsed exhausted when on the march. His wife, Biddy, known throughout the brigade, dragged him to a bank and struggled to get him on to her shoulders. Then she carried her husband, with his rifle and knapsack, two miles to the regimental bivouac.

A fight was sometimes less arduous than a long march on which suffering could be extreme. Yet the infantry bore their hardships with, generally, uncomplaining stoicism.

During the Peninsular campaigns one officer wrote: 'I have often seen the blood soaking through the gaiters and over the heels of the soldiers' hardshoes, whitened with the dust.'

Many men left the ranks because they had no shoes and marched on the softer verge or in the fields. In the end so many shoeless men were out of the ranks that they were formed into detachments. Their feet were often a bloody mess, cut and bruised by stones, sticks and thorns. When bullocks were killed they were given the hides to make into rough moccasins.

Sweat-soaked, exhausted men would sometimes fall, to lie, conscious, but unable to summon another ounce of will. When a man was badly wounded, he usually lay in the field until he died; if he could walk he dragged himself to the rear, hoping to find a doctor to help him. Wounded men sometimes tramped for hundreds of miles under dreadful conditions.

During the Battle of Talavera a man of the 43rd was shot through the middle of the thigh, and lost his shoes in crossing the marshy stream. But he refused to quit the fight, limped under fire in the rear of his regiment, and with naked feet and streaming with blood from his wound, marched for several miles over a country covered with sharp flints.

In another action a private, William Dougald, was hit in the thigh by three spent balls in the course of five minutes; and although all of them were severe Dougald never quitted the field. A few days later another engagement with the French seemed inevitable, and Dougald, now so lame he could scarcely walk, was told he could to go the rear. 'No,' he said, 'I will rather die than leave my comrades.' With great pain and exertion he kept up with his company, reached the army and fought bravely. In fifteen minutes he had again been wounded, this time mortally.

Stocqueler recounts the extraordinary story of a trooper named Wilson 'the most quiet and inoffensive creature of the troop . . . remarkably sober' who was one of a cavalry screen protecting an infantry withdrawal. 'I saw him engaged hand to hand with a French dragoon; I saw him – for I was by this time disabled by a severe wound, and stretched at length beside others of my suffering comrades – give and receive more than one pass, with equal skill and courage. Just then, a French officer delivered a thrust at poor Harry Wilson's body, and delivered it effectually. I firmly believe that Wilson died on the instant; yet, though he felt the sword in its progress, he, with characteristic self-command, kept his eye still on the enemy in his front, and raising himself in his stirrups, let fall upon the Frenchman's helmet such a blow, that the brass and skull parted before it, and the man's head was cloven asunder to the chin. It was the most tremendous blow I ever saw struck; and both he who gave, and his opponent who received it, dropped dead together. The brass helmet was afterwards examined by order of an officer, who, as well as myself, was astonished at the exploit; and the cut was found to be as clean as if the sword had gone through a turnip, not so much as a dent being left on either side of it.'

Often, a man's sufferings only began when he was carried or when he staggered into the barn or church being used as a hospital. Here surgeons in shirt sleeves wielded saw and knife and probed with more enthusiasm than skill, amid a foul mess of blood, rags and dirt. Most surgeons were kind and well-meaning, but medical knowledge was faulty.

Less than 50 per cent of wounded could expect to survive gangrene, loss of blood or tetanus. Operations were performed without anaesthetic, hence surgical shock was severe and often fatal. The wonder of it is that any wounded man survived. Generally, the French did not rely on amputation as much as the British did.

Vinegar was the only antiseptic, disinfectant and dressing for wounds. Typhus, caused by lice, killed many soldiers who had survived wounds, while dysentery and ague (probably malaria) was common.

'G.B.', wounded in action in Egypt in 1801, suffered from infection after a musket ball had been extracted. The wound became inflamed, and his foot and ankle swelled considerably. 'I was suspicious that the dirty water with which it was sometimes washed was the occasion of the inflammation. An erroneous opinion was entertained, that salt water would smart the wounds; and as fresh water was not in plenty on board the ship, only a small quantity of it was allowed for washing them. *A great number of wounds were washed with one basin-full*,* and, as many of the wounds were foul, this was calculated to infect those that were clean. Had salt water been used, a basin of clean water might have been taken to every one.'

Cooper tells in his *Seven Campaigns* how he suffered from fever and dysentery at the close of 1809 and was taken to a convent where he was put in a corridor with about 200 others. 'My case was pitiable; my appetite and hearing gone; feet and legs like ice, three blisters on my back and feet unhealed and undressed; my shirt sticking in the wound caused by the blisters, my knapsack and necessaries lost; and worst of all, no one to care a straw for me.' At Elvas he was one of twenty men put into a room with no ventilation; eighteen died.

Somehow surviving, Cooper was moved to another hospital, but it was so crowded he was accommodated in the charnel house. At Celerico he was squashed into another crowded room. At no time did he see soap or towel and he existed on biscuit, salt pork and wine.

* Author's italics.

True, Wellington, unlike many other commanders, saw that if a sick, injured or wounded man could be returned to fitness he could also return to the line. In the Peninsular War two notable doctors served with him – Sir James McGrigor, the Inspector-General of Hospitals and James Guthrie, a great surgeon of the day. With their help Wellington organized a medical system, which, though far from ideal was an ambitious humane step. After a time medical supplies were more readily available, transport was obtained for the wounded and pre-fab wooden huts were made into hospitals. The energetic Guthrie visited these hospitals and imposed – with difficulties and against obstruction that can only be imagined – a certain standard of surgery. The result was that 5,000 men previously wounded returned in 1814 to serve again during the closing stages of the campaign.*

Red tape killed many soldiers of Wellington's armies as it has killed English troops of all eras. Wounded men often claimed compensation for equipment lost, abandoned or sold after a battle. The official mind being what it was – and is – each claim had to be approved by a board and while it was tardily considering the evidence the wounded were detained on ships in harbour. 'Many die that might be saved,' Wellington wrote in anger.

In summer, when not campaigning, the men had little organized entertainment or recreation apart from those initiated by the few compassionate officers. In bivouac in winter their only comfort was a fire, around which they sat to smoke, drink and yarn. The old soldiers were full of adventurous stories, none of them outstanding for their modesty or reserve, or truth. A few soldiers were lucky enough to go to a dance or a ball, but Spanish dancing –

---

* But lessons are quickly forgotten and no system was in preparation for the Waterloo campaign. The medical chaos which followed the battle spurred Wellington to call in Guthrie again. Wellington wrote, 'The same reckless sacrifice of arms and legs has again taken place and nothing could undo the irretrievable mischief insufficient care occasioned in the first few days.'

particularly exhibition dancing – was expressively sexual and was apt to unsettle the soldiers who watched it.

English troops have never had much respect for holy relics and in Catholic Spain they mocked it in several ways; they had to have *something* to laugh at. Some troops, quartered in a chapel, found out that the 'miracle' eyes of a saint were moved by an elaborate contraption of strings which they worked with hilarity until they broke it.

Towards the end of the campaign several divisions or brigades held concerts and even presented plays – the Light Infantry Division put on Sheridan's *The Rivals* – but often enough performances were ruined by the performers or the orchestra (the regimental band) becoming drunk.

At Buccellas in September 1810 the light company of the 28th Regiment gave a party to which they invited a number of officers from other companies and units. Late in the evening they ran out of wine and the junior subaltern was ordered to the vat for a fresh supply. He turned the cock, but no wine ran, so he let down a camp-kettle by a rope through a trap door in the top of the vat. The kettle bumped an obstacle so the officer brought a lamp to investigate. He found a British drummer in full regimentals, pack, haversack, and all, floating in the wine. He had been missing for some days, and was supposed to have deserted. 'Drummer's wine', was long a byword with the 28th.

Britain was heavily committed in many places by 1811 and recruiting was being pursued with enthusiasm by enterprising recruiting officers. One with a vivid imagination supported by a facile pen was Lieutenant G. James, recruiting for the 69th Regiment, James knew how to appeal to a man's pocket, as is shown by one of his posters.

> 69th or South Lincolnshire Regiment of Foot, 1811, Commanded by General Cuyler, an officer to whose distinguished merit no language can do justice.
>
> Wanted for this line Regiment, a few dashing, high-spirited young men, whose hearts beat high to tread the path of glory. Young men of this description know the opportunity offered to them, which may never again occur,

of enlisting into one of the finest Regiments in the Service, the 1st Battalion of which (1,300 strong) is most probably at this moment, with others of their most gallant countrymen, laying siege to the Island of Java, in the East Indies, *where their prize-money will be almost incalculable.** The 1st Battalion was also employed at the reduction of the Island of France (Mauritius), where I had the honour of governing it, and likewise of returning to England with several of the men, who had, by their increase of pay and prize-money, saved enough to purchase their discharge, and provide themselves with a comfortable independence for life in their own country.

Such, my fine fellows, are the advantages of a soldier's life, independent of the honour of serving the King, whose indescribable virtues render him an inestimable blessing to the country. Besides all these advantages, young men shall receive a bounty of sixteen guineas for volunteering into this fine regiment, and may make application to me, Lieutenant G. James, at my quarters next door to the George Inn, High Street, or to either of my sergeants, at my rendezvous, the Flying Horse, Watergate. An early application by young men of any education will ensure immediate promotion.

I trust I need say nothing further to induce you to come forward to tender your services, but if after this any of you should remain in a lethargic state recollect that you are called upon to defend the cause of a lawful sovereign against an inveterate enemy, a common usurper, a Corsican pirate. You will find me, as above stated, ready to receive you with a bottle of wine in one hand and sixteen guineas in the other, and before you join our regiment I intend to treat you with a supper and ball, when you may have the enthusiastic pleasure of dancing with the object of your affection.

Whatever Mr James's regiment was doing, other English soldiers were treading the 'path of glory' against the

---

* It was probably 19s 10d.

'Corsican pirate'. Many paths led to glory in the Peninsula but none to more glory than that won at the Battle of Albuhera on 16 May, that year. Albuhera was a prime example of the stand-up-and-fight-it-out battle which for so many years dominated wars and in which Tommy Atkins, by virtue of his steadiness, excelled.

Eight

1808–15(2)
Heroes at Albuhera; Hoodlums at Badajoz

Albuhera, one of the finest battles in Tommy Atkins's history, is also an outstanding illustration of discipline and training prevailing over weight of numbers and sheer force. Discipline is a weapon, the weapon with which the British Army in particular was chiefly armed. Never was it better used than at Albuhera. This battle also demonstrates the ordeal of the soldier on active service. It brought fame and glory to British arms, a new word to the English language – and death to 7,000 British and French soldiers.

In May 1811 Napoleon had reason to be proud of his success in Europe, but the campaigns in Spain irritated him constantly. Here the British, after initial setbacks, were holding down massive French forces. In the south at this time, General Sir William Beresford was laying siege to the great fortress of Badajoz, but on 12 May he heard that Marshal Soult with an army of 25,000 was marching south from Seville to relieve Badajoz.

Wellington sent word to Beresford to abandon the siege, for the moment, and to intercept the French, but not necessarily to engage them. Beresford had only 7,000 British troops, nearly all untried in battle.

They had not been engaged in recent great battles fought by Wellington and they were in a mood to fight *somebody*. Many officers impressed this on Beresford, who himself was spoiling for a fight.

He also had 23,000 German, Portuguese, and Spanish troops, the latter most unreliable and semi-trained. He marched from Badajoz and seven miles away took up a position along the ridge overlooking the tiny village of Albuhera, with his left flank fairly secure on the Albuhera River, but his right flank wide open.

Soult's 4,000 cavalry, 20,000 infantry and his artillery batteries were all veterans, battle-tried and hard, with a profound contempt for the Spanish and Portuguese troops. Soult studied the British position and saw at once that the hill in the centre was the key position. But he was too wily a general to make straight for it.

About 8 a.m. on 16 May, after some preliminary skirmishing, he set two columns in motion. A left thrust was his feint, vigorously punched home by lancers and hussars. They crossed the river but the British 3rd Dragoon Guards, with sword and pistol, drove them back into it.

The assault on the right was made by an infantry column of 8,000, supported by many squadrons of cavalry, including the formidable Polish lancers whose ability and driving during the battle so impressed the British that in 1819 lancer regiments were introduced into the British Army.

The French attack hit the awkward Spanish battalions. Beresford tried in vain to bring them to the charge and in desperation he grabbed an ensign by his uniform and carried him, flag and all, to the front. When not a Spaniard followed, Beresford dropped the ensign in disgust and the man scuttled to safety.

Beresford repeatedly dragged Spanish officers to the front and compelled them to lead their men. When it came to actual conflict some Spaniards stood firm, but they were steadily being pushed off the hill. To support them and to stop the retreat from developing into a rout Beresford hurried his 2nd Division, under General Stewart, from the secure left flank.

The British troops had been living on horseflesh and nothing else for several days and they were hungry, but the leading brigade, led by Colonel Colborne, went at the double through the Spaniards and up the hill.

Suddenly, through heavy mist on their right, came the frightening thunder of cavalry. Then thousands of steel points appeared as lancers and hussars, having turned the Spanish flank, caught the British in open order.

In five violent minutes two-thirds of the brigade were trampled out of existence. The men of the 31st Regiment (East Surrey) ran into square and stood fast. Edged with steel and flame they were an island within a sea of rampaging enemy horsemen, who rode to and fro across the hill spearing the wounded. The Buffs (East Kent Regiment) suffered severely.

When British cavalry drove off the enemy cavalry French artillery opened up with grape shot from most of their forty guns. To compound the disaster many demoralized Spaniards were firing blindly on their British comrades.

The Spanish dragoons were ordered to charge and made a half-hearted run before they wheeled and bolted. In the confusion six British guns and hundreds of men were captured.

There was so much bravery that no particular act was outstanding, but one incident which survivors recollected later was the refusal of thirteen-year-old Ensign Thomas of the Buffs to surrender the colours of his regiment to the enemy. He was cut down and killed on the spot.*

A lancer attacked Beresford, but the general was one of the strongest men of his day; he wrenched the lance from the Pole, unhorsed and killed him.

The 29th Regiment (Worcestershire) advancing to help Colborne's brigade saw a mass of fleeing Spanish infantry rushing toward them, pursued by enemy cavalry. The Spaniards would have disorganized the British regiment and left the men to be picked off by the cavalry, so the regiment fired at both Spaniards and French and continued their advance.

The two other brigades of the 2nd Division were now coming up – one under Hoghton, the other under Abercrombie. The 57th Regiment (later the Middlesex Regiment) was with Hoghton.

---

* 'Every ensign has his dignity, although he is wholly to be at the captain's command; yet in justice no captain or other officer can command the ensign-bearer from his colours, for *they are man and wife, and ought not to endure a separation*; nor can he be commanded with his ensign to any safe (dishonourable) place or action.' Grose, *Military Antiquities*, 1801. Author's italics.

Cheering, the two brigades swept up the hill to the crest of the ridge and there they formed a two-deep 500-yard line of six battalions. And everybody on the battlefield knew that if that line were broken the French would win the day.

The British were outnumbered now by more than two to one – 3,000 against 7,000 – but for the moment their line was long enough to overlap both flanks of the French infantry mass. Between the two forces was a gap of less than sixty yards; at this range the steady British volleys were devastating.

The French had three advantages:

They were spread over a downward slope and the rear men could fire over the heads of the soldiers in front, thus adding to the hail of lead which smote the British.

Marshal Soult had placed heavy guns on a strategic height. These guns, some of them at a range of only fifty yards, pounded away at the British lines. The French infantry suffered less from the British artillery.

A thunderstorm had broken and rain and hail were beating against the British troops.

British infantry leaders, mounted on their horses, were easy targets and early in the battle General Hoghton was hit by a musket ball. He stayed in the saddle and gave orders until he had been seriously wounded three times; then he died and fell to the ground.

Command of the brigade devolved on Lieutenant-Colonel Inglis, CO of the 57th. Inglis was in front of his battalion and had his horse shot from under him, but he went on giving orders with the traditional calmness of the British officer. His battalion was taking terrific punishment. Men fell all along the line, but no gap was left for long. The troops closed up, but as they did so the line shrank in width. Under the onslaught they steadily loaded and fired, and even advanced a few steps.

Among the steadiest were the boy drummers and fife-players of the regiment, who stood fast near the flank and waited, under constant fire, for orders.

Grapeshot hit Colonel Inglis in the breast and he staggered and fell, badly wounded. A young ensign and two men wanted to carry him to the rear, but Inglis told them to leave him where he was.

In full view of the remnants of his battalion, he shouted to them, 'Die hard, 57th! Die hard!'

About the time that Inglis was hit, Captain Fawcett of the same regiment was also seriously wounded, but he, too, refused to leave the field. He ordered his bearers to place him on some high ground and from here he controlled his company – what was left of it. 'Fire low!' he shouted many times. 'Conserve ammunition!'

As usual, the most dangerous spots of the field were under the King's Colour and the Regimental Colour. They drew enemy fire like magnets, for they were rallying points for the regiment and their loss usually had a sharp effect on morale.

The staff holding the King's Colour of the 57th was broken and the Colour itself was riddled by seventeen shots. Ensign Jackson was wounded three times while carrying it and passed it over to Lieutenant Veitch, who was then himself twice wounded.

Jackson retired briefly to have his wounds dressed and then, missing all the fun, returned to the fighting line and asked Veitch for the Colour. Veitch told him to go to hell. He now had the honour of carrying the Colour and carry it he would until he dropped.

Ensign Walsh of the Buffs had been seriously wounded and as there was nobody to whom he could hand the Colour, tore it from its staff and hit it against his bleeding breast. Lieutenant Latham saw that Walsh had been surrounded, wounded and taken prisoner. He dashed in to grab the Colour and in an astonishing fight was slashed, lanced and beaten down. His left arm was cut off and the left side of his face was practically severed. But somehow he managed to tear the Colour from the dying Walsh and hide it inside his uniform. After the fight a sergeant of the Seventh Royal Fusiliers found the almost lifeless Latham and dressed his wounds. His brother officers awarded him a gold medal and he lived for many years despite his multiple serious wounds.

Within a few hours Hoghton's brigade had lost all its field officers, most of the company officers and four-fifths of its men. But the tiny force that remained, though bloody and battered, was unbroken.

The men had fought in every imaginable order; they had resisted cavalry in square, deployed into line and somtimes into column. They had inched forward to within twenty-five yards of the French. But the French had held their ground with stubborn bravery and at this point the odds were strongly with them.

Beresford, fast losing his nerve and aware that the fighting men's ammunition had almost gone, told his staff he would withdraw his troops from the ridge.

At this point a staff officer, Colonel Hardinge, using Beresford's name without permission, ordered up General Cole's division – the reserve. This consisted of the Fusilier Brigade – two battalions of the 7th (Royals) and one of the 23rd (Royal Welsh) – and a Portuguese brigade, in all about 5,000 men.

Cole ordered the Portuguese to hold off the French cavalry while the Fusiliers attacked the infantry.

The 7th and 23rd, in a line as straight as a parade ground formation, appeared suddenly through the smoke of battle and startled the French. Their artillery poured grapeshot into the Fusiliers to give the French infantry time to open out and expand the front. Most of the officers were hit and many fell, but the Fusiliers continued the advance with such relentless steadiness, firing by volleys, that the French could not hold their ground.

Soult himself rode into the battle and tried to whip up the spirits of his men. The entire French reserves were thrown in. Groups of veterans made suicidal assaults on the Fusiliers. Polish lancers launched headlong charges.

But 'nothing could stop that indomitable infantry'.* They broke the French and bayonet-swept them down the hill. The French had lost the battle which by every rule of war they should have won.

The battle had lasted for seven hours. Left on the crest were 1,500 unwounded men – the triumphant remnant of six thousand who had gone into action.

When the Buffs were mustered it was said that only three privates and a drummer answered the roll call.

* Napier.

A captain brought Hoghton's brigade off the ridge. Corporal Thomas Robinson led a company of Royal Welsh Fusiliers. A lieutenant led the survivors of the 57th. The day after the battle, a boy drummer of a company of the 57th reported to the quarter-master for the day's rations.

'How many men?' the QM asked.

'No men,' the drummer said. 'Just me. I'm the only one left.' And he held out his cap for the food.

His regiment had lost its CO, twenty-two officers and 400 of the 570 men who had gone into action on that bloody ridge. That night of the battle, after the pickets had been posted, not enough men remained to carry off the wounded and bury the dead. The 7,000 men who were killed lay within a space of about 300 square feet.

On 19 May General Stewart, commander of the 2nd Division, said, 'The situation on which the 57th fought was the key to the whole position and the regiment's gallant conduct was the chief means of ensuring victory at Albuhera.'

Officers who visited the battlefield immediately after the French retreated were impressed by the way in which the 57th men had fallen – in ranks, with every wound to the front. Wellington himself wrote that 'this action is one of the most glorious and honourable to the troops of any that have been fought during the war'.

Eleven infantry and two cavalry regiments won the right to show Albuhera on the battle honours.[†] One historian called it 'the most noble of all Peninsular blazons on a regimental flag'.

It was after this battle that Marshal Soult said: 'There is no beating these troops, in spite of their generals. I always thought them bad soldiers, now I am sure of it. For at Albuhera I turned their right, pierced their centre, broke them everywhere; the day was mine, and yet they did not know it, and would not run.'

---

† The British Military General Service Medal 1793–1814 commemorates the Peninsular War. Twenty-one bars were awarded for various battles on the Peninsula, but many more than this were fought.

No battle in which Tommy Atkins has fought can excel the glory of Albuhera.*

The battles of Barrosa, Fuentes d'Onor, Arroyo Dos Molinos and Ciudad Rodrigo were other victories. Then came Badajoz, a strong fortress town stubbornly defended. The taking of this fortress was one of the toughest tasks British soldiers have ever faced and its conquest provides both a proud and shameful picture.

Badajoz had a strong outfort, Fort Picurina, which was assaulted on the night of 24 March 1812. In the furious hand-to-hand fighting the British lost twenty officers and three hundred men killed and wounded while the French would not surrender until only eighty-six remained on their feet. The way was open to storm Badajoz and as Marshal Soult was advancing with a strong French force to relieve the city time now became important.

No fewer than twenty-two officers of the 95th (later the Rifle Brigade) alone were killed or wounded leading forlorn hopes at Badajoz.

One officer, Major O'Hara, said before the attack, 'Well, in a few hours I will be a lieutenant-colonel or cold meat.' He was killed.

Yet Ensign Joseph Dyas if the 51st Light Infantry (later the King's Own Yorkshire Light Infantry) survived two forlorn hopes. When the first attack failed Dyas volunteered to lead a second, but because of his extreme youth his commanding officer refused permission. Dyas then obtained authority from the brigade commander. The ensign collected another band of volunteers and this time he carried the position. His regiment today commemorates his bravery in the officers' mess toast of 'Dyas and His Stormers'.

---

* The last 57th survivor of the men who held the ridge was Henry Holloway, a drummer. He lived near Lydd, Kent, and when the regiment's first battalion was passing through in 1888 they halted and saluted the old man. He bequeathed his medal, with five bars, to the regiment. It forms the stem of the Loving Cup that is taken from the Officer's Mess to the Sergeant's Mess of the 1st Bn every Albuhera Day and from which the toast is drunk to those who fell at Albuhera.

Wellington gave the order for an attack on 5 April. That storming and the subsequent battle and sacking of the town produced frightful scenes. The men, led by gallant young officers, dashed forward under fire, raised storming ladders against the castle walls and ran up them, though for a long time not many reached the top. The French were alert and ready on the ramparts, with great mounds of shells; each man had three loaded muskets beside him. The French let water into ditches where one hundred British soldiers were drowned; they had fixed many hundreds of sword blades into beams as a barrier and they had hammered thousands of spikes into planks. Mines were exploded under the massed attackers. By midnight more than 2,000 British soldiers had fallen and little progress had been made.

Eventually, amid the shocking carnage and the fantastic noise the British troops broke through the defences. Badajoz was won – at a cost of 5,000 British casualties, many of whom fell in an area of 100 square yards.

Men, women and children were shot in the streets for no other apparent reason than pastime; every species of outrage was publicly committed in the houses, churches, and streets, and, said Captain Robert Blakeney of the 28th, 'in a manner so brutal that a faithful recital would be too indecent and too shocking for humanity'.

No discipline or order could be maintained and most officers dared not interfere, though several risked their lives to rescue Spaniards, whether or not they appealed to them for help.

Blakeney went on:

> The infuriated soldiery resembled rather a pack of hell-hounds vomited up from the infernal regions for the extirpation of mankind than what they were twelve short hours previously – well organized, brave, disciplined and obedient British Army, and burning only with impatience for what is called glory.
>
> Whatever accounts may be given of the horrors which attended and immediately followed the storming of Badajoz, they must fall short of the truth . . . it is impossible to imagine them. . . . The frenzied military mob . . . were ferociously

employed in indiscriminate carnage, universal plunder and devastation of every kind. . . . I beheld the savages tear the rings from the ears of beautiful women who were their victims, and when the rings could not be immediately removed from their fingers with the hand, they tore them off with their teeth. . . . The sack continued for three days without intermission; each day I witnessed its horrid and abominable effects. . . . I shrink from further description.

The barbarity of the soldiers extended to such a pitch that they would not for two days carry off their own wounded men at the foot of the walls of Badajoz. They also stripped them naked, the officers as well as the men who were wounded.

Wellington finally restored order by marching in fresh regiments. He threatened to hang men who continued in their violence, did indeed string up a few, and the insane wildness subsided. Not every soldier lost his discipline at Badajoz but those who did left a black page in British military history and a sour taste in the mouths of Spaniards. Unfortunately in 1813 troops were guilty of similar frenzy at the taking of San Sebastian. After the bloody five-hour battle there was a thunderstorm which, wrote Napier, 'seemed to be a signal from hell for the perpetration of villainy which would have shamed the most ferocious barbarians of antiquity. At Ciudad Rodrigo intoxication and plunder had been the principal objects; at Badajoz lust and murder were added to rapine and drunkenness; at San Sebastian, the direst most revolting cruelty was added to the catalogue of crimes; one atrocity, of which a girl of 17 was the victim, staggers the mind by its enormous, incredible, indescribable barbarity . . . a Portuguese adjutant, striving to prevent some ruffianism, was put to death in the market place not with sudden violence but deliberately. Many officers exerted themselves to preserve order, many men were well-conducted, yet the rapine and violence commenced by villains soon spread . . . and the disorder continued until fire, following the steps of the plunderer, put an end to his ferocity by destroying the whole town.'

Those who take Wellington to task for his opinion that his men were the 'scum of the earth' must remember that the British Army did include some of the vilest scum ever to disgrace a uniform. Wellington's error was in giving the impression that the army at large was inferior in moral qualities. Wellington was prone to spread his criticisms too widely, as Johnny Kincaid observed on one occasion. 'Lord Wellington had been adored by everyone,* but in consequence of some disgraceful irregularities . . . he immediately issued an order . . . a sweeping censure of the whole army. . . . It excited a feeling against him . . . which has probably never been obliterated. It began by telling us that we had suffered no privations, though this was hard to digest on an empty stomach . . . many regiments were not guilty of any irregularities. . . .'

In October 1812 Wellington had criticized the British soldier's inability to march well. In a letter to Earl Bathurst he wrote: 'Our soldiers are not sufficiently exercised in marching. . . and they become sickly as soon as they are obliged to make a march.' Immediately afterwards the Duke issued an order instructing all his commanders to give their men three route marches a week. In May the following year he started his greatest march of the Peninsular War. In six weeks his men marched more than 600 miles, crossed six rivers, gained a decisive victory at Vittoria, captured two fortresses and drove 120,000 veteran French troops out of Spain.

Wellington's victorious troops fought their way over the Pyrenees and into France. Their march through France helped to make up for the atrocities at Badajoz and San Sebastian, though nothing can ever wipe out their memory. The troops marched 300 miles without a charge of misconduct being made against them by the civil authorities – a remarkable record of behaviour for the time. It is interesting to sum up the achievements of these men, as Napier did in his historical account. They had won nineteen pitched battles and innumerable combats; they had made or withstood ten sieges and taken four major forts; they had twice thrown the French out of Portugal and once from Spain; they had brought off some of the most remarkable river

* Extravagant, perhaps. Not *everyone* 'adored' Wellington.

crossings in history – the passage of the Douro in 1809 was a classic operation of its type. They had finally invaded France itself. In doing all this they had killed, wounded or captured 200,000 enemies. Their own losses were 40,000 dead.

If the infantry seem to have been given more space than other arms in this account it is only because they bore the brunt of the fighting. However, the cavalry did well when it had the chance and the new Horse Artillery performed brilliantly, as at Fuentes d'Onor when Captain Norman Ramsey with his two guns went full gallop through a French cavalry brigade.

One of the most remarkable testimonies to the influence of the English soldier was given in Paris, when the Allied armies reached and occupied it in 1814. The citizens and government of Paris were apprehensive about the fate of their famous bridge, the Pont d'Iéna. At Jena in 1806 the French had worsted the Prussians in battle and Blücher had boasted aloud and oft that he would destroy any bridge to wipe out the humiliation. Blücher put engineers to work on demolition charges – Wellington countered by mounting a single English infantry sentry on the bridge. He calmly marched his beat and the Prussians, morally and psychologically bested, abandoned plans to blow up the bridge.

Napier ended his great account of the Peninsular War with this sentence: 'Thus the war terminated, and with it all remembrance of the veteran's services.' Nothing could be more damning. It was the same old story.

When the Peninsular War ended in 1814 the Government at once, as always, began the melancholy business of reducing the army. The consequence was that when Napoleon threatened Europe after his escape from Elba in 1815 the force given to Wellington was 'the worst army I have ever commanded'. This was another unjustifiably vehement criticism and this 'worst army' showed spirit and devotion to duty that was pure Crécy in quality.

Wellington seems to have had second thoughts, for two or three weeks before the battle of Waterloo, he was discussing with Thomas Creevey whether Blücher and he could defeat Napoleon. Pointing to an English infantryman he said, 'It all depends on that article whether we do business or not. Give me enough of it, and I'm sure.'

It is said that somebody asked Wellington how he could account for having so consistently beaten the French marshals. 'Because,' said Wellington, 'their soldiers always got them into scrapes, mine always got me out of them.'

Still, one charge against Tommy Atkins of 1815 was true. He had no thought for the future even when it touched his own survival. This was possibly due to his lack of education and here again the vicious circle is evident, for Wellington violently opposed any plans for educating the army. Wellington was frustrated and exasperated when soldiers burnt as firewood the doors and windows and even the roofs of buildings in which they had been cantoned in poor weather. Soldiers were apt to burn roofs even when icy rain or snow was falling. The most insane example of such thoughtlessness occured during the night of 17–18 June 1815, when troops broke up the great door of the barn at the farm of La Haye Sainte, Waterloo; the lack of a door made defence of the place much more difficult the following day.

The Battle of Waterloo has been too much written about to appear here. The victory is generally accorded to Wellington, with Blücher and his Prussians accorded honourable mention. In fact, Waterloo – 'the nearest run thing that ever you saw' Wellington called it – was won as much by the steadiness of the common soldiers as by the Duke. Napoleon had made the mistake of under-estimating his enemies; he thought little of the British as fighters. But at Waterloo they broke his Imperial Guard, those fine men who had vanquished Austrians, Russians and Prussians. In line and in square Tommy Atkins had proved himself indomitable at Waterloo.

To show the spirit of all it is only necessary to tell the story of Corporal John Shaw, in the words of Charles Dickens 'the model of the British Army itself'. Shaw was born in 1789 at Wollaton, Nottinghamshire. Magnificently built, he became famous as a pugilist but later was even better known as a fighting man. Macaulay says, seriously, that Shaw did more to win the battle of Waterloo than did Wellington himself. In *Bleak House* Dickens wrote, 'Old Shaw the Life Guardsman, why, he's the model of the British Army itself. Ladies and gentlemen, I'd give a fifty-pound note to be such a figure of a man.' Shaw was hardly 'old' but Dickens is right about his figure. He was something over six feet, weighed fifteen stone and was powerfully built. The idol of the many sportsmen of London, Shaw, like many other men of the Household Cavalry of the early nineteenth century, was a sought-after artist's model and sat for Landseer, Haydon, Hilton and Etty. At Waterloo Shaw charged into action under Lord Uxbridge and by the farmhouse of La Haye Sainte he met his first opponent, whom he killed in a duel. He rode at a French standard-bearer, but could not get through to him. Soon after this, in another charge, Shaw cut down nine enemy. As the British cavalry returned, disorganized into small parties and out of hand, Napoleon sent two cavalry brigades to intercept them. Shaw and Major Kelly teamed up, charged the French ranks and cut their way through. During the ebb and flow of battle the ranks of the Heavy Brigade were further depleted, but Shaw still sat his horse. In the late afternoon, again near La Haye Sainte, he was attacked by ten French horsemen. In a furious fight he slashed five Frenchmen from their saddles – and then his sword snapped. So he used his heavy helmet as a weapon. Soon, however, he was brought down and, according to Victor Hugo, a French drummer boy pistolled the big man. With more than thirty wounds, Shaw dragged himself to the farm and there on a dunghill he bled to death. The 'model of the British Army' indeed he was.

An editorial writer in the *Navy and Army Illustrated** aptly summed up the hectic years of the Napoleonic and Indian Wars. In this era, he said, 'the soldier's happiest time was when he was on active service. He suffered horribly, it is true, was shamefully fed, shockingly tended, and often died miserably of wounds and ailments from which under modern conditions he would recover in a fortnight. But he led the life of a full-blooded

* Issue of 6 July 1901. The *Navy and Army Illustrated* has been challenged as an authoritative source of reference, but the comments of some of its writers are interesting.

man, he had his fill of "sumpshuous fightin", and he lived in a constant atmosphere of change. Now and then he came in for something pretty handsome in the way of loot, and he was naturally not hampered by many scruples as to laying his hands on anything in the way of 'portable property' or temporary refreshment. Opportunities for personal distinction were pretty frequent, and a really brave soldier would probably be spared many of the discomforts and much of the bullying which less bold spirits had to endure without a murmur.'

Opportunities for personal distinction might have been frequent, but there was no official issue of campaign medals or decorations to show that a soldier had seen service or had distinguished himself in action. Cromwell had issued a medal for the Battle of Dunbar in 1650, but it was not a campaign medal in the modern sense, and the idea was not followed up. Long before the Crown issued medals the officers of many regiments, at their own expense, conferred medals on their men for long service, bravery, marksmanship and efficiency. A few medals were struck for the Carib War of 1773 and again for the war against the French and Caribs in 1795. Officers were given medals for the Peninsular battles.

The first medal given to British troops in the field was the Seringapatam Medal, for the capture of a fortress in 1799 – but the men did not receive royal permission to wear the medals until 1815. The Seringapatam Medal was issued by the Honourable East India Company.

In 1816 the Waterloo Medal established the precedent for granting the same medal to officers and men alike. Wellington approved this medal, but did his best to see that the practice was not continued. Due to his obstruction it was not until 1 June 1847 that the Government sanctioned a Military General Service Medal to cover services between 1793 and 1814, although no bars were issued for service before 1801 and none between that date and 1806. In all, twenty-nine bars were issued for battles in the Peninsula, Egypt, Italy, North America and the West Indies. Many men who would have been entitled to the medal had died before it appeared in 1848.

Still, after that time medals were issued for most campaigns and Tommy Atkins came to covet them and to be proud of them. The medals and the bars are historic reminders of actions fought in hundreds of places. For instance, the India General Service Medal of 1854 has twenty-three different bars for campaigns spread across India from the Khyber Pass to Burma between 1854 and 1895.

Despite the pride with which Tommy Atkins wore his campaign medals, his long service and good conduct medal and, later, his decorations for bravery, they have never played a major part in his martial psychology. They always meant more to an officer than to the man in the ranks. Other nations, notably the French and Germans, have made great play on the soldier's emotions and mentality with medallic adornment and badges and insignia – and with great success. Soldiers have gone on service and into action consciously wanting to win these adornments.

With Tommy Atkins they have been wholly incidental. The large number of soldiers who have sold their medals and the even larger number who have not bothered to apply for medals to which they are entitled seems to prove the point. There is, of course, the point that the medals struck for the two world wars are cheap and shoddy; this may explain why some men have not bothered to apply for them.

Until 1914 the main purpose of a medal, in Tommy Atkins's view, was to attract the girls. Such an attitude reveals much about the man who wore the medals. During Victoria's reign the proudest medal was the Long Service and Good Conduct Medal, for this identified the veteran. And Tommy Atkins attaches great importance to being a veteran.

Nine

Punishment: 'Europe's Most Barbarous Martial Laws'*

Probably the greatest cross Tommy Atkins was ever called upon to carry was that of vicious punishment. The various punishments inflicted on British soldiers were as diabolical, ruthless and degrading as any torture invented by such experts as the Chinese, the Spaniards and the Nazis. The only difference lay in that British officers were not so disgustingly ingenious as the other foreign torturers. But what the British army punishment lacked in variety it made up for in volume and enthusiasm.

An historian must if he is honest, look at everything in the context of the times about which he writes. So one must recognize that at certain periods some soldiers were little better than animals and that only harsh punishment could have any salutary effect on them. Some brutalized louts – brutalized, perhaps, by the Army itself – were contemptuous of any punishment other than the lash. The layman must also realize that the object of military law was not – and is not – to make men virtuous by punishing moral default, but to produce

---

* Material for this chapter has come from many sources, most of which are quoted here. Contemporary writers all tend to corroborate one another's evidence on punishment and flogging, but it is probably true that the whole truth can never be known. I have deliberately kept the 'sensational' from this chapter and have given mostly the stark facts and contemporary observers' comments.

instant and complete obedience. Therefore a military offence is not necessarily a crime in its moral sense.

However, making allowance for history and for the exigencies of Service life, it must still be admitted that the punishments meted out to British soldiers were often vindictive, vengeful and vile. Just how far these punishments were responsible for producing Tommy Atkins's unique brand of discipline is open to debate. If they were in part responsible for his steadiness under fire and in adversity, then similarly they were responsible for destroying whatever initiative and enterprise was latent in the common soldier.

Scott Claver says: 'It is a sobering thought to reflect that possibly as much blood from drum-head floggings has stained the barrack squares and decks of ships as was ever spilled upon the battlefields of Europe and Empire'.* This is a hyperbolic estimate, but the thought is indeed sobering. And it is true that more, many more, soldiers were flogged than were wounded in action.

The foundation of all subsequent Articles of War seems to have been *Lawes and Ordinances of Warre*, published by the Earl of Essex in 1642, when commander of the Parliamentary Army. Nearly fifty delinquencies were punishable by death. Secondary punishments included having the tongue bored with a red-hot iron.†

Twenty years later another set of regulations laid down some of the duties of the Provost-Marshal – the army's police chief. The Provost-Marshal was to have charge of 'all manner of tortures, as gyves (fetters), shackles, bolts, chains, belobowes (iron bars with sliding shackles), manacles, whips and the like'.

At the same time it was evident that the Provost-Marshal and his underlings had already become the soldier's protectors as well as disciplinarians because his duties included looking 'to the proportions of the true weights and measures' of merchants selling victuals in camps.

---

* *Under the Lash*, 1957.
† Until 1710 this punishment could be awarded even to an officer, for blasphemy, but I can find no record of its having been inflicted on an officer.

These merchants – more correctly, sutlers – were subject to certain types of discipline of which the most obnoxious was the whirligig, a circular wooden cage turned on a pivot. A defaulter was placed in the cage which was then spun so violently that, as Grose says, 'the delinquent became extremely sick and commonly emptied his or her body through every aperture'.

The rules of 1642 also laid down that 'the Gentleman which should be elected to this place of Provost-Marshal, would be a man of great judgment and experience in all martial discipline, well seen in the laws and ordinances of the camp, and such a one as knows well the use, benefit and necessity of all things belonging either to food or raiment. He should be a lover of justice, impartial to his dealings, and free from the transportations of passions; . . . have an ear that could contemptuously beat back, not furiously drink in, slander and railing languages: . . . an eye that could gaze on all objects without winking; and an heart full of discreet compassion, but not touched with foolish or melting pity. . . .'

It was his duty to 'discover the lurking subtleties of spies, and by learning the true interpretation of men's words, looks, manners, forms and habits of apparel, to be able to turn the insides of their heart outwards, and to pull out that devil of malicious deceit, though he lie hid in never so dark a corner; and truly a better service cannot be done, nor is there any Art sooner learned if a man will apply his knowledge but seriously thereto.'

It might well be said that provost-marshals, general officers and other officers turned the insides of many soldiers' hearts outwards, breaking their hearts sometimes. They had the holier-than-thou attitude that a defaulting soldier could show virtue by being executed. Sir James Turner, in his *Pallas Armata*, published 1683, discussed military punishments and concludes that 'the most honourable death for a delinquent soldier is beheading, the next to that is shooting, with pistols if he be a horseman, with muskets if a foot soldier'.

Where a few men were condemned to die for the sake of example, the entire group, be it platoon or company, were ordered to cast dice on the drum-head and their names and the number they threw were noted by the Provost-Marshal.

As many as it had been decided should suffer were then taken from those who had thrown the lowest numbers. If any two happened to throw the same number they threw again until one had lost. From a manuscript in the British Museum it seems that this method of 'winning death' was practised in Ireland during William III's reign.

During one of William's campaigns, the Provost-Marshal submitted a bill for £307 10s for executing soldiers convicted of crimes. The cost, per victim, included 10s for 'hanging and taking down', 6s for 'extraordinary treats after the sentence of death', and even 2s 6d for 'reading the sentences'. In those days a convicted man was known as 'the patient'.

From the mid-seventeenth century until the mid-nineteenth century flogging was the most common form of punishment in the army, although several other 'minor' punishments existed. Corporal punishment had not been so much in use in earlier times in England because private soldiers in those days generally had some property and were punished by forfeitures and fines. 'Soldiers of the present times,' wrote Grose in 1801, 'have nothing but their bodies and can only be punished corporally.'

For many years flogging was carried out with a rod, but early in the eighteenth century the cat-o'-nine-tails* ousted the rod.

Properly to understand what Tommy Atkins had to endure from his own countrymen, it is necessary to study the ritual of flogging in detail, but first the 'minor' punishments deserve mention. In 1717 secondary punishments included branding on the forehead, cutting off of ears, degradation to the duties of a pioneer-scavenger. Other military defaulters – I cannot label all of them criminals – were picketed, that is, they were suspended by one wrist from a tree-branch or something

---

* The cat did not always have nine tails, though I can find no record of its having fewer than six. Dr Henry Marshall, Deputy-Inspector General of Army Hospitals in the 1840s, noted that in his time six tails was the normal number. There was no uniform cat; some were made of whipcord and others of leather. The tails were usually two feet long – but could be as short as 16 inches – and often tied into three large knots, to cause even further agony.

similar while they stood with a bare heel resting on a pointed stake. At Maidstone in 1722 the 1st Horse Grenadiers mutinied in protest against this torture being inflicted on one of their number. Torture it was. To relieve the pain in his foot, the sufferer could only take the weight on his wrist, which was just as agonizing.

As late as July 1750 a soldier of Okey's Regiment was sentenced by court-martial to be bored through the tongue, and to run the gauntlet (then the gantelope) through four companies, for uttering blasphemous words. According to the record he was at the time of the offence 'in a ranting humour with drinking too much'.

In 1754 it was officially stated in orders that, 'When any Man is absent from the Parade of the Morning he is for Guard, he shall go forty-eight Hours to the *Savoy* (a euphemistic term for the cells) on Bread and Water, and 14 to the Drill for the first offence, and for the second, be brought to the Court-Martial.'

'It is very difficult,' wrote Lieutenant-Colonel Dalrymple in 1761, 'from the kind of men we get to avoid frequent and severe punishment, especially in time of war'.

Some of these severe punishments were inflicted without court-martial sentence; they included tying neck and heels, riding the wooden horse and picketing. Appalling as these punishments were, they were inflicted for minor offences. To have his neck and heels tied a soldier was made to sit on the ground, with a musket under his hams and another over his back. Then the muskets were tied together with straps, so that the poor devil had his chin between his knees. In this position many a man sat until blood 'gushed out of his nose, mouth and ears, and some men suffered ruptures'.*

The gantelope was used mostly in cases of theft or some offence that was reckoned to have damaged the character of the unit. At first the method was to form the regiment into rows, facing inwards, with each man holding a switch. The defaulter, stripped to the waist, was made to walk through the ranks

* The recollections of an 'Old Officer', in *Cautions and Advices to Officers of the Army.*

while each man lashed him. So that he could not move too fast a sergeant preceded him, holding the point of his halberd at his breast. For some reason the method was changed. The offender was tied to crossed halberds as if to be conventionally flogged; then each man in the regiment would take the cat from a sergeant stationed at the halberds and give the offender a lash. This, too, was abandoned – the gantelope was not used after 1805 – because 'it degraded soldiers to executioners'.

This reason is pathetically and tragically laughable, for nobody gave a damn about the degrading effects of orthodox flogging on the victim, the spectators or the drummer who administered the punishment. Nor, apparently, were any of the other punishments considered degrading.

The wooden horse was one of the most disgusting of punishments, and it crippled some men for life. The wooden horse was a plank of wood standing on four legs and sometimes graced with a carved horse's head. The plank – the back of the horse – was quite thin, perhaps an inch thick. The defaulter, his wrists tied behind him, was made to mount this abomination and to sit astride it for as long as his tormentors had decided. To make the position even more painful, weights, generally muskets, were tied to his ankles 'so that the horse could not throw him'. The pain, of course, was excrutiating.

The strappado was another diabolical punishment. The victim had his arms fastened behind his back and then was hoisted high into the air by a system of pulleys, before being suddenly dropped with a jerk. This happened three or four times and he was lucky if his shoulder joints were not dislocated.

Most of these corporal punishments were abandoned during the last few decades of the eighteenth century, not for reasons of humanity, but because simple flogging was so much easier and had become the vogue. Still, in 1786 Grose noted that 'booting' was a common unofficial punishment in the cavalry. A defaulter found guilty by his own comrades – not by court martial – was flogged with a belt on the soles of his feet.*

* When done with a stick it is more commonly known as bastinadoing.

The men organized 'troops' courts martial among themselves – a practice condoned by authority – and their punishments were often more severe than those of a formal court martial. The main punishment was cobbing. A defaulter was held down by some soldiers while others cruelly whipped him with a belt, canteen strap or rope.

At the end of the century and on into the nineteenth century ingenuity again showed itself and it became standard practice to punish soldiers in a variety of ways. Usually the CO awarded the punishments, but many other officers passed impromptu sentence on their own initiative. There were innocuous punishments such as extra guard-duties and drills, confining to barracks, further parades, wearing the uniform jacket inside out, stopping a man's grog ration or diluting it with water. There were more punitive inflictions, such as drinking salt water, bread and water diet, gagging, holding heavy weights for long periods. And there were the stocks, the log, the dry-room and the black-hole.

The stocks need no explanation. Often enough a soldier had to sit in them for many hours, but at that was more fortunate than civilians suffering the same sentence; they were pelted with filth and with abuse.

When a man was awarded the log, a heavy log or a large round-shot was attached by a chain to his leg. He had to drag or carry it with him at all times, except when on guard duty. Lord ('Daddy') Hill, a more humanitarian general than most, said 'I think the log is a punishment more for a beast than a man. . . .'

The dry-room derived its name from its inmates being deprived of their liquor ration. Defaulters were kept in this room, often on a diet of bread and water, except when escorted out for drill. Often forty men might be in the room at the one time, with all the inevitable risk of further corruption.

The black-hole was a practically lightless and generally small cell in which a defaulting soldier – perhaps he had committed the heinous crime of 'wiping his nose on a chilly morning' as Shipp tells us – was kept for forty-eight hours at a time. He would be released for twenty-four hours, not for compassionate reasons, but merely to make him more apprehensive about returning for his second, third and fourth spells of forty-eight hours.

A relatively minor punishment at the end of the eighteenth century was a fine of 5s for contracting venereal disease. This money went directly into the Medical Officer's pocket, so statistics for VD in the army at this time may be viewed with suspicion, since many a doctor was not above reporting a soldier to have VD for the sake of the fee.

At this point we should look at military execution, which was usually carried out with protracted ceremony, the better to impress upon the watching soldiers that, they, too, might well face a firing squad if they misbehaved. There is a notion that executions were carried out only on active service, and then for some serious crime, such as desertion in the face of the enemy. But 'riotous and disorderly conduct' in England could also lead to execution. This was the fate of the two men of the Oxfordshire Regiment at Brighton on 14 June, 1795. The *Annual Register* of that year noted:

The Oxfordshire Regiment marched on Friday night from Seaford . . . to attend the execution of the two men. . . . The hour of four after midnight was the time appointed to assemble. On the march the regiment halted and twelve of the men who had taken part in the riot were called out. 'This was done to demonstrate to the men that state of obedience in which the officers were determined to hold them and by this measure they felt more pointedly the folly of their former conduct [for] those whom they had made their leaders were not to suffer death at their hands. . . . On rising ground . . . three thousand cavalry were posted; they were followed by the Horse Artillery. The guns were pointed and matches lighted. From the . . . arrangement of the troups a more magnificent and awful spectacle were never exhibited in this country. [After two lesser offenders had been flogged by torchlight the condemned men were brought in under strong escort.] They were accompanied by a clergyman . . . and were fully prepared to meet their fate. They approached the fatal spot with resignation . . . kneeled down upon their coffins with cool and deliberate firmness, when the one who was to drop the signal said to his comrade, 'Are you ready?' Upon the reply . . . he dropped a prayer book and the party did their duty at six yards distance. One of them not appearing to be dead entirely was instantly shot through the head; the same ceremony was performed on the other. After this the whole line was ordered to march round the dead bodies.

In the East Indies some troops of the Honourable East India Company sentenced to death were shot from the mouth of a cannon. The soldier was bound to the gun with his breast against the muzzle. Grose calls it 'both a military and a merciful death'. Grose thought, but was not certain, that it was adopted by Sir Eyre Coote and used by him on some of the King's troops. Certainly, during and after the Indian Mutiny many sepoy mutineers were 'blown from the guns'.

Despite all these punishments and their severity it must not be thought that service penalties were necessarily more harsh than those imposed by civil courts. This was an age when man's inhumanity to man was inescapably obvious, when civilians were transported for life as punishment for some offence such as stealing a loaf of bread. It must also be remembered that at the time when some offences in the British Army were punished by flogging, the same offences in the French Army would result in sentence of death. Most soldiers bore their frightful floggings stoically and accepted them as a fact of existence.

One soldier diarist has recorded that until he had been flogged with the cat he felt he had not become a man. It is significant to find that few of the many soldiers or officers who have recorded their attitude to the cat objected to flogging for serious offences, but nearly all spoke out violently against flogging for trivial offences. Many preferred flogging to gaol, where conditions were appalling. Solitary confinement was so dreadful that most soldiers, given the choice of this or of light or medium flogging, would not have hesitated. Even an ordinary gaol sentence was a frightening prospect. Conditions and diet were so bad that few men came out without serious decline in their physical condition.

It was the unreasoning viciousness and inhumane number of lashes that were so grotesque. Dr Hamilton, a reliable observer, recorded that Private Anthony Gregory of the 10th Foot was given 100 lashes, 'well laid on', for allowing the queue of his hair to drop off when on duty. A man who brushed a fly from his face while on parade could also expect to be flogged.

In his biography, Bombardier Alexander Alexander tells the story of a young private of the 9th Regiment, found asleep at his post at Chatham in 1801. The boy's reputation was sound and his officers – some of them, anyway – tried to have his sentence of flogging quashed. But the general responsible, Sir John Moore, incredibly enough, was adamant, and before the regiment the lad was triced up in a bitterly cold wind and driven sleet.

'I saw the Drum Major strike a drummer to the ground for not using his strength sufficiently,' wrote Alexander. 'The man's back became black as the darkest mahogany and greatly swelled.' The MO had the victim taken down after 229 lashes and he was sent to hospital, where he died a week later.* 'I have witnessed 700 lashes inflicted, but I have never seen a man's back so black and swelled,' Alexander noted. Perhaps conscience about the incident made Moore the humane leader he undoubtedly became.

Even the lads in boy regiments were flogged, and we have it on the authority of the Revd Best that one boy died a few days after a flogging and that the officers tried to ascribe his death to some other cause.

Shipp records that two boys of his experimental unit, aged 13 and 11 were sentenced to be flogged because they had deserted – if that is the word for childish homesickness. Each boy was given about six dozen vicious lashes and they

* In 1866 Herbert Compton of the 14th Hussars saw a gravestone in a churchyard near Hounslow, on which was the inscription 'A.H.' followed by the number of a cavalry regiment and underneath FLOGGED TO DEATH. Compton found out that the man had been punished for taking his horse out of stables without orders. *A King's Hussar*. (Compton was editor and compiler.)

shrieked in pain. The older boy was courageous enough to offer to take his younger brother's punishment, but even this had no effect on the CO Said Shipp, 'In little more than a year after this there were not two greater reprobates or vagabonds in the whole corps. The elder boy soon died. Of the fate of the younger I cannot speak with certainty, but I think he was found drowned in Table Bay at the Cape of Good Hope.'

Southey, in *Espriella's Letters*, said that in 1807 the martial laws of England were the most barbarous in Europe.[†] The offender is sometimes sentenced to receive a thousand lashes – a surgeon stands by to feel his pulse during the execution and determine how long the flogging can continue without killing him. When human nature can stand no more he is remanded to hospital. His wound, for from shoulders to the loins it leaves him one wound, is dressed, and as soon as it is sufficiently healed to be laid open in the same manner, he is brought out to undergo the remainder of his sentence. And this is repeatedly and openly practised in a country where they read in their churches, and in their houses, that Bible, in their own language, which saith, "Forty stripes may the judge inflict upon the offender, and not exceed".'

Shipp, in Jersey in 1808, said that the sentence of 1,000 lashes was rigidly enforced 'with the additional torture which must have resulted from the number five[*] being slowly counted between lashes . . . as though 1,000 lashes were not themselves a sufficiently awful sentence without so cruel and unnecessary a prolongation of misery. Many of these poor creatures fainted several times. . . . Numbers of them were taken down and carried from the square in a state of utter insensibility. The spectacle . . . created disgust and abhorrence in the breast of every soldier who was worthy of the name of man.'

The mechanics of flogging were simple. In the centre of the parade ground or area set aside for punishment were the

† They were no more barbarous than in other countries. Some contemporary writers and others since have said that Prussia's military laws were harsher than those of Britain. And it must be emphasized that civil punishment was equally harsh.
* Other observers speak of ten drum taps after each stroke of the lash.

triangles; originally they comprised of sergeants' halberds – long pikes – lashed tripod-style. The defaulter, when lashed to them, had his arms and his legs apart. In permanent stations or barracks timber triangles were kept ready for use. Sometimes two or three would be in use at the one time. Being tied for some time to the halberds (or to a tree or any other convenient structure when in the field) was in itself a severe physical punishment and strain. The ropes were often so tight that a man's hands turned black and were numb for several days. The hands-high position was also damaging to the criculation and threw great strain on the heart. Occasionally, if a man were so tied that he would twist about in pain, or if the cat-wielding drummer[†] was inaccurate, the thongs would twist around the victim's neck and damage his face. It seems likely that some men lost their eyes while being flogged.

Corporal punishment was always administered publicly, the idea being that the example might deter others from similar offences. Every available man was forced on to parade in ranks facing inwards in square. When the commanding officer, the adjutant, the medical officer, the drum major and the drummers were in position the prisoner was marched in, stripped to the waist and bound to the triangles.

The drummers relieved one another after twenty-five lashes, so that their arms would not become too tired. Napier noted that 'It is to be observed that when men are charged with the infliction of any punishment, no matter how revolting . . . they generally become desirous of adding to its severity; their minds grow hardened by seeing such punishments inflicted and they erroneously believe that the bodies of their fellows grow equally indurated.'

Unually only a few lashes from the leather thongs would draw blood and by fifty a man's back could be a jelly, though there were those tough characters who could stand a lot

† Drummers had many duties and were odd-job men. One very odd job concerned a drummer and a trumpeter of the Oxford Regiment of Horse. They posed, in disguise, as a parson and clerk and officiated at the 'marriage' of the Earl of Oxford and a London actress. The Earl paid them well for their services.

without showing more then bruises. Frequently the defaulters sucked a musket ball or chewed a piece of leather to stifle their cries of agony.

If the adjutant believed that the drummers were not putting their weight into the flogging he would speak sharply to the drum major or even lash him with his rattan cane. The drum major would then cane the drummers and incite them to renewed ferocity. While the flogging was going on one drummer or an NCO would stand by to call aloud the number of each stroke and write it down.

The surgeon was supposed to stop the punishment if he considered it excessive, but only rarely did this happen. Even when a soldier showed signs of collapse the surgeon would merely bring him round, so that the flogging could continue. If for some reason the flogging was interrupted – and to their anonymous credit some surgeons did interfere – the respite was only temporary. When his wounds had healed the man was brought out for the punishment to be completed. A drummer who rose to commissioned rank wrote: 'It was my duty to flog men at least three times a week for eight years. . . . There was no possibility of shrinking. . . . Immediately after the parade I used to run into the barrack-room to wash away traces of blood and so to escape from the observation of the soldiers.'

Nobody was ever sentenced to less than 25 lashes, but such a low number was rare. Even 100 lashes was considered, even by the victim, as light punishment. Sentences of 300 to 500 lashes was fairly common and others of 800 to 1,500 lashes not infrequent. Remember that four hours were needed to inflict 1,000 lashes and you get a faint idea of the victim's ordeal. I believe that 1,500 was the maximum number of lashes a court martial could legally award, but I have not personally seen a record of this number. I had in my possession for some years a log book of the Royal Marines in which 800 lashes was the maximum sentence awarded. However, it is on record that in India in 1788 a man was awarded 2,000 lashes.

There were COs – on the evidence of Napier – who 'distributed lashes from the poll of the neck to the heel, thus flaying the shoulders, posteriors, thighs and calves, multiplying the punishment enormously. They [the victims] will often lie as if without life, and the Drummers appear to be flogging a lump of raw, dead flesh.'

Sometimes the soldier was flogged on the buttocks, either to make it more painful or more shameful or both or perhaps because his back was already raw from a previous flogging. Sometimes, for the same reason, he was flogged on the calves. It was said that flogging on the buttocks occasionally caused an erection 'sometimes to such a degree as to attract the attention of men in the ranks and to excite their suppressed laughter'.

At least one commanding officer ordered twenty-five lashes on each shoulder alternately, and there are records of similar left and right punishment on the buttocks, with a left-handed and a right-handed drummer wielding the cat or cane. 'Being late and general slovenly marching' were crimes sufficient to merit this punishment.

I could give stroke-by-stroke details of a flogging, but they are unpleasant at best and revolting at worst and are probably best left to the reader's imagination. It is enough to say on this theme that sometimes the ends of the cat became so heavy from coagulated blood that they had to be washed in water, but in some regiments this was not done so that the punishment would be all the more severe. In one regiment cats were soaked in brine before being used, but it was found that the CO Lieutenant-Colonel Bayly, 98th Regiment, had no knowledge of this.

Some commanders were utterly pitiless about flogging – or so it seemed. On the retreat to Vigo – part of the general withdrawal during the Corumna campaign – General Robert ('Black Bob') Craufurd saw two men leave the ranks. He shouted to his brigade to halt and though the French were not far behind, he ordered a drum-head court martial. The soldiers were each condemned to 100 lashes. A private in the ranks near Craufurd growled, 'Damn his eyes! He had better get us something to eat than badger us this way.' Craufurd overheard and at once had this man court martialled, too. His sentence: 300 lashes. It was too dark to carry out the floggings – though one account says that one man was punished before the column moved on. The men, starving, ice-smeared, ragged, and bloody, some shoeless, pressed on all night.

At dawn Craufurd ordered the brigade into the square.

'Although I shall obtain neither the goodwill of the officers nor the men by so doing, I am resolved to punish these three men. Begin with Daniel Howans.'

Howans, the man who had spoken from the ranks, now said, 'Don't trouble about tying me up. I'll take my punishment like a man.' And he took the whole 300 without sound. His wife watched the infliction of the lashes and when it was over she covered his bleeding back with his greatcoat. Howan's colonel asked to forgive the other two men on account of their fine record as soldiers.

'I order you, sir,' Craufurd said, 'to do your duty. The men shall be punished.' But as preparations were being made, Craufurd said, 'Stop. On your colonel's intercession I will allow you this much. You shall draw lots and the winner shall escape. But one of the two I am determined to make an example of.'

The loser stripped and took seventy-five lashes before Crauford stopped the flogging. 'Rejoin your company,' he told the men. Then, to the brigade, 'I give you all notice that I will halt the brigade the very moment I see any man disobeying my orders, and try him by court martial on the spot.'

A soldier who saw all this wrote later, 'No one but one formed of stuff like General Craufurd could have saved the brigade from perishing altogether; and if he flogged two, he saved hundreds from death.'

Captain John Kincaid, a capable, humane officer with a sense of humour, proportion and reason saw something in favour of flogging – at least as practised by Craufurd – and he must be listened to. 'Where soldiers are to be ruled, there is more logic in nine tails of a cat than in the mouth of a hundred orators. It requires very little argument to prove, and I'll defy the most eloquent preacher . . . to persuade a regiment to ford a river where there is a bridge to conduct them over dry-shod, or to prevent them drinking when they are in that river if they happen to be thirsty, let him promise them what he will. . . . With the soldiers [there was] this difference, that Craufurd's cat forced them to take the right road whether they would or no. . . .'

Kincaid spent a chapter in his *Random Shots From a Rifleman* showing that Craufurd was cruel to be kind, that by flogging a few he was benefiting all. 'Punishment for disorders were rarely necessary after the first campaign; for the system, once established, went like clock-work, and the soldiers became devotedly attached to him.'

There is proof of their devotion – or at least of the thoroughness of their training at Craufurd's hands. He had inherited command of the famous Light Division, but in 1810 was killed. Marching back from his funeral near Badajoz, the Division encountered flood water across the road. The men paused, looking for a way around. Then they instinctively remembered Craufurd's training – Keep straight ahead, regardless of obstacles. The column plunged into the water, kept formation through it and reached the other side in silence. It was magnificent testimony to Craufurd's personality.

There was nothing stupid about wading through water. Craufurd had not taught them to do this from sheer cussedness; he had not flogged them in fury. Hesitation is fatal in war. Among other things it sows the seeds of panic. It was not much safer to cross bridges in his day than it is now, with enemy in the locality; bridges are good targets and they can be death traps. No man led by Craufurd lost his head in panic; no man obeying his orders was ever caught in a trap, though Craufurd was nearly caught during an action on the Coa River in 1810. There was method in Craufurd's severity and no doubt this applied to other leaders of Craufurd's type.

Whatever Craufurd's motives in flogging, there is no doubt that some commanding officers took an unholy and unhealthy delight in it. So many soldiers' and officers' memoirs bring this to light. One colonel was so perverted that he ordered that every man flogged had to wear a yellow patch on his left sleeve. For each subsequent flogging a hole was made in the patch. As a result the regiment lost its spirit and morale broke down completely. A sense of shame and futility permeated every activity. The CO was relieved and his successor abolished the detested patches, but the men needed months to recover.

One of the most puzzling aspects of flogging is that everybody concerned must have known that excessive punishment damaged a man irreparably as a soldier. Many became so ill or weak that they had to be discharged; others needed up to a year to recover. Yet others contracted pneumonia, lockjaw, asthma and other diseases. 'We sometimes find the body melt away into a spectre,' wrote Dr Hamilton. Even a light sentence on service meant that a soldier could not carry his pack and weapon for some days. At one time in 1811 – a year of battles – no fewer than thirty-two men of one regiment were in hospital recovering from the lash, though another regiment, Northamptonshires,* acquired one of its nicknames, 'The Steelbacks', from the stoicism with which its men endured flogging.

Perhaps the greatest insult of all was that the victim was compelled to pay 6d or 1s for the use of the cats, an iniquitous charge shown on the soldier's account as 'Drum Major's charge'.

Sometimes after a flogging a soldier would be drummed out of the service with a halter around his neck. After the flogging the prisoner, with an escort of a corporal and six men, would be paraded before the regiment, the halter would be put around his neck and often a label would be pinned on his back stating his crime. A drummer would then take the rope and lead the defaulter before the regiment, while the other drummers would follow beating the *Rogues March*. If the unit was quartered in a town the procession would parade right through it and on the outskirts the drummer would kick the defaulter 'on the breech, leaving him the halter for his perquisite'.

A few commanding officers managed their regiments efficiently without recourse to flogging. One such commander was Sir Robert Wilson, CO of the 20th Light Dragoons. His regiment was always smart, well disciplined and well behaved, yet Wilson never flogged and later in parliament became an outspoken opponent of flogging. In the early years of the nineteenth century parliamentary agitation, by Wilson and others, came to nothing in the face of stubborn opposition from men such as Castlereagh, Secretary of State for War. In 1809 William Cobbett was sentenced to two years in gaol for taking up in his *Political Register* the case of soldiers given 500 lashes for alleged mutiny. In 1811 another editor was found

---

* This was the last British regiment to carry colours into battle – at Laing's Nek in the Boer War of 1881.

guilty of seditious libel, also for caustic comments on the use of the lash, and was gaoled and fined.

By 1812 flogging was virtually the only major army punishment – a panacea for every crime, sin, fault and misdemeanour. In that year, the average number of lashes inflicted in a regiment serving in India was 17,000.

On 16 November 1812 Wellington, an advocate of the lash, hanged two men for shooting pigs in the woods, that 'shameful and unmilitary practice'. True, shots of pig-hunters had given him the impression that his flank skirmishers were in touch with the enemy, but the punishment seems harsh.

Even after 1812, when the Duke of York issued his confidential circular to all commanding officers limiting the number of lashes to 300, the more brutal officers simply awarded extra doses of the lash. If a man were absent at tattoo he would get 300 strokes. One officer said that in 'conscience' he could not and would not comply with the order if he felt convinced that a man deserved 600 lashes.

In 1814 three men of the Bengal European Infantry were sentenced to 1,500 lashes each, and one victim in desperation grabbed the drum major's sword and shouted to his comrades in the ranks to rescue him. But fear kept them in their places and the poor devil was overpowered by sergeants. He received every stroke of the 1,500 and almost immediately after, court martialled for mutinous conduct. He was taken out and shot and perhaps was glad to go.

On 10 June 1816 Wellington himself signed an order that a soldier guilty of passing a counterfeit two-franc piece to a woman at Versailles be given 999 lashes.

Occasionally even a monarch felt moved to protest. George III, commenting on a sentence of 1,500 lashes awarded to a private of the 54th Regiment, was 'graciously pleased' to express his opinion that no sentence for corporal punishment should exceed one thousand lashes. One thousand lashes and he was graciously pleased! Yet five months later a soldier of the 67th Regiment serving in Bengal was sentenced by court martial to receive 1,500 lashes. The sentence was approved and confirmed by Headquarters, Bengal Army.

In India in 1820 a private soldier named Gilling was

sentenced to 1,000 lashes for having in his possession, without entitlement, three white shirts, a white jacket and a white capcover, as well as being absent from his quarters for one night. At Dinapore, India, in 1825, a soldier was sentenced to receive 1,900 but the commander-in-chief reduced this to 1,200.

Of massive punishment Napier wrote, 'As the hundreds of lashes mounted up the faces of the spectators assumed a look of disgust, there was always a low whispering sound, scarcely audible, issuing from the apparently stern and silent ranks – a sound arising from lips that spoke not; but a sound produced by hearts that felt deeply. The punishment had become excessive . . . the culprit had disappeared and the martyr had taken his place.'

Sergeant Teesdale in 1835 said that frequently when his regiment was stationed at Bremen there was a punishment parade each morning and evening and that at every parade from fifteen to twenty were flogged for petty reasons. On one occasion, after standing to attention for two hours to watch the agonies of his comrades, one soldier of blameless reputation suffering from a cold aggravated by bitter weather could not stop himself from coughing. The CO instantly held a drum-head court martial; the man was found guilty of 'being unsteady in the ranks' and given fifty lashes.

Dr Bell, on duty in the West Indies in 1838, was able to write with apparent pride, that flogging proved 'a useful remedy' for a man who had convulsions when marched to the triangles. Previously the convulsions had been sufficient to cause his sentence to be cancelled, but the CO and the doctor agreed that this unsatisfactory state of affairs could not continue, so convulsions or not they gave him 300 lashes – after threatening him with burning with red-hot irons if he dared to have a fit. 'While I remained in the regiment,' wrote Dr Bell, 'I never heard of his being attacked by any convulsive disorder. . . .' Bravo, Dr Bell!

Flogging anecdotes are innumerable because there was no shortage of witnesses and the act was apt to leave a vivid impression on even the most bovine of brains. So we know that most men received their punishment with outward calmness and with courage that, exhibited in battle, would bring commendation. Some made so light of the experience that they could joke when they were taken down. One tough old soldier grinned at the officers as he was being escorted from the square and said, 'Now, gentlemen, I've got my three thousand a year the same as you.'

Many officers were inured to flogging and unmoved by watching it. There is the classic case of the major with a pronounced northern accent who was one day holding a church parade. He was reciting the creed and had noted that Christ had 'suffered unto [sic] Pontius Pilate' when a bored and irreverent soldier whispered loudly, 'What's Ponchews Peelatt?'

'At yer auld tricks again, Jock?' the major said. 'Come here.' He convened a drum-head court martial, had Jock sentenced to 100 lashes and saw them inflicted before he calmly carried on with the service. Christ might have suffered unto Pontius Pilate, but many a soldier was crucified unto the triangles.

Occasionally there was grim humour in a flogging ceremony. Sergeant Lawrence of the 34th, when a private, received a stiff sentence, endured 175 without difficulty but then became irritated, restless and impatient. As he twisted, the triangles came loose from their fastenings and Lawrence moved slowly with them about the square, with the attending adjutant and his party following. The situation became so undignified and incongruous that the whole parade laughed and the commanding officer stopped the proceedings and remitted the rest of the sentence. But on more than one occasion, when the triangles collapsed and fell with the victim the punishment was completed with him lying on the ground.

Sometimes men felt compelled to resort to irregular protest. At York a deputation of four men paraded themselves to the CO, Colonel Long, at his office window, and demanded that he treat them more humanely. They must have known that this would lead to trouble – as indeed it did. Long called the guard, had the men arrested and tried and supervised their punishment – 800 lashes each.

The purpose of the Royal Commission of 1835–6 – granted only after many years of agitation – was to decide 'Whether, after a careful reference to all the circumstances and conditions under which the British Army is governed, and all the services which it is called upon to perform, it may be practicable to dispense with the power of inflicting corporal punishment, or to make any other changes or modifications in the punishment now applicable . . . without detriment or danger to the paramount consideration of maintining strict discipline and effectually repressing crime in the ranks of the British Army throughout all the various contingencies of military service to which our troops are necessarily liable.'

A colonel was asked, 'Are we to understand that . . . corporal punishment should be resorted to in cases of necessity only, but that the power of inflicting it should be retained?'

'Most decidedly,' said the colonel. 'I conceive that if you were not to retain the power of punishing men by flogging, the officers might as well pull off their hats to the regiment and wish them goodbye.'

Surgeon Parkin gave some of the most interesting evidence. He claimed that charges that flogging was degrading were specious because it would be almost impossible morally to degrade most of the men sentenced to the cat. 'The man who is picked up drunk from the kennel, kicked out of a bagnio, bleeding from wounds in the head and face, and brought almost insensible into the barracks and hospital; or has been one of five, three of his own comrades, and two prostitutes, wallowing in the same bed together for a night, cannot suffer a moral degradation from the lash.'

Parkin's evidence was one-sided, since he implied that nearly all men flogged were of this low type. This was not the case.

Wellington told the Commission that he was 'inclined to believe that there is less punishment now', and added pointedly, 'But then, on the other hand, I am inclined to believe that there is now a great deal more crime. I do not see how you can have an army at all unless you preserve it in a state of discipline. How can you have a state of discipline unless you have some punishment . . . There is no punishment which makes an impression upon anybody except corporal punishment . . . By not enforcing your discipline and not enforcing your own orders, and not punishing when those orders are not obeyed, you are doing the grossest injustice to those who do obey your orders . . . In hundreds of instances the very threat of the lash has prevented very serious crimes . . . I declare that I have not an idea that can be substituted for it.'

The Duke said that he had never heard of a soldier being so cowed in spirit after severe flogging as to be unfitted for active service, nor did he think that flogging made a bad soldier worse. In lengthy questioning, during which many suggestions were made to him about better barracks, awards of merit and pensions and other things that might be done to improve army life, Wellington persisted that there could be no discipline in the British Army without flogging.

In defence of Wellington's views about his army it is only fair to say again that many men who enlisted in the British forces at this time were vicious, idle, dissolute, drunken and depraved. This applied more to those who came from manufacturing districts and large towns.

A sergeant-major questioned before the Commission said emphatically that 'with the class of men that we have it is impossible to do without corporal punishment', but was forced to qualify this in that his regiment had only about forty 'really bad characters'.

In publishing its finding, the Commission noted that, 'In considering therefore the subject of the punishments by which the discipline of the British Army has been created and maintained up to this time, it is well to see how far they have answered their purpose. To the superior discipline of the British Army when on service . . . strong testimony will be found in the evidence . . . more especially that of the Duke of Wellington, Sir Henry Fane and Sir Henry Hardinge. . . . Undoubtedly the only ground upon which the continuance of any punishment inflicting severe pain must consist in its efficacy as an example and . . . its effect in the way of reformation of the person undergoing it must be considered a secondary object . . . It is admitted to have great effect in deterring other soldiers, and especially the younger, from committing offences which will subject them to it.'

The Commission examined the system of punishments in the French Army – which at that time had no corporal punishment – but stated confidently that 'after all . . . the

French code does not produce, even in times of peace, a discipline in any degree equal to that which is enforced in the British Army.

'Officers of all ranks speak of flogging as an evil, rendered necessary by the description and prevailing habits of our soldiers, and more especially the vice of drunkenness which is, we fear, far from being confined to the ranks of the army, but pervades the population of the country. . . .'

Speaking about ways of making Service life more attractive to better types of men, the Commission recommended that 'every facility should be given in barrack yards for the enjoyment of many games by soldiers, such as fives courts and rackets, and by providing additional space for cricket and football. . . .'

The Commission, an honest one, confessed that friendship and familiarity between officers and men, an 'astonishing feature' of the French Army, could not work in the British Army. It could not recommend that it be made easier for common soldiers to win commissions because a man who had spent many years in the ranks would never become socially fitted as an officer, nor would he be happy as one.

Finally, the Commission stated bluntly that 'the opinion of almost every witness whom we have examined is that the substitution of other punishments for corporal punishment upon actual service and in the field is impracticable and, if practicable, would be sufficient for the maintenance of proper discipline'. One witness who did not agree with this was the Commander-in-Chief at that time, Lord Hill.

However, in 1836, the Articles of War limited a general court martial to a sentence of 200 lashes, a district court to 150 and a regimental court martial to 100. In 1868 flogging supposedly ceased in the British Army, but not until 1881 did an Act of Parliament formally abolish it.

At no time while flogging was on the way out or after it disappeared did Tommy Atkins's discipline and morale show signs of collapse. The far-sighted opponents of flogging had known that this would be the result, but in no country have military conservatives put up such a stubborn, senseless resistance to reforms as in Britain.

In the meantime, in 1840 a new punishment for desertion had been introduced. It was a cold instrument which rammed a set of needles into the skin to a depth of a quarter-inch, leaving the letter D. Gunpowder was rubbed into it to leave an indeible stain or tattoo. The regiment was paraded to see the infliction of this degradation, which often preceded a flogging. Little pain was involved in the punishment but the shame was considerable.

In 1946 a major twice decorated for gallantry was charged on two counts of having ordered his RSM to flog two privates of the Yorks and Lancs Regiment for being asleep on sentry duty far behind the Japanese lines in Burma. They received twelve strokes each. It was said at the officer's court martial that General Wingate, leader of the Chindits, favoured corporal punishment in circumstances where no other form of punishment was possible. A brigadier said that flogging was inflicted for severe offences in the Burma command. The major was acquitted, largely on the grounds that his superior officers had condoned his action.

Ten

1815–59 (1)
Some of Those Finest Hours

Some years after Waterloo Sir William Napier published his heroically dramatic and lengthy account of the Peninsular War in which, though sometimes critical, he generally found Tommy Atkins to be a good soldier. At one point he was fairly outspoken about it.

That the British infantry soldier is more robust than the soldier of any other nation, can scarcely be doubted by those, who in 1815, observed his powerful frame, distinguished amidst the united armies of Europe; and, notwithstanding his habitual excess in drinking, he sustains fatigue, and wet, and the extremes of cold and heat, with incredible vigour. When completely disciplined, and three years are necessary to accomplish this, his port is lofty, and his movements free: the whole world cannot produce a nobler specimen of military bearing; nor is the mind unworthy of the outward man. He does not indeed possess that presumptuous vivacity which would lead him to dictate to his commanders, or even to censure real errors, although he may perceive them; but he is observant, and quick to comprehend his orders, full of resources under difficulties, calm and resolute in danger, and more than usually obedient and careful of his officers in moments of imminent peril. . . . Napoleon's troops fought in bright fields, where every helmet caught some beams of glory; but the British soldier conquered under the cold shade of aristocracy, no honours awaited his daring, no despatch gave his name to the applauses of his countrymen; his life of danger was uncheered by hope, his death unnoticed.

Simultaneously on sale with Napier's volumes was a less pretentious book by Captain John Patterson who had served in the Peninsula with the 50th Regiment. Said Patterson: 'The soldier was at that time, and still is, I apprehend [in 1840] looked upon as a mere machine, to be moved and wheeled about at will, having no right to exercise the reasoning or corporal blessings wherewith kind nature had endowed him.'

Patterson's profile was more realistic. Napier, for all his historic judgement, was something of a romantic. But even he must have realized that he erred when he said Tommy Atkins was 'full of resources under difficulties'. The common soldier was neither expected nor permitted to show resource and he was, indeed, a 'mere machine'. And, in the years after Waterloo, he also became a clothes horse, as we shall see.

After Waterloo England became weary of war and soldiers. Parliament grew meaner than ever in financing the army. Within the army, too, reaction set in. True, in India the Honourable East India Company's troops were fighting a series of wars punctuated by many gallant actions, but all this was too remote in an age when news took months to reach home. Peacetime soldiering in England was tedious and without the impetus of war no improvements occurred in any part of army structure. The old hands at the Horse Guards resisted any changes on the ground that what had worked before would work again. Tradition was paramount – a fine sentiment, but one bound to kill progress. The army was trapped in a maze of red tape and petty regulations and in forty years resolutely advanced absolutely nowhere. Fortescue summed it up with unusual acidity: 'The troops were infamously housed, abominably over-crowded and senselessly fed.' The traveller and military observer Kinglake noted that the Duke of Wellington's methods tended to divorce the country and the army still further. Colonel de Watteville went so far as to say that in this unfortunate period 'the army tended to become the laughing stock of the nation'.

Probably he was referring mainly to the astonishing array of uniforms now to be seen in the country. Military dress was certainly colourful, but it was about as impracticable and unserviceable as possible. Not, I suppose, that this mattered much for an army which rarely saw action. Cavalrymen suffered more than other soldiers. The head-dresses they were obliged to wear make wonderful collectors' pieces today because of their fantastic shapes. The horsed soldiers were loaded with all kinds of 'dashing' trappings – dolmans, pelisses and jackets cut so exquisitely and slung so elaborately that even women's tailors would be envious of their line. The cavalry officer needed to be quite wealthy to outfit himself in the style and luxury that the cavalry regiments demanded; this was the real reason for the exclusiveness of the various cavalry regiments. Writers like Dickens and Thackeray, and the press and the public ridiculed the gorgeous and at times bizarre uniforms. The infantry soldier was issued with, among other things, a large shako in the shape of a bell. Musketeers of the Civil War period, two centuries before, had worn a much more useful hat.

The soldier was still an inveterate drinker and the problem of drunkenness plagued army commanders. Sometimes pay days were so arranged that neighbouring units received their money on different days – in the hope that fewer brawls would result. Pay-day fights between regiments were really serious as the men, wild with drink, used stones, sticks, iron bars and bottles. Nearly always serious casualties occurred before patrols could restore order. Not that the men needed to be drunk to start an inter-regimental fight. Some regiments were at loggerheads for years over some real or imagined grievance long since forgotten. The men of X regiment knew, simply, that 'those bastards from Y regiment are our mortal enemies'. No reason was necessary. A garrison town was not exactly a tourist attraction, for men were continually reeling back to barracks with street urchins sniping at them with stones and insults.

The men's behaviour was bad, but really they were not to blame. They lived in squalid surroundings with no amenities, amusements or social life. They did not even have anything to read. Books were banned because the army authorities were scared that political matter might unsettle the men. Actually, from 1825 just twenty-eight titles were allowed into barracks –

and the books were only for sick men. As the books had been selected by a censorship bench of bishops it is not surprising that even the sick soldiers rarely read them. Wellington at this time actively discouraged education for soldiers.

Once in a while some public-spirited person or group would make a breakthrough in improving the lot of the troops – and then the troops themselves would ruin the effort. Once somebody secured an increase in the number of issue blankets. But old soldiers had been racketeering in blankets for a long time; a syndicate of three would sell one blanket and then cut and sew two other blankets into three.

The pay sergeant was a menace to Tommy Atkins's contentment. He knew every trick for keeping back part of a soldier's pay, often with the excuse that he must hold funds for any future stoppage for loss of or damage to uniform or equipment. In those days a soldier could die from disease at any time and the pay sergeant would 'inherit' the money he held for stoppages. Pay sergeants' iniquities and the refusal or indifference of officers in dealing with them deeply offended the men.

If Fortescue's comment that the troops were infamously housed was true – and it was – then the conditions of soldiers' wives and children were doubly infamous. When the first barracks were built, about 1792, the married soldier was allowed a corner of a barrack room for himself and his wife, but only at the rate of six wives a company, that is, a proportion of one wife to twelve infantrymen. Behind a screen of blankets or canvas Tommy and his wife owned two single beds and virtually nothing else. Here they had their entire being, without privacy other than that provided by the screen. Here the woman had her children, here the children grew up. They slept on the floor, although small boys could usually find a bed left vacant for the night by a soldier on duty or absent. These small boys were the only ones who might have been said to enjoy barrack life, for the men usually made pets of them.

A new bride, especially one from a quiet, decent home found her introduction to barrack life a traumatic experience. Some contemporary writers say that the presence of a woman lessened profanity, but the women would still be exposed to a horrifying amount of it. When the men were drunk, and sometimes when they were not, a woman might be molested, unless her husband was known to be a tough man with his fists and boots.

Boredom menaced women in these surroundings. Many of them, no matter how decent when they joined the regiment, had not the strength of character to fight off boredom and the evil influence of their surroundings. They became hard and callous and they drank heavily. They were then difficult to handle and made life hell for the men in the room.

Other women were kept busy in the earlier days by cooking for the room, washing and mending clothes and keeping the place clean. For all this a woman was paid a very small sum out of the men's stoppages. The right type of woman could be a blessing to a barrack room by writing letters for illitertate soldiers, listening to their complaints, tending them when they were unwell. Not for many years would life improve for soldiers' wives.

Not infrequently a soldier married 'off the strength', that is, without official permission. His wife could not then find accommodation in the barracks and life for her and her husband was miserable. Some COs were highly intolerant when it came to giving permission to marry. At one time a man went away without leave for two hours to be married and on his return was arrested, charged and given twenty-eight days in prison.

When a soldier who had married off the strength was transferred to another station his wife had to come to him as best she could. One woman slogged all the way from the south of England to Edinburgh and arrived with bleeding feet. If the unofficial husband had children and had amassed furniture and belongings then his worries multiplied. Some soldiers were driven to suicide or to desertion by the intensity of their family problems.

Distribution of food was another constant source of annoyance and frustration. For one thing, there was never enough food; after all, not until the 1820s were breakfast messes introduced. There has never been a truer military dictum than 'an army marches on its stomach'. How the

British Army managed to perform its grandly heroic deeds when half starved is one of the major mysteries of the service.

Food was shared out most unfairly, especially to recruits before they woke up to the tricks of the trade. During the pre-Crimea period the carver or server would put a certain amount of food on a plate and call out, 'Who shall have this?' to a man known in some regiments as 'the namer'. Recruits did not know that the words 'Who shall have this?' could be spoken in several ways, according to a code. Emphasis on a particular word meant that the meal was a poor one and that 'the namer' should award it to a recruit.

In 1826 the troops did get one break. With the creation of the Metropolitan Police Force soldiers were gradually relieved of police duties, which they detested. However, in Ireland soldiers continued to act as police for many years more.

Thackeray (as Michael Angelo Titmarsh) pilloried the soldier. 'The whole system of the army is something egregious and artificial. The civilian who lives out of it cannot understand it. It is not like other professions which require intelligence. A man one degree removed from idiocy, with brains sufficient to direct his powers of mischief and endurance, may make a distinguished soldier. As to the men, they get the word of command to advance or fall back, and they do it; they are told to strip and be flogged, and they do it; to murder or be murdered, and they do it; for their food and clothing and twopence a day for their tobacco.'

Comments like these were typical. Many people saw the army as a useless extravagance. It was the eternal British attitude to its soldiers. There was no war, so what was the use of keeping them? What did they do to pay for their keep? The idea of a deterrent force, of one trained ready for an emergency never entered the public mind. I am, of course, being flattering when I refer to a 'trained' force. There was virtually no training apart from the perpetual and much-damned drilling on the barrack square. This instilled a certain type of discipline and uniformity of movement, but it did not prepare men for the changing face of war. Of course, as the decades went by before the Crimea very few and finally none of the men with real European battle and active service experience remained in the army; this meant that the army had no genuine instructors. It was a case now not of the best leading the worst, but of the ignorant leading the ignorant.

It is not strictly true to say that troops at home saw *no* action. In 1818 they were in action at Winchester College, when the boys rebelled against a tightening up of school discipline.* They seized the school keys, locked the gates and turned out all the school servants, except the cook who was to keep working for them. Then they locked the Warden inside his house.

A tutor was sent to tell the boys that the Riot Act had been read, and that soldiers were on the way. If they would surrender the keys, the tutor said, all the boys could go home for a fortnight. The boys accepted the terms and rushed off towards the town. But the authorities had no intention of keeping their side of the bargain. As the boys passed through a narrow part of the Close called the Slype (slipway) they met soldiers with fixed bayonets, headed by an officer.

The officer was knocked down, but the bayonets were too much for the boys, who turned and ran. The soldiers chased them, enjoying the job because they had recently quarrelled with the boys over a bathing place. The officer joined in the chase, pricking with his sabre one of the big college boys who afterwards became a distinguished clergyman.

The rebel boys raced past the College, only to come face to face with another company of soldiers with fixed bayonets. Hemmed in, they had to go back to College and surrender. Punishment included expulsion for twenty boys.

It was no easy job putting down a school rebellion in those days, either for schoolmasters or soldiers. Some boys had pistols, the others swords and bludgeons. It was a pistol shot, fired in the yard of his boarding house by a schoolboy, that started a rebellion at Rugby in which soldiers were involved in 1797. The offender was flogged and in the riot which

---

* Winchester also had rebellions in 1770, 1774, 1778 and 1793, in none of which soldiers were involved. Eton, Harrow and Rugby had similar outbreaks about the same time. Historians blamed the spirit of the French Revolution.

followed windows were broken. The headmaster, Henry Ingles, known as 'Black Tiger', ordered the fifth and sixth forms to pay for the damage. Outraged, the seniors incited the whole school to pile up desks and benches in the Close and set them on fire. The headmaster's books were thrown on to the bonfire for good measure.

There was a recruiting party of soldiers in the town and they were called in. The boys retreated to an island in the Close, which had a moat around it. The Riot Act was read and while the boys were being called on to surrender the soldiers crept round behind them and took them prisoner. Many expulsions and floggings followed. Some of the ringleaders distinguished themselves as officers under Wellington.

But taming schoolboys was mere diversion. For troops and their families on their way to the hell that was India there was no diversion – certainly not until troopship accommodation improved a little after the 1850s.

The English race is indeed a peculiar thing. It teaches its young about the horrors of the Black Hole of Calcutta (for instance) but never tells them a word about the more protracted and no less acute miseries suffered by British soldiers and their families on troopships. Perhaps because in the latter case the torments were inflicted by British upon British.

A troopship was a floating hell. The men and their families were packed into decks too low for a man to stand upright, with no space, no furniture or fittings and no privacy. The food was appalling and as the trip went on it became worse; fruit and vegetables were only obtainable on the rare occasions when a ship put into a transit port. Such accepted modern amenities as baths, reading and recreation rooms were non-existent. When diesease broke out – which, inevitably, was frequently – men died in hundreds.

Mrs Sherwood, wife of a captain in the 53rd Regiment, spent four months *en route* to India and lived to write about her ordeal: 'Our cabin was just the width of a gun over which the cot was slung, but it could not swing, there being not sufficient height. On entering the cabin, which was formed only of canvas, we were forced to stoop under, there not being one foot from the head or the foot of the cot to the partition. . . .

We were in constant darkness [because her canin was on the lee side] and we have much putrid water on board, which is pumped up every four hours near our cabin door, so that we are occasionally floated by it. Hence our cabin was not altogether tolerable in the day, and not over agreeable at night.' But Mrs Sherwood travelled in luxury compared to the conditions of the wives and children of ordinary soldiers.

Of his voyage to India John Shipp had written:

It would be difficult to picture a set of men more deplorably situated . . . but our distresses were not yet at their height; for, as though our miseries still required aggravation, the scurvy broke out among us in a most frightful manner. Scarcely a single individual on board escaped this melancholy disorder, and the swollen legs, the gums protruding beyond the lips, attested the malignancy of the visitation. The dying were burying the dead . . . Every assistance and attention that humanity or generosity could dictate, was freely and liberally bestowed by the officers on board, who cheerfully gave up their meat and many other comforts . . . but the pestilence baffled the aid of medicine and the skill of the medical attendants. My poor legs were as big as drums; my gums swollen to an enormous size; my tongue too big for my mouth; and all I could eat was raw potatoes and vinegar. But my kind and affectionate officers sometimes brought me some tea and coffee, at which the languid eye would brighten, and the tear of gratitude would intuitively fall, in spite of my efforts to repress what was thought unmanly . . . Thus passed the time; men dying in dozens, and, ere their blood was cold, hurled into the briny deep, there to become a prey to sharks. It was a dreadful sight to see the bodies of our comrades the bone of disputation with these voracious natives of the dreary deep. . . .

Service in India was fraught with dangers, some inflicted by the authorities. Reginald Heber, Bishop of Calcutta, was moved to protest about one evil in 1826:

Nothing can be more foolish, or in its effect more pernicious, than the manner in which spirits are distributed to European troops in India. Early every morning a pint of fiery, course, undiluted rum is given to every man, and half that quantity to every woman. If half the quantity of spirit, well watered, were given at a more seasonable hour, and, to compensate for the loss of the rest, a cup of strong coffee allowed to each man every morning, the men would be quite as well pleased, and both their bodies and souls preserved from many dreadful evils. Colonel Williams of the 'Queen's Own' has tried this experiment with much success, and it might, with a little resolution, be universal throughout the army.

The Indian Campaigns – and there were to be scores of them – were arduous. That in Burma in 1824–6 was especially trying, but it brought out one of Tommy Atkins's most dominant traits and one which has drawn many comments from observers and historians.

Tommy had to fight a clever, ruthless and cruel enemy who usually operated from strong emplacements. When the Burmese caught a soldier they tortured and mutliated him. The climate and vegetation were not much kinder. Only one man in about seven endured the tough campaign, which ended in complete victory for the British. The Burmese expected reprisals. They were astonished to be shown friendship 'by a big, kindly creature who welcomed them with a smile', as Fortescue put it. This friendship was not the result of any order. Tommy Atkins was incapable of bitterness that lasted for long. Fortescue says, 'In a very few weeks the deserted towns and villages were again swarming with happy, docile and contented people; and the British soldier was completely – sometimes rather too completely! – at home with them and intensely popular with them all.' The same process of fighting first, friendship after, occurred in several other parts of the world, notably in New Zealand after the Maori wars.

In 1837 Victoria became Queen but her accession made no immediate difference to the life of Tommy Atkins. Certainly in the very early years of her reign she did not inspire men to join the Colours. Sergeant J. MacMullen of the 13th Regiment made his own analysis of why men entered the army in the 1840s and published it in *Camp and Barrack Room: or, the British Army As It Is.*

Indigent – Embracing labourers and mechanics out of employ, who merely seek for support	80 in 120
Indigent – Respectable persons induced by misfortune or imprudence	2 in 120
Idle – Who consider a soldier's life is an easy one	16 in 120
Bad characters* – Who fall back upon the army as a last resource	8 in 120
Criminals – Who seek to escape from the consequence of their offences	1 in 120
Perverse sons – Who seek to grieve their parents	2 in 120
Discontented and restless	8 in 120
Ambitious	1 in 120
Others	2 in 120

But in 1842 an English regiment – no doubt with its quota of perverse and idle as well as restless and ambitious men – gave Britain and her Army one of their finest hours. It was also one of the most disastrous and tragic hours, but the two often go together in British history. The place at which it happened can still be identified, for on a low hill near Gundamuck, on the side of the Kabul Road, is one of those lonely memorials, rarely seen by Englishmen, which mark a place of combat.

The preliminaries started in November 1841 when the supporters of Dost Mohammed, a fiery leader, violently revolted. The British military commander, General Elphinstone, vapid and sick, could have held out in Bala Hissar, a stronghold in Kabul, but in the end he agreed to withdraw his troops and all his people and take them back to British territory by way

---

* A selection of the worst types seemed to be present at the Bull's Head, Nottingham, early in 1844 when young Mr Ryder arrived to join a group of recruits destined for the 32nd Regiment. He was 'ashamed of being among them; for they were a dirty, ragged lot of blackguards – some of them nearly drunk'.

of the Khyber Pass. In deep snow, on 6 January 1842 the 44th Foot (The Essex Regiment) led out from Kabul 4,500 troops, mostly Indian, many British women and children and a rabble of 12,000 Indian camp followers.

The withdrawal was a nightmare, with savage Afghans hovering on the flanks and in the rear, pouncing at every opportunity. The situation was so dangerous that the 44th was sent to the rear to protect the column. But their numbers were too small. Within four days 9,000 camp followers were dead from Afghan bullets and knives or from frostbite and exposure. Akbar, son of Dost Mohammed, offered to keep safe the woman and children if they were surrendered to him. This was a desperate decision to make, but this time the promise was kept and the women and children were ultimately rescued unharmed.

Before long Elphinstone's force was reduced to 150 sowars of the Fifth Native Cavalry and 250 men of the 44th, commanded by Colonel Shelton, a veteran of the retreat to Corunna, thirty years earlier. The men had a brief rest at Jagdulluck and went on, with a patrol under Captain Soutar, leading the way through the rocky, treacherous country. The others tried to shepherd the rest of the survivors as they fought off Afghan attacks. The job of carrying the wounded was especially difficult. Every soldier present must have known the inevitable end of the retreat, but discipline and morale remained high. On the sixth day of the march Captain Soutar wound the regimental colour around his waist, under his uniform.

On 13 January came the last stand. On the hill near Gundamuck forty-five men of the 44th, with about twenty officers – survivors of other units – defied the Afghan hordes, at odds of one hundred to one. When the ammunition ran out they fought with sword and bayonet – and so they died. Only Soutar survived the fight, because the Afghans found the colour around his wounded body and believed he must be somebody of high rank and worth a ransom. Of the column that set out from Kabul only one man reached Kandahar – Brydon, the surgeon of the 44th, and he was in a bad way.

Months later, when a British punitive column arrived the Afghan tribesmen told them of the desperate courage of the Redcoats on the little hill of Gundamuck. The colour which

Soutar saved came back to England and its shreds for ever hung in the regimental chapel at Warley.

The heroism of Tommy Atkins at Gundamuck cannot disguise the immensity of the disaster or its cause – senile generals, gullibility, mediocre weapons and a stupidly large baggage train. The men did not even have muskets with the newly-introduced percussion caps, an innovation which practically eliminated misfires. In short, Tommy Atkins fought on his guts. It was not the first time; it would not be the last. The sort of guts these men had was shown after the Battle of Hyderabad in the Scinde (or Sind) War of 1843, when ten badly wounded men of the 22nd Regiment (Cheshire) marched all the following day, in burning heat and over sandy desert, because they believed another battle might be imminent. For this reason soldiers have often concealed their wounds.

But neither guts, determination, steadiness nor any other quality absolved English soldiers from the strictness of discipline in India and executions were not rare. Sergeant MacMullen was a spectator at a military execution in 1844. Nothing, he said, could be more impressive or solemn.

All the troops at the station were drawn up so as to form three sides of a square, the gallows occupying the centre of the vacant side. When every preparation was made, a guard proceeded to the criminal's cell, who was dressed in a white gown, and has his irons knocked off. He was then placed in a dooly (litter), and borne to the left flank of the troops, where the procession was already formed. First went the band, playing the 'Dead March', with drums muffled, next a portion of the guard followed by four soldiers bearing a coffin. After these came the criminal, accompanied by a friend in lieu of a clergyman; the rear was brought up by the remainder of the guard. Thus marshalled, the procession moved slowly along the side of the square, till it reached the gallows, at the foot of which the coffin was placed, the band then filing to the rear of the regiment. The criminal, left alone with his guard and executioner, now mounted the platform with a firm step. The rope was adjusted round his neck. 'Mother, mother!' exclaimed the unhappy man, 'what will you say to this!' The next moment the drop fell, and he was swinging in mid-air.

The wars in the 1840s against those redoubtable fighters, the Sikhs, provided the most desperate series of battles the British ever fought in India – and gave Tommy Atkins further opportunities to show his stuff. But it was not all glory – as the more romantic writers would have it – and it is just as well to realize this before we look at the bloody actions. Soldiers themselves are the most honest reporters. One such was Corporal Ryder of the 32nd, who described a day's march in Indian conditions – and what it could do to men.

We struck camp at 11 o'clock. This was a very long day's march, over sandy deserts and plains, the water being short and the horrors past describing. We drew near to a well some time in the morning, and the confusion all round was fearful – the men rushing and pushing to get at it, some letting their caps fall into it, and some their bayonets; and I quite expected some of the men would go in. One poor fellow, endeavouring to get up, had fallen, and was begging most pitifully that some one would give him a draught to save his life; but, God help him! He spent his breath in vain. The doctor seeing him in this deplorable state, asked a man to give him a drink, but was refused. Every one must take care of himself: all respect for one another was gone. I was very nearly done up myself.

The Battle of Ferozeshah, in the first Sikh War, was a classic example of the maxim that a battle is never lost until it is won. In few other battles was final victory snatched so dramatically from looming disaster. The events leading to the battle began in December 1845, when a Sikh Army of 50,000 men, with 100 guns, under the command of Lal Singh, crossed the Sutlej River and invaded British territory with the object of sacking Delhi. The most formidable part of the Sikh Army was the Khalsa, the Praetorian Guard of the Punjab. The whole force was well equipped, especially with heavy artillery, and had been well trained and disciplined by French officers.

Crossing the Sutleg, Lal Singh detached part of his army to besiege Ferozepore, where the British had established a fortified post with a garrison of about 7,000 British and native Indian troops. Sir Hugh Gough, Commander-in-Chief in India, a Peninsular veteran who always wore a white coat in action to make himself conspicuous, marched with about 10,000 men from Umballa to the relief at Ferozepore. He had only a few light guns.

On 18 December at Moodkee, Gough repelled a Sikh assault, at heavy cost to both himself and the enemy. At 4 a.m. on 21 December he moved against the entrenched camp at Ferozeshah were a large part of the Sikh Army was in position.

Gough decided to attack at once. He had reliable reports that Ferozepore garrison had escaped and was on the way to join him, and he wanted to strike before the thwarted besiegers could reinforce the Sikhs at Ferozeshah. But Sir Henry Hardinge, another Peninsular veteran – we saw him at Albuhera – and the Governor-General of India, for political reasons ordered the British advance to be postponed.

Late in the afternoon the attack was launched, and in the brief period of daylight British troops and Sepoys advanced through semi-jungle, fighting a confused battle to reach the entrenchments and get in with the bayonet.

The Sikhs worked their guns with great efficiency. The Horse Artillery had hit back as best it could with its light pieces before the 62nd Regiment (Wiltshire) with the two native Indian battalions of its brigade charged the enemy guns. In a few minutes, the British battalion lost 260 all ranks; 18 of the 26 officers were casualties, and sergeants found themselves in charge of companies. Their attack broke down. Elsewhere the 9th Regiment (East Norfolk) suffered even more severely with 330 casualties.

Time after time the British had been repulsed and when night fell they had only a tenuous position, close to the Sikhs.

Soon a Sikh heavy gun opened fire on the British lines, mainly on the 80th Foot. Sir Henry Hardinge called out: 'Eightieth, that gun must be silenced!' The weary, battered Staffordshire men went into action again – knowing the attack was a desperate gamble. In the darkness they quietly formed line, and disappeared in the direction of the gun flashes.

William Hodson, legendary founder of Hodson's Horse, said of the action: 'The 80th is a splendid corps; well behaved in cantonments and first-rate in action. I lay [near] them on the memorable night when Lord Harding called out: "Eightieth, that gun must be silenced!" They jumped up . . . advanced through the darkness, and soon we lost the tread of their feet while they gradually gained the front of the enemy's battery whose fire had caused so much loss; when suddenly we saw the blaze of the Sikh battery, followed at once by a thrilling cheer from the 80th, accompanied by a murderous fire as they sprang upon the battery and spiked the guns. In a few moments they moved back silently and laid down as before on the cold sand, but they had left 45 of their number and two captains to mark the exploit by their graves.'

Next morning at first light Gough attacked again, surprising the Sikhs and driving them out of their earth-works, capturuing prisoners, guns and stores.

The rest of the Sikh Army now appeared from Ferozepore. Had the commander, Tej Singh, realized that the British had been in action for about forty hours, without food or water and suffering also from the intense heat, and that most of their small arms ammunition and all the gun ammunition was spent, he might have pressed his attacks with more determination. When he saw the indomitable 3rd Light Dragoons apparently preparing to make another charge he retired in disorder, leaving most of his guns, stores and baggage. The Dragoons would have gone into action, but they were so exhausted they scarcely had the strength to mount their horses, which were almost as spent as their riders.

The Sikh forces lost 73 of their guns and many men. British casualties totalled 674 killed and 1,721 wounded.

In England the Duke of Wellington was impressed by the victory at Ferozeshah. He asked in Parliament: 'Who but old soldiers could have done what the 80th did at Ferozeshah, when they stormed at night the batteries which were plunging shot and shell into their bivouac?'

Hardinge's report to Parliament said in part: 'I found myself with . . . that Regiment which has earned for itself immortal fame in the annals of the British Army – Her Majesty's 80th Regiment . . . The British Infantry as usual carried the day.'

On 10 February, 1846 British troops were again in action against the Sikhs, this time at Sobraon, a battle which provides another example of the steady resolve which has become the hallmark of Tommy Atkins. The regiment that perhaps distinguished itself most in this encounter was the 10th (Lincolnshire Regiment) on the extreme left of General Sir Hugh Gough's army. The 10th advanced in a dressed line, in silence so complete that it unnerved even the fierce Sikhs. A Sikh gunner, Hookhum Singh, is reliably reported to have said later, 'A creeping feeling came over me . . . they appeared as demons. . . .'

The massed Sikh artillery was ordered to fire into the English ranks and for a few minutes smoke covered the battlefield. When it cleared the Sikhs saw that the approaching regiment had been badly hit, but that the survivors were still silently advancing. Other cannon balls tore further holes in the lines, but the advance seemed remorseless. At last the Lincolnshire CO, close to the guns, ordered a short halt to take breath. Then the men rushed into the protective ditch, scrambled up the other side and rushed the guns, bayoneting the gunners and their protecting infantry. It was all over in ten minutes – a ten minutes, according to Charles Napier, which were full of 'deeds of gallantry which ought to be recorded in letters of gold and engraved in the memory of all British soldiers'.

Eleven

1815–59 (2)
The *Sarah Sands*; The Crimea; The Mutiny

One episode engraved on the minds of most British soldiers* was the magnificent bravery shown when the troopship, the *Birkenhead*, was wrecked in 1852. The story of how the women and children were saved by the few boats available while the officers and men stood in ranks on the deck of the sinking ship is too well known to be recounted here. The tale of the *Birkenhead* has tended to overshadow that of the *Sarah Sands*, though in some ways the latter is the more remarkable of the two.

The *Sarah Sands* was another of the horrible, ill-crewed tubs in which the War Office of the mid-nineteenth century was content to ship British soldiers and their families. About half the size of a modern Cross-Channel ferry, the *Sarah Sands* left Portsmouth for India on 15 August 1847 with 350 officers and men of the 54th Regiment – the Dorsetshires. On 11 November, between Cape Town and Ceylon, fire broke out and the crew, all foreigners, took to the boats. The end should

---

* And on those of other nations. An account of the British soldier's bravery on the *Birkenhead* was read to every regiment in the Prussian Army. The disaster took place in the last year of Wellington's life. Speaking about it in the House of Lords, Wellington said nothing about the courage of the doomed men but repeatedly referred to their discipline. Perhaps the two, in his mind, were inseparable.

have been inevitable, but again discipline thwarted fate. The men went to work in relays as fire-fighters and as one party was burnt and beaten back another took over. After a fourteen hour battle the flames were out, but the ship was in a desperate state – the rudder gone, the stern half of the ship twisted and leaking, the whole ship foundering. The only drinking [sic] water was a filthy fluid from the engine-room condensers. On top of all this a barrel of gunpowder had blown a hole in the side and the sea swarmed with sharks. But somehow, with soldiers acting as seamen, the *Sarah Sands* limped into Mauritius two weeks later. The Horse Guards issued a General Order praising all ranks of the regiment for their conduct – but they did not improve the standard of troopships.

About this time, however – in 1850 to be precise – the army did something quite revolutionarly: it introduced and enforced a two-hour daily school lesson for all recruits. This was fully twenty years before the introduction of compulsory civil education. The Army had official certificates of education in 1854 but the more progressive regiments had issued their own certificates long before this.*

In 1851–2 the British Army was again fighting the Kaffirs of South Africa – a campaign which deserves to be more memorable than it is, though not for any military reaons. Bully beef makes its first appearance here and was apparently well received. It was issued again during the Crimean War of 1854–5 and once again, in a better form, during the Ashanti Expedition of 1873. After that it cropped up everywhere, to become in the end one of the most reviled – but one of the most necessary – of all army issues.†

---

* Some army schools date from about 1750. In 1811 the Duke of York appointed Army School Sergeants and in 1803 he had founded a school for the sons of soldiers. During the Peninsular Wars Wellington ordered that regiments should introduce facilities for schoolmastering. Little schooling went on, but the awareness for its necessity was at least present.

† As early as 1813 a Bermondsey catering firm had experimented with preserving meat in tins and in 1818 the results of these experiments appeared in Royal Navy lists as *boeuf bouilli*.

Bully was not strictly a British innovation, but then at this time the British Army was all too ready to adopt foreign ideas, without first making sure they were right, physically and psychologically, for British troops. In 1852 Lieutenant-Colonel John Luard fired a broadside at army dress – and not without good reason: 'Unfortunately, we are too apt to adopt every novelty we see, regardless of utility. We have introduced the large-topped, overweighted shako from the French; we have had the large trowser [sic] from the Cossack; the front of the coat passed and stuffed like the Russian. We have changed from one extreme to the other, without good reason; and we still have tight coats, stiff stocks, high caps and tall plumes, all of which it is to be hoped, for the comfort of our soldiers and the efficiency of our army, will shortly be got rid of.'

But in the 1850s the army was about as inefficient as an army could be – though this is not intended to be a reflection on the common soldier or on the junior officers. Officialdom, and in analysis, public opinion were to blame. The men who were shipped to the hell that became the Crimea were mostly hardened – not from battle experience, but from long service and barrack life. Their language was probably as foul and as blasphemous as in the time of William III. There was less drunkenness than in most other places where British soldiers fought, but mainly because cheap wine was not available.*

Perhaps oddly, the Crimean Army was inferior to Wellington's Peninsular Army in that fewer educated men served in it. The general standard of intelligence was inferior, too. It is significant that fewer soldiers left diaries of the Crimean War than of the Peninsular War. Still, the new postal service helped to rectify the balance and many officers and men wrote home from the Crimea.

In the Crimea, as elsewhere before and after, the soldier suffered from poor food and poor clothing. The clothing was good enough for parades in Britain, lamentable for field service. Some units did not even possess greatcoats and

---

* For eighty years after the battle of Balaclava, 1854, great mounds of British beer bottles were conspicuous near Sebastopol. They finally vanished only after the German-Russian holocaust of World War II.

suffered terribly from the intense cold. Most uniforms were in rags and tatters within a few months.

Often the food was literally rotten or in other ways not fit to be eaten. The whole catering system was inept and inadequate and was even worse in the hospitals than in the camps. But the troops had a saviour as important in his way as Florence Nightingale – though unhappily less publicized. He was a Frenchman, Alexis Soyer, a chef from London. He arrived to help Miss Nightingale and he had the same sort of missionary zeal. Despite blind obstructionism, Soyer managed to impose his will on the army's system of cooking and introduced many fresh ideas. He also introduced a new stove – the Soyer – which is now better known than its advocate. It made a vast difference because the army was still using iron kettles of ancient pattern. Charming, energetic, unmilitary, Soyer first improved matters for the hospital patients, then moved into the trenches.

Officialdom, in the form of General Eyre, said, 'Soldiers don't require such good messes as these while campaigning. You will improve the cook but spoil the soldier.'

But *Punch*, changing, though only briefly, from its traditional caustic attitude towards the soldier, noted:

> A cook can defy, you see,
> A Commissariat's knavery.
> The soldier who saves a nation free
> Should have a ration savoury.

Red tape was rampant. On one memorable occasion Lord Cardigan refused to allow some horse lines to be moved from muddy slush to dry ground. The lines were filthy and dangerous for man and beast but his Lordship was adamant. His reason: To move some of the lines would spoil the symmetry of the whole.

At Scutari, where Florence Nightingale laboured for the troops, it was said with bitter irony that red tape would let twenty men die rather than infringe a single regulation.

Private Robert Browning Parsons of the 17th Regiment, who arrived at Balaclava in November 1854 left a simple and honest account of life – and death – in the Crimea.

Then began our experience of the soldier's life whilst on campaign. The weeding out of the weaklings commencing in real earnest – in our tent alone we were reduced from 19 down to eight in the first three months – and this, not by the hand of the enemy, but by those companions of active service – exhaustion and disease – for it was no unusual sight in the morning to see the dead bodies of two or three men taken out from the tents, the men having passed away during the night, owing to the ravages of exhaustion or dysentery, and no wonder at this, when the food we had to live upon is taken into consideration, for raw beef and pork were delicacies at this time, occasionally washed down with coffee – the coffee being previously prepared by us by being put into a piece of old biscuit bag and pounded. Chocolate also used to be sent out to us, this reaching us made up in shape something like a big flat cheese. This chocolate we found would burn, so breaking it into pieces and piling stone around, we then would set fire to it, place our canteen on the top and then wait for something warm; this being the only way we succeeded in doing so for the first few months.

My impression of the first sights of our men before Sebastopol I shall never forget, their appearance being appalling. The men were unshaven, unkempt, dirty-looking, ragged, and filthy; and as I saw them wading about up to the knees in mud and 'slurry', I could not discern whether they were British, Turks, or Russians, until speech disclosed that they were British; but soon we were as bad as they.

The rifle with which we had to defend ourselves was not like the modern magazine rifle, but the old-fasioned 'Brown Bess' with round bullet, the charge having to be rammed home in the rifle with the ramrod. Many a night when our duty and need for the rifle came, it was found impossible to use it, the ramrod being frozen to the rifle and quite immovable, the bayonet and butt end of the rifle having then to be brought into use.

Sergeant Thomas Gowing of the Royal Fusiliers, wrote to his parents from Sebastopol: 'Once more a few lines from this miserable camp – mud! mud! mud!!! We arrived here on the 8th, at once marched up the front; a number of my poor comrades I hardly knew – what a change! The old Fusiliers, once one of the finest corps in the service, now poor, half-starved, miserable-looking wrecks of humanity. The older hands had still that unconquerable look about them, that it would be far cheaper for the enemy to build a bridge of gold for them to pass over, than to try and take them prisoners.'

But, as always, much of Tommy Atkins's suffering was his own fault – or rather the fault of a system which had never trained him in survival. Stocqueler, writing at the time, noted that: 'With all their indomitable courage and energy in action, and all their fortitude and high moral bearing, most of them [English soldiers] were in some respects, very helpless fellows. Few of them could handle a spade or a mattock with any dexterity; fewer still an axe or a saw, a hammer or a trowel. Few of them could even mend their own clothes tolerably, and fewer still could mend their own shoes; they were bad cooks, and all, except the old soldiers, bad hands at lighting a fire. . . . A part, and not an inconsiderable part, of the sufferings of the British Army in the Crimea, arose from this. . . .'

In short, the army was suffering for the sins of omission and the lack of foresight by its leaders during the previous centuries. That the Crimean War was considered successful was entirely due to the dogged courage of the men in the ranks. The Nation, the Government, the War Office and the leaders in the field could claim no credit at all. Many decades of neglect and parsimony killed many British soldiers, and so lowered British military prestige that foreign powers believed right up to Word War I that Britain was a second-rate power with an army fit only for fighting savages. This was not true; the soldiers were splendid, but leadership counts more in the minds of statesmen.

The Crimean War is too sorry a tale to be dwelt upon, but the Battle of Inkermann – the 'Soldiers' Battle' – proved that Tommy Atkins had the same old fortitude. The Russian advance took place in darkness, drizzle and fog on the morning of 5 November 1854. Lord Raglan found himself committed to a surprise engagement, with massive Russian columns overwhelmingly superior to his own few men. He had no way of deploying his men. As British units came up they were simply pushed piecemeal into the battle in an attempt to hold up great rivers of men. Over and over again these rivers loomed out of the fog and desperate fighting took place with bayonet, butt and even fist. In small and larger parties the British infantry attacked at every opportunity, but the battle swayed to and from all the morning, for the Russians had great reserves. It is possible that more than 50,000 Russians were involved, while not more than 8,000 British troops were engaged. At one point Colonel Egerton with 260 men routed and pursued 1,500 men of the Tomsk Regiment, a crack Russian unit.

Charles Rathbone Low, a military historian of the nineteenth century believed that, 'Never in history, not even at Albuhera . . . did British soldiers fight with more desperate bravery or display the bull-dog tenacity which knows not when it is beaten.'

The battle was fiercest around the Sandbag Battery, the scene of one of the bloodiest hand-to-hand combats in history. A worthless entrenchment, it was some yards in advance of the British position and it was taken and retaken fourteen times, until it was heaped with dead and dying. Kinglake, the historian of the Crimean War, said, 'The Sandbag Battery is a monument of heroic devotion and soldierly prowess, yet showing the vanity of human desires. Supposed, although wrongly, to be a part of the British defences and fought for accordingly, with infinite passion and at great cost of life, the work was no sooner taken than its worthlessness became evident . . . to those particular troops which chanced to be posted within it.'

'Men! Remember Albuhera!' shouted young Captain Stanley of the 57th – the Diehards – and a moment later a bullet hit him in the heart. But soldiers of the times were inspired by such battle cries and Stanley's company fought with renewed courage. And for most of the time an artillery duel was in progress, with the Russians alone firing 100 cannons.

Some French troops were thrown in to help the British and by three o'clock that afternoon Mount Inkermann was cleared of Russian troops – except for the dead and wounded. How many Russians died at Inkermann has never been accurately established, but the minimum number was 11,000 and it is possible that 20,000 died. British casualties amount to 2,600. Inkermann might have been a soldiers' battle, but generals fought, too. Three of them were killed, six others were wounded or had their horses shot under them.

The scandals resulting from mismanagement of the Crimean War and from the maltreatment of British soldiers had a salutary effect on army administration and on the public's attitude to the army. Just after the war Charles Dickens admitted that Tommy Atkins had been maligned and misunderstood. In a prologue to his story *The Uncommercial Traveller* he wrote: 'Any animated description of a modern battle, any private soldier's letter published in the newspapers, any page of the records of the Victoria Cross, will show that in the ranks of the Army there exists under all disadvantages as fine a sense of duty as is to be found in any station on earth. Who doubts that if we all did our duty as faithfully as the soldier does his, this world would be a better place? There may be greater difficulties in our way than in the soldier's. Not disputed. But let us at least do our duty towards *him*.'

In a way, Dickens was reflecting a changing public opinion towards the soldier and the change was largely brought about by other writers – the new race of official war correspondents who were at last able to reveal something of the hardships, miseries and dangers of a soldier's life.

Many army reforms were set in motion, such as the establishment of an Army Clothing Factory and a Small Arms Factory – at Enfield. Proper instructional camps were set up at Colchester, Aldershot and Curragh. A School of Musketry was founded at Hythe and a School of Gunnery at Sheerness. The Army Medical Service was revitalized and army hospitals were built. And there were other changes which did not directly affect Tommy Atkins.

In 1857 and 1858 Tommy's courage and endurance were tried to the limit during the Indian Mutiny. Only a handful of British troops were available at the beginning of the Mutiny and they had to do much hard fighting before reinforcements could arrive. They captured Delhi and some of them, mostly artillerymen, held out for twenty days at Cawnpore.

Cawnpore is emotionally important in British history but its military implications have been strangely ignored. Never in British conflict – *not even at Fontenoy, Albuhera or Rorke's Drift – has a force fough so bravely and so successfully against odds*. For Cawnpore *was* successful until the apparently inevitable surrender, long delayed.

Some of the defenders of Cawnpore were civilians turned soldier; they showed, therefore, that soldierly qualities are latent in most Englishmen and that the regular soldier is merely an Englishmen who happens to be in uniform. Qualities common to English civilians and soldiers came out at Cawnpore, although the man who dominated its defence was an army officer, Captain J. Moore of the 32nd Regiment. He was one of the finest field soldiers who ever served England; he is also one of the most disgracefully ignored by historians.

Tall, fair and blue-eyed, Moore was full of energy, dash and courage and stood out above the other brave men in Cawnpore. Thousands of mutinous sepoys and irregular troops, under the command of the vicious and infamous Dhundu Pant, commonly called Nana Sahib, surrounded the small area held by the British.

The officer in command at Cawnpore was Major-General Sir Hugh Wheeler, a veteran soldier aged 75 with more than fifty years of Indian service behind him. He still rode and walked like a soldier, but he was now too old to think and act like one. He was not the man to command a besieged outpost or for the responsibility for the lives of 1,000 people, made up of 465 men of every age and profession, 280 women and about as many children, including Moore's own wife and child. Only 400 of the men were able to fight.

Despite warnings from Captain Moore and others General Wheeler did not believe that Cawnpore was threatened until the place was surrounded. It was largely due to Moore's insistence that any effort at all was made to prepare for trouble. But probably even Moore did not foresee the sufferings to which the tiny garrison would be subjected. History has called it 'the massacre of Cawnpore'; it should be 'the victory of Cawnpore'. For three weeks these English people held out against tremendous odds, suffering cruelly from heat, thirst, starvation and heavy enemy fire.

Cooped within the small space, the women and children were exposed to the concentrated fire of thousands of muskets and twenty heavy cannon. Before the end of the third day every window and door had been beaten in; next went the screens, the piled-up furniture and the internal partitions and soon shell and musket ball raked through the naked rooms. Some women were killed outright by grape and roundshot; others were killed by bullets; many were crushed beneath falling debris or mutilated by splinters.

In this wreckage, amid this carnage, Captain Moore was everywhere visible. Under the rampart, at the batteries, in some outpost, or a corner of the hospital, he encouraged, exhorted and sympathized.

British artillerymen helped by civilians had to stand out in the open to fire and gradually they died there. By the end of the first week all fifty-nine artillerymen had been killed or wounded at their posts or had died from sunstroke.

The temperature varied from 120 to 138 degrees in the shade. Fever and apoplexy, cholera and dysentery killed people almost daily. There were no drugs, no surgical instruments.

One night the thatched roof of one barrack was set alight by the rebels, a calamity to the defenders for it deprived them of shade. Captain Moore decided to show the mutineers that the garrison's spirit was not broken. In the early hours of the following night he took fifty picked men and raided the enemy. They killed a number of gunners, spiked and rolled over several 24-pounders and generally made nuisances of themselves, for the loss of one man.

On 18 June Moore wrote a brief, cheerful letter to an official at Lucknow. 'Sir Hugh Wheeler regrets you cannot send him the 200 men, as he believes with their assistance we could drive the insurgents from Cawnpore and capture their guns. Our troops, officers and volunteers have acted most nobly and on several occasions a handful of men have driven hundreds before them. Our loss has been chiefly from the sun and their heavy guns. . . . We, of course, are prepared to hold out until the last. . . . We trust in God, and if our exertions here assist your safety, it will be a consolation to know that our friends appreciate our devotion. Any news of relief will cheer us.'

But there was to be no relief.

One day a marksman shot a fat Brahmin bull at 300 yards. Moore led a party of eight volunteers across the open ground under enemy fire to drag the bull back to the stockade, where it was cooked and eaten. This cheered the garrison immensely.

By day and night the fire never ceased; the round-shot crashed and spun through the windows, raked the earthwork and skipped about the open ground; the bullets pattered like hail; the shells rolled hissing along the floors and down the trenches; then, bursting, they spread mutilation and destruction.

On the night of 22 June, when a major attack was expected, Lieutenant Thomson, in command at the outposts, sent for reinforcements. Moore replied that he could spare only himself and Lieutenant Delafosse – Delafosse with a sword, Moore with an empty musket. Moore shouted 'Number One Company to the front!' The enemy fell for the bluff, broke and ran.

Eventually, after three weeks, when the garrison's food and ammunition had almost gone, Nana offered and poor doddering General Wheeler accepted safe conduct to the boats on the Ganges. The ragged survivors marched to the river and were in the middle of embarking when they were murderously attacked by thousands of enemy. Only one boat got away from the shallows and drifted down the channel. On it was Captain Moore, his wounded arm slung in a handkerchief. The boat grounded many times and once when this happened Moore was helping to push off when a musket ball went through his heart.

Moore's gallantry was well recorded by the survivors of the gallant band at Cawnpore – just four of them, two officers, a private and a gunner. Four out of 1,000. One of them said, 'Captain Moore was the spirit of the defence; he was the inspiration. No braver man ever lived.'

The men who survived the onslaught at the river's edge were massacred soon after and later Nana Sahib had the 200 surviving women and children slaughtered.

The atrocity of Cawnpore brought out something grim in Tommy Atkins. He had always been a champion of women and children – despite his occasional aberrations – and every man of the 2,000-strong army which marched towards Cawnpore was full of hate and vengeance.

Day after day as they marched from Allahabad the heat was intense and in scores men dropped from heatstroke and cholera, but the little force could not be stopped and at Cawnpore the men charged the enemy guns and sent the rebels flying. Many Indians were hanged in those bitter days – often on mere suspicion. After the Mutiny was quelled many others were tried and executed at the cannon's mouth.

Other Tommies of the 32nd Foot (Cornwall Light Infantry) held Lucknow, more of them relieved this beleaguered city, which was again held until relieved a second time. On 16 November the second relief force was held up by a fortified building called the Sikander Bagh, garrisoned by 2,000 rebel sepoys. The Tommies made a breach in the wall and stormed the place with the bayonet. These men had seen the well into which Nana Sahib's butchers had thrown the bloody corpses of Cawnpore's women and children and they showed no mercy; they killed every rebel in the building, except for a few who jumped from the roof. It was a rare thing for Tommy Atkins to be so bitter and ruthless and it showed the depths of his revultion for the Cawnpore atrocities.

On 28 November the Commander-in-Chief, Sir Colin Campbell, reached Cawnpore, where another battle had been in progress, with the British troops faring badly. As Campbell arrived at the bridge of boats across the Ganges an officer said to him, 'Thank God you have come, sir. The troops are at their last gasp.'

Campbell glared at him. 'How dare you say, sir, of Her Majesty's troops that they are *ever* at their last gasp!'

A good line, it was sufficiently well-delivered to survive for posterity. But in fact, for quite some time – order in India was not restored till the end of 1859 – many a soldier was at his last gasp. Some of them belonged to that splendid regiment the 43rd Light Infantry (Oxford and Bucks). From April to July 1858 – in the hottest part of the hottest year for fifteen years – the Regiment marched 1,300 miles from Bangalore to Calpee, halting only occasionally for brief rests at hill stations. The heat was so intense that three officers and forty-four men died, many from sunstroke. This was one of the most gruelling marches in military history.

Khaki had put in its appearance during the Mutiny. Captain Medley, Bengal Engineers, wrote in his book *An Early Campaign in India*, published in 1858: 'The well known British scarlet was now a rare sight indeed [at Delhi]. The European regiments wear white clothing in the hot weather; but white is not well suited to campaigning and most of them had died their coatees the well known khakee [sic] or dust colour. This khakee, which before May 1857, was only seen across the Indus was . . . adopted by the Frontier troops for their hill fighting, being nearly of the colour of the desert of the bare stony hills in these parts. . . . Directly these troops marched to join our camp the advantages of the colour were seen and it quickly became fashionable for everybody, which it has pretty well since remained.'*

Tommy Atkins's scalp and facial hair had changed almost as frequently as parts of his uniform. At the beginning of the century Hussars had worn moustaches and Heavy and Light Dragoons adopted them in 1810 or 1811, though after the Peninsular War they were moustache-free. Hussars wore them the entire nineteenth century and Lancers similarly except for the period 1830–9. William IV in 1830 banned moustaches in the Horse Artillery and in the cavalry except for the Household Cavalry and Hussars. In 1839, Victoria ordered that all mounted men including the Horse Artillery were to wear moustaches. At the beginning of Victoria's reign, too, the infantry wore their hair very short and had it cut once a month. Every man cultivated a little curl on each side. So highly were these ornaments valued that when a man emerged from prison, or the cells, with his head looking like a worn-out scrubbing-brush, he frequently attached false curls to the

*But the red jacket remained in general use in action until the Boer War, 1899–1902. However, it was cut more sensibly in later years.

inside of his forage cap, in order that he might be able to walk out without exposing the brand of punishment and disgrace.

In 1854 the growing of beards and moustaches by all arms in the East was sanctioned – and men made most of the opportunity. The beards were ordered off at the end of the war, but during the Mutiny and for some years later beards were worn by troops in the East. Many illustrations of the period show soldiers with very full beards.

In 1857 an order stated that, 'The fashion of the day is not to be permitted to influence the practice of the army in a particular which is considered alike essential to health, and cleanliness, and military appearance of the soldier; and a certificate that this order has been complied with will be sent to the orderly room by officers commanding companies, on the 1st of each month. Moustaches and whiskers are permitted to be worn at the option of the men, but the whiskers must be shaved away two inches from the moustache. Soldiers when out of barracks are expected habitually to appear dressed when walking in the streets, that they keep the step and preserve on all occasions a soldier-like carriage. No smoking or chewing tobacco is permitted in the barracks or in the public streets.'

In 1856 the price of a soldier's necessaries had been deducted from the gross amount of his bounty, but in 1857 the amount was paid in full – 'a wise and liberal decree' Stocqueler calls it – and the Government provided the kit, which comprised a pair of trousers, a pair of boots, three shirts, a fatigue jacket, three pairs of socks, a stock and clasp, a pair of braces, a knapsack with strap, a forage cap and number, two shoe brushes, a sponge, a comb, razor, soap and shaving-brush, a pair of mitts, knife, fork and spoon, mess-tin and cover, and two towels. All this made a totel weight of 48 lb 13 oz.

Perhaps the most hopeful sign of better things for the common soldier was that better married quarters were on the way. Of course, it had been a long job getting them and they were far from ideal. Agitation for better married quarters commenced about the time of Victoria's accession. Public morals were becoming a little more respectable – there was still a lot of room for improvement – and many sensitive people were appalled at the lot of the married soldier and his wife.

They bombarded the authorities with petitions and pleas, but all were evaded with the stock excuse, 'No money available.' By the 1840s some regiments on their own initiative gave married men separate quarters. The 11th Hussars was one of the first to set an example, and in 1852 the officers of the Brigade of Guards went even further. With commendable charity they raised £9,000 to build the Victoria Lodging House in London for fifty-four of their married privates and their families, at a rent of 2s 6d a week for each man. The officers' action caused a contretemps about the legal position of serving officers becoming landlords of the men they led. The stock cliché about its being 'highly irregular' was trotted out. In the end the War Office solved the problem by buying out the 'syndicate'. Disgracefully, the War Office refused to pay more than £8,000 for the building, as petty an example of profiteering as could be imagined.

Much publicity given to many deplorable incidents during the Crimean War led to more agitation. Married women taken to the Crimea were in a dreadful state. Many, as Miss Nightingale noted, were 'in rags and covered with vermin'.

In 1855 a commission was set up to investigate the barracks problem. It discovered, among other things that there was only one barrack bath in the whole of the United Kingdom and that in some married quarters there were still four families to one room. The Commission's work was, extraordinarily enough, rapidly productive, for separate married quarters were authorized. Unhappily the job was botched and though the families were together they had no more privacy than before. The married people's barracks were shockingly overcrowded and as each room had only one fire-place the women quarrelled incessantly over cooking priorities. When they moved into even better quarters they became bored and many clubbed together to buy drink. Some soldier writers noted that there was now more sexual licence among married people than ever before. Disease in these conditions spread rapidly.

Truly, life for Tommy Atkins could still be much, much better. He needed a humane, far-sighted man of authority to reform and transform the army and give the common soldier the benefits he deserved.

Twelve

1860–1902
The Glorious Years

The army of the Queen from the 1860s to the end of the century was a fabulous force, for all its shortcomings. In many ways this was the period of Tommy Atkins at his most heroic and at his best. This was the glorious age of empire building, of punitive expeditions, of rescue-our-people forays into mountain and jungle fastnesses. These things had been going on for a long time, of course, but in the second half of the nineteenth century activities were more hectic, more numerous. This was a great era for soldiering, though no big wars occurred. And the troops, collectively as regiments and individually as men, went out of their way to seek action. When they found it they showed the dogged devotion to duty and the steady courage that came to be synonymous with the name Tommy Atkins. The army was permeated by a spirit of adventure, and adventure was there to be had, in the form of dozens of 'small wars', in India, Africa, China, New Zealand, Burma. Officership was sometimes faulty, occasionally downright poor, but if the officers failed the men, the reverse was not true. The men were as good as the officers allowed them to be.

The soldier still had lowly social status, despite a more general acceptance of his job. Caricaturists were cruel in their humour – especially in *Punch*, which never wearied of its persecution. No doubt some of their comments were legitimate, but the artists showed no balance, no sense of fair play. The colonel or major was always half-witted and irritable, junior officers were officious and ridiculous, non-commissioned officers were big-chested and big-headed and the common guardsman was obviously a moron.

It was true enough that the army itself regarded its private soldiers as pretty dull-witted. Throughout the nineteenth century no soldier was trusted to perform the simplest task without supervision. For a long time a lance corporal was sent to the railway station to check the departure of a lone soldier on leave. This refusal to recognize that the common soldier might have common sense was one of the great obstacles to the development of initiative and enterprise in the ranks and it had frightening effects until recent times. The attitude that no soldier could be trusted was understandable and explainable, of course. For two centuries the army had been largely a crude amalgam of the sweepings of England. Perhaps one man in a hundred could be trusted with money; only some could be trusted not to sell equipment to turn it into liquid refreshment. Tradition dies hard in an army and even when the standard of many men in the ranks had risen considerably they were treated collectively as not worthy of trust or reliance. And standards *were* rising, mostly as a result of moves within the army itself. In 1859 a soldier could not be made a corporal – short of outstanding service in the field – unless he had reached a certain elementary standard of education. In 1860 the Army Certificate of Education was introduced and in some regiments the CO made it a necessary step towards promotion. But progress was slow and for nearly ten years some COs had to resort to 'rewards' – bribes, really – to induce men to attend army schools.

But in this era nearly every soldier had a great sense of pride of regiment. As Wolseley said in his *Soldier's Pocket Book*: 'The soldier is a peculiar thing that can alone be brought to the highest efficiency by inducing him to believe that he belongs to a regiment that is infinitely superior to the others round him.'

It is not too much to say that the regiment was a family. It was a family of strict discipline and the regimental 'father' might be something of a bullying bastard, but its close-knit unity gave its members a sense of security and purpose. The most terrifying days of a soldier's life were when he was, perhaps by compulsory retirement, evicted from his regimental home.

173

Tommy Atkins managed to preserve his *esprit de corps* even when vilified and derided by the public, as he often was. In sharp contrast, the officer – *Punch* cartoonists notwithstanding – was regarded as a superior being. The public seemed to think that a man able to control those crude inferior beings, the ordinary soldiers, was worthy of respect.

In 1860 the Tommies were in China for the second of three wars they fought there. The war is notable for two things: the sacking of the Emperor's summer palace at Peking and the winning of the Victoria Cross by Hospital Apprentice Andrew Fitzgibbon – the youngest ever to receive the award.

The outbreak of the Indian Mutiny had held up the settlement of a dispute with China which had been going on since 1856. The real difficulty was the old Chinese attitude which still refused to have any dealings with the 'Outer Barbarians', even though they had signed a treaty in 1858 agreeing to receive British and French ministers at Peking. After a rather pointless attack in June 1859, an expedition under General Sir Hope Grant was sent from India. During the earlier part of September 1860 there was no serious fighting and the diplomats thought they were settling matters, then the Chinese turned on them and seized them and their escort. Most were tortured and half their number died under their ordeal. Grant's force at once attacked the city. Andrew Fitzgibbon's moment of destiny had arrived.

Born at Peteragurgh in Bengal on 13 May 1845, Andrew was the son of a quarter-master sergeant in the Kumaon Battalion, later to become a battalion of the Gurkha Rifles. On 15 July 1859, when only 14 years of age Andrew joined the Bengal Medical Service and when the expedition left for China he was attached to the 67th Regiment – the 2nd Battalion Royal Hampshire Regiment. He had his fifteenth birthday on the voyage.

The 67th had to attack the Taku Forts, the key to the formidable defences of Peking. The forts, about ten score of them, were so sited as to give one another covering fire. In front of each was a deep, dry ditch, then an open space blocked by an abattis – a fence of sharpened stakes pointing outwards – then a water-ditch behind which was 20 feet of ground thickly planted with sharp bamboo stakes. Beyond this was yet another water-ditch, also staked, And when the attackers passed all these obstacles they came across strongly built and heavily defended forts.

The men and boys of the 67th took up a position only 500 yards from North Fort, and as they waited for the order to attack they must have mentally despaired of ever penetrating through the fiendish defences. The order came. They rose to advance and at once the Chinese opened up with musket-fire.

Andrew Fitzgibbon, though unarmed, was one of the first to leave cover. He attended a wounded Indian soldier, then, under heavy fire ran across open ground to dress the wounds of other wounded. While doing this he was himself severely wounded. For a boy of fifteen he showed remarkable bravery and devotion to duty. I do not belittle his performance when I say that in modern war his act would certainly not warrant an award of the VC.*

The Summer Palace at Peking was packed with priceless works of art of all kinds: some writers have said that it contained treasures equal to those of the Vatican. British and French troops were allowed to run wild in the Palace and to loot what they fancied. Some of them took jewels worth thousands which they later sold for shillings. Their orgy of plunder finished, they burned the place down.†

Wolseley, writing of the China War, found himself easily able to accept the infamy. 'Soldiers are nothing more than grown-up school-boys. The wild moments of enjoyment passed in the pillage of a place live long in a soldier's memory. . . . Such a time forms so marked a contrast with the ordinary routine of existence passed under the tight hand of discipline that it becomes a remarkable event in life and is remembered accordingly.'

In 1863 Tommy Atkins took part in the tough hill-country

---

* Little is known about Fitzgibbon's later life, except that he held several appointments, civil and military, in Bengal.
† In a sale catalogue for 25 October 1965 Christie's listed a pair of beautiful vases of rouleau from the K'and Hsi period. An explanatory note read: 'From the Summer Palace, Peking, 1860, looted by General John Hackett, whose collection was sold in these rooms on 23 July, 1891. . . .' One can admire the honesty of the wording.

expedition to Umbeyla (Ambeyla) at a cost of nearly 1,000 casualties, and in 1867 he was in the fastnesses of Abyssinia. Between 1860 and 1866 yet other Tommies were in New Zealand coping with those intelligent and courageous warriors, the Maoris. The thin red lines were reaching out to all parts of the globe.

But the most significant military act of the 1860s took place in Britain and was not warlike at all. In 1868 Edward Cardwell became Secretary of State for War. The date and the man are important. Cardwell was the man who faced up to and carried through reform of the army, surely one of the most difficult tasks ever undertaken by a British minister. The practical, humane and logical Cardwell breathed sanity into the whole business.

Cardwell had the Short Service Act passed in 1870. The Act brought into being the Army Reserve and did away with the long-service soldier; it wiped out the enlistment bounty and at one stroke eliminated many malpractices, and it made provision for the discharge of the villains who were a disgrace to the uniform they wore. The act, in fact, gave the army a much needed face-lift. In 1871 Cardwell achieved something even more spectacular – by obtaining a royal warrant he put an end to the purchasing of rank. No longer could some fool or exhibitionist buy himself into the position where he held men's lives in his hand. By this step Cardwell brought about the beginning of real professionalism.

The purchase system had begun in the mercenary companies which replaced the feudal levies of the Middle Ages. Each officer's commission had a certain pecuniary value. In 1720 a Royal Warrant had fixed the price of a first commission at £450 and each step upwards meant a higher price, unless a vacancy occurred by death, when promotion by seniority usually applied.*

* An original letter in the author's collection.

Camp Weymouth
Sept. 4th 1796

My dear Lee!

If your engagement with the Lieut. Col: of the 29th is not gone too far now is your moment to get promotion for nothing, the fatal accounts of the loss of so many Lieut. Cols in the West Indies will give you this

Prices varied according to regiments and a cavalry or guards commission was dearer than one in an infantry of the line regiment, but, for instance, in 1856 a man would have to pay £2,400 to promotion to captain, while a lieutenant-colonelcy would cost £7,000. It was no easy task, therefore, for Cardwell to put an end to a system in which so much money was involved.

The abolotion of the purchase system cost the Government £7,000,000 in compensation but this was, as Cole and Priestley have said[†] 'a small sum to redeem the army out of pawn from its officers'.

Among many other things, Cardwell reorganized the War Office, reframed the duties and system governing the militia, brought in new equipment, made reforms in pay, housing and catering and brought reason to the length of time a soldier might be expected to serve abroad. Never again would a regiment in a foreign station be 'forgotten'.

Cardwell's reforms had the important effect of making the army a competitive employer of labour. But not too competitive, for rates of pay were still relatively low. Although the scum of the nation could not now get into the ranks, most of the men who enlisted did so because they were not trained for anything that would pay better money. This remained true for many years. As Sir Henry Wilson said, 'Jack Frost (harsh reality) was the best recruiting sergeant.'

During the Egyptian campaign of 1882 a padre, the Revd E.J. Hardy, asked a man, gaoled for striking a sergeant, why he had done such a thing. The soldier said, 'We were expecting to be attacked by Arabs next day and as I had been in one engagement and did not like it, I determined to do something that would get me out of another, so I struck the sergeant, knowing I would be made a prisoner.'

---

chance. Lieut. Col. Payne of the Royals is to be promoted to the Lieut. Col. of the 17th Light Dragoons; the Duke of York gave him this appointment yesterday.

Yours very Sincerely
Samuel Hawker

† An Outline of British Military History, 1936.

Hardy told the man that he hoped he was a unique specimen of British soldier. The defaulter said, 'It's no use talking to me, sir. . . . I admit that I am a coward, but I can't help it. A battle is not to my taste and whenever my turn comes I shall try some means to get out of it.'

'Then why did you become a soldier?' Hardy asked.

'Starvation,' the man said.

Nevertheless, pay reforms in the sixties and seventies made some amends for the gross abuses of the past. In 1836 good conduct pay had been introduced, beginning at 1d a day after three years' service. In 1867 basic pay was increased by an extra 2d a day and in 1870 a man could win good conduct pay after two years. Three years later a daily ration of free food was introduced, resulting in a man now having 1s clear per day, although he did not now get beer money. In 1876 a wise if inadequate step was taken to give a discharged soldier some means of settling into civilian life. Each soldier received 2d a day deferred pay, to be paid on discharge.

In 1881 the 'Cardwell system' was introduced, although Cardwell had left office in 1874. In a revolutionary step – and as usual after violent opposition – two battalions were linked into one regiment, one battalion to serve at home while the other was abroad. The idea was partly so that the home battalion could train young soldiers until they were ready to be sent abroad.

However, the main reason for virtually all the Cardwell reforms had been to have in Britain an adequate force for Home Defence. As a result of Cardwell's plans the number of battalions at home would be more in balance with those abroad. For instance, in 1868 only 47 of the Army's 141 line battalions were in Britain. The linked regiments had a common territorial connection, a common depot and recruiting area. Two militia battalions were allotted to each brigade district. At this time, in 1881, regiments assumed Territorial Titles and ceased to be known by numbers. The storm of protest over the changes lasted a long ten years, but the effect in the end was harmonious and efficient.

By establishing for each infantry regiment a fixed depot. Cardwell gave it a permanent home. This produced invaluable security if only because a regiment was able to have a museum, where the recruit could learn much. Also, a depot made the regiment more acceptable to civilians of the district.

Sir Garnet Wolseley took Cardwell's reforms about officers to logical conclusion in the field. Not the least of Wolseley's many achievements was the issue on 1 April, 1883, of the order *Squadron, Battery and Company Training*. This revolutionary order marked the beginning of systematic and efficient training for officers and indirectly led to a closer bond between officers and men. Until the order of 1883 the gulf between them was deep and wide, especially in peace time. War was rather different because the British officer had never been lacking in spirit, courage or initiative. But during times of peace an officer rarely appeared on parade. On some major occasion, such as full regimental parade, officers would arrive in cabs or coaches, do whatever was required, and would vanish within seconds of the command 'Fall out the officers!'

Wolseley insisted that every officer, no matter the size of his command, was wholly and personally responsible for its training. Wolseley had bitter personal experience of inefficient officers, as he wrote after his campaigns in Egypt in 1882–5. 'I have seen splendid battalions kept in the rear while others of inferior quality were sent to the front because the general commanding did not dare employ against the enemy a corps whose commanding officer was manifestly incompetent . . . I hold that it is criminal to hand over in action the lives of gallant soldiers to men who are deplorably ignorant of the elements of their profession. . . . It is but right that the nation should . . . expect . . . that none but competent and properly educated officers should be selected for the position of lieutenant colonel. . . .'

The comments of a young soldier named William Robertson who at the age of 17½ joined the 16th (Queen's) Lancers in 1877 give a vivid picture of Army life at the time and hint at the reforms brought about by Cardwell. He wrote:

The system introduced by Mr Cardwell under which men enlisted for twelve years' regular service, had not yet had time to get into full swing. Regiments were, therefore, still composed mainly of old soldiers who, although very admirable comrades in some respects and with a commendable code of honour of their own, were in many cases addicted to rough behaviour, heavy drinking, and hard swearing. They could not well be blamed for this. Year in and year out they went through the same routine, were treated like machines – of in inferior kind – and having little prospect of finding decent employment, on the expiration of their twenty-one years' engagement, they lived only for the present, the single bright spot in their existence being the receipt of a few shillings – perhaps not more than one – on the weekly pay-day.

These rugged veterans exacted full deference from the recruit, who was assigned the worst bed in the room, given the smallest amount of food and the least palatable, had to 'lend' them articles of kit which they had lost or sold, 'fag' for them in a variety of ways, and finally, was expected to share with them at the regimental canteen such cash as he might have in the purchase of beer sold at 3d a quart. . . .

On return to quarters, if not before, old quarrels were revived or new ones were started, and some of them had to be settled by fists. One of these encounters took place on and near the bed in which I was vainly trying to sleep, and which was itself of an unattractive and uncomfortable nature. Argument and turmoil continued far into the night, and I began to wonder whether I had made a wise decision after all. I continued to wonder for several nights afterwards, and would lie awake for hours meditating whether to see the matter through, or get out of bed, put on my plain clothes (which I still had) and desert. Fortunately for me another occupant of the room removed the temptation these clothes afforded, for, having none of his own, he one night appropriated mine, went off in them, and never came back.*

Barrack-room arrangements for sleeping and eating were poor. The brown bed-blankets were rarely washed: clean sheets

* It was just as well the young cavalryman did not desert: he became a Field-Marshal.

were issued once a month and clean straw for the mattresses once every three months. The only other furniture consisted of four benches and two deal tables. Tableclothes there were unknown and plates and basins, bought by the men, were the only crockery. The basin was used as a coffee-cup, tea-cup, beer-mug, soup-plate, shaving-mug, and receptacle for pipe-clay.

The food ration consisted of 1 lb of bread and 12 oz of meat. Groceries, vegetables, and all other requirements were paid for by the men, through a daily deduction. The regulation meals were coffee and bread for breakfast, meat and potatoes for dinner, and soup or pudding once or twice a week; tea and bread for tea.

At this point, 1878–80, Britain became involved in a second Afghan War. I cannot become involved in its complexities, for Tommy Atkins was not interested in them. However, 7,000 men under Sir Donald Stewart won a battle at Ahmed Khel in 1880. After this Stewart left 4,000 men under General Primrose to hold Kandahar and marched on to Kabul. In July a large enemy force, of Ghazis, moved towards Kandahar and Primrose sent Brigadier-General Burrows with 2,500 men to deal with them. However, Burrows got into a serious position and fell back towards Kandahar. On 26 July he heard that a rebel leader Ayub Khan, was at Maiwand, only eleven miles away and was heading for Ghazni (Ghuznee, Ghusni) where he would be able to cut the Kandahar-Kabul road. At dawn on 27 July Burrows marched to meet Ayub Khan, thus initiating another magnificently gallant and hopeless action.

General Burrows's force included 490 men of the 66th Foot (Berkshire Regiment) a troop of the Royal Horse Artillery (six guns) and elements of various native regiments, foot and cavalry.

At 10 a.m. the brigade, with bands playing, came upon the whole of Ayub Khan's rebel army, a great force stretching for miles across the plain. The British soldiers knew at once they were in for a fierce fight. Burrows prepared for battle. He advanced well into an open plain beyond Maiwand, placing his men in one long, two-deep line, with five companies of the 66th Foot on the right; and the other company of the regiment was guarding the baggage in a deep water-course closer to the village. The position was poor and almost everybody other than General Burrows knew it. They should have been in the water-course or behind it.

Ayub Khan had 6,500 regular troops and 3,500 wild Ghazi tribesmen. His artillery opened the battle and soon showed that he had as big an advantage in guns as he had in men. The fanatical Ghazis made one sweeping attack after another and were beaten back by rifle-fire. Then Afghans opened fire from Maiwand village behind the British soldiers and some of the baggage guard was detached to deal with this attack.

After hours of attacks, the Indian native regiments were forced back and before long the British force had been forced into a triangular shape. Masses of enemy, horsemen and infantry, swarmed around them while the Ghazis made the battle hideous with their wild screaming.

'Retire by companies to the Kandahar road,' was the order and the Brigade moved back, fighting off enemy cavalry attacks. Though hemmed in, the Royal Horse Artillery broke through with their guns.

The Berkshire men retreated to the water-course in front of Maiwand. Here their CO, Lieutenant-Colonel Galbraith, and several of his officers were killed.

The colours were carried by young second lieutenants, named Barr and Honywood. Barr fell dead across his colour, but Honywood, wounded early in the engagement by a bullet in the leg, managed to struggle into temporary safety.

Forced away from the water-course, the survivors held out for a time in an enclosure then they retreated to the Kandahar Road and finally they made a stand in a garden. For every minute that they could hold out they stopped the enemy from chasing the rest of the Brigade, including some men of their own regiment. Honywood was shot again and mortally wounded while holding the colour high above his head, shouting, 'Men what shall we do to save this?'

The others fought on, standing back to back surrounded by the whole Afghan Army and knowing that death was all they could hope for. Inflicting great losses on the enemy, they fought until only eleven men remained on their feet.

Then these eleven men did an incredible thing. They charged!

And, as if to encourage them, a little white dog, the regimental mascot, followed barking at their heels. Out into the open they ran, as if daring the Afghans and the Ghazis to attack them. But the 10,000 enemy would not accept the challenge and held back, not daring to approach that deadly little band, now dropping one by one.

Four survivors continued to fire steadily and calmly until every man had been shot down. And only when the last man had fired his last shot did the enemy approach.

Many people refuse to see anything in the least glorious about war, but surely the stand of the last eleven at Maiwand was an act of almost sublime glory. Nobody knows for certain the names of these last eleven soldiers, but Tommy Atkins would be a suitable name for all.

The Afghans chased the remainder of the brigade to Kandahar, but the delay at Maiwand had given the brigade time to get clear, although about half the total force were casualties. The Berkshires lost 276 killed and missing.

Associated with Maiwand is the name of Gunner James Colliss, of the Royal Horse Artillery. During the retreat Collis was walking by the side of his gun on which were placed ten wounded men. When the Afghans began to fire on these helpless men, Colliss went to the front and fired in return. He attracted the fire of the Afghans to himself until the gun was taken out of range.

It was for this act that he won the VC, but Colliss performed other acts of gallantry. He was getting water for the wounded, when he saw Afghan cavalry approaching. He opened fire from cover and so accurate was his fire that the Afghans apparently assumed that the force against them was too strong to be attacked. It was said that Colliss's action saved the wounded from being discovered.

A month later at Kandahar, Colliss was standing by his gun when he heard some officers talking about the urgent need of getting a message to an officer who had led a patrol out against the enemy. Colliss volunteered to deliver the message. Under fire, he was lowered forty feet down the wall of the fort, delivered the message and returned to his post.

For some reason not publicly divulged Colliss forfeited

his VC by Royal Warrant in November 1895, when he had long been a civilian. But the disgraceful withdrawal of his decoration could not cancel out Colliss's gallantry and he remains to history a brave man.*

Sir Frederick Roberts's relief force marched from Kabul to Kandahar, a distance of 297½ miles, in intense heat and across unfriendly mountainous country, in nineteen days. There were few roads worthy of the name, and the soldiers carried most of their rations. A special star was struck to commemorate this march.

Tommy Atkins was marching and counter-marching through many parts of Africa and India at this time – 'Boots, boots, boots, boots marching up and down again,' as Kipling said – in jungle, desert, river and mountain columns. He was not always successful, as some war correspondents were quick to perceive. Few of these correspondents were as frank and impartial as Archibald Forbes. Forbes, trained as a soldier himself, covered many campaigns and saw as much as anybody has seen of Tommy Atkins at war and on service.

Forbes commended where he saw the commendable; he criticized where he saw the crass, the callow and the cowardly. He did not glorify the English soldier; he set him down realistically. 'Shoulder to shoulder is long dead,' Forbes wrote, 'and its influences have mostly died with it, but in the present days of swarm-attack human nature remains unchanged. The soldier of today has to wrest with or respond to his own individualiy.'

Forbes meant that public opinion no longer touched the soldier on each of his elbows, as it did in shoulder-to-shoulder fighting. Here a man damned himself immediately and irrevocably if he broke. In any case, breaking was physically difficult in tight formation; a man bent on breaking would have to fight his way through the ranks behind him.

Forbes wrote:

---

* Anyone who has received the VC, but who is afterwards convicted of treason, cowardice, felony 'or any other infamous crime', may have his name erased from the list of recipients. There have been eight such forfeitures, the last in 1908.

Today's soldier is tried by a much higher test than in the old close-quarter days . . . he often fails in the higher morale which his wider scope of individuality exacts of him if he is to be efficient. . . . The officer gives the forward signal but the consequences of not obeying it do not come home with so swift vividness to the reluctant individual man. He is behind cover . . . how dear that cover is! . . . So he lies still . . . and his own particular wave goes on and leaves him behind. He may join the next or he may continue to lie still.

Forbes compared Tommy Atkins with the German soldier in the new open order – it was new at the time – and found him wanting. 'They [the Germans] know that it is good for soldiers to die a little occasionally.' Forbes reported the Franco-Prussian war from the German side and stood with a German general watching a skirmish near Metz. The German battalion consisted chiefly of young soldiers and they were unsteady. The old General shrugged and observed, 'Dey vant to be a little shooted; dey will do better next time.'

Forbes believed that all young soldiers need to be 'a little shooted'. He said, 'It is only by exposing them somewhat instead of coddling them for ever behind cover, as if cover, not victory, were the aim of the day's work, that this experience can befall them.'

Forbes, indeed, was critical of English troops of the 1880s and 1890s. He thought that the Zulus' massacre of troops at Isandlwana, 1879, could have been averted by a 'vigorous attempt at a rally', and the ignominious defeat at Majuba Hill, 1881, at the hands of the Boers was due to the British soldier's being 'so much a creature of cover and of dodging that he went all abroad when he saw a real live enemy standing up in front of him at point-blank range . . . the Boer had better nerve'.

Quite outspoken, Forbes revealed what dispatches tried to cover up, that pickets and sentries were too often running from their posts. 'The young soldier . . . does not make a bolt for it because he is a coward, or rather a greater than average coward, but simply because his training has not furnished him with a reserve of purposeful presence of mind. . . . He is unfamiliar in advance with his obligation to die serenely at his post. . . . The British soldier of 1882 was a creature of the "get-to-cover" period.'

Still, Forbes like many other correspondents of his day tended to equate victory, or at least courage, with heavy casualties. He extols the casualties of Inkermann (2,487 out of 7,464) but finds the loss of a mere 258 at Tel el Kebir, 1882, cheapened the victory.

Rudyard Kipling, Tommy Atkins's greatest champion, took a more romantic view of him. The British soldier and the British Army owe much to Kipling, who, born in 1865, grew up in the imperialistic days of glory. Through his ballads, Kipling made Tommy more popular. Appearing on the stage, Tommy Atkins became the bright symbol of popular imperialism. Dozens of songs were written about him – songs like 'Soldiers of the Queen' and 'A Little British Army Goes a Damned Long Way'. Artists like Caton Woodville almost mass-produced colourful, stylized but popular illustrations of Tommy Atkins in all his splendour. And through all this the soldiers of the Queen did indeed go a damned long way. They were, ultimately, marching towards military catastrophe, but during the years of marching with the flag, of outpost and fortress fighting, of skirmishing in the African bush, or up-river patrols Tommy Atkins did not think of the future, even though it was no further away than 1899.

Kipling expressed to the essence the private's irritation.

I went into a public 'ouse to get a pint of beer,
The publican 'e up and sez: 'We serve no redcoats here.';
The girls be'ind the bar they laughed and giggled fit to die,
    I outs into the streets again an' to myself sez I:
    Oh it's 'Tommy this, an 'Tommy that, an 'Tommy go
    away,'
    But it's 'Thank you, Mister Atkins' when the band begins
    to play.

I went into a theatre as sober as can be,
They gave a drunk civilian room, but 'adn't none for me;

They sent me to the gallery or round the music 'alls,
But when it comes to fighting, Lord! they'll shove me in the
    stalls!
    For it's 'Tommy this, and Tommy that, an' Tommy wait
    outside';
    But it's 'Special trains for Atkins' when the trooper's on
    the tide.

As Kipling said, concluding his poem, 'It's a thin red line of heroes when the drums begin to roll.' That thin red line was clannish in its exclusiveness and within its own circle of comradeship did not really care a lot about what outsiders thought.

In the 1890s Kipling prophesied that 'about 30 years hence, when we have half-educated everything that wears trousers, our Army will be a beautifully unreliable machine; a little later, when we have educated it up to the standard of the present officer, it will sweep the world.'

For the officers, the latter part of the nineteenth century was a wonderful time. They enjoyed army life, but many officers could hardly be called keen in the professional military sense. Despite Wolseley's plans, it was possible for an officer in say, 1890, to be absent for about 250 days of the year, many of them spent in sport or travelling abroad. Often the only officer within a regiment's lines was the orderly officer, left to supervise nominally, the drilling, training and various duties, all capably handled anyway by the senior NCOs. Neither the NCOs nor the men resented the officers' absence. They took for granted that the officer's superior social status entitled him to do exactly as he pleased. Officers were beings apart, personages who spoke, dressed, acted and ate differely from the masses. Most men had an affectionate regard for their officers, as is clearly seen by the number who risked their lives under fire to rescue wounded officers. And despite the gulf which remained between officers and other ranks they had one strong link in common – courage. Soldiers can smell courage or cowardice in an officer. The Victorian soldier rarely smelled cowardice.

But the army was still not impressing foreign observers – perhaps because many officers still did not know their business sufficiently well. Some time in the 1890s Padre Hardy, accompanying a division on manoeuvres in Britain, asked the German military attache – foreign observers were often present at manoeuvres in those days – what he thought of the British Army. 'It is excellent for fighting savages,' he said. 'Just as ours is excellent for fighting the French.'

Hardy had some criticisms of his own.

When trade is bad we get good recruits and when good, bad ones. The army is still recruited mainly from the class of manual labour. Men enlist for the queerest reasons. . . . Once a patient in a military hospital told me he did so in order to have a military funeral, an honour that the poor fellow soon obtained. Another man gave to me as his reason for enlisting that he wanted to learn to read. . . . He grew up quite illiterate and . . . thought he would learn something quietly in a military school. . . . Only 49 recruits in a thousand can be described as well educated.

Several inferences, including one about the standard of education could be drawn from the way in which Hardy discovered that a military prisoner was shamming madness. This man would lie on the floor and pretend to be totally deaf and dumb. At last, something Hardy said 'caused him in an unguarded moment to give just the least suspicion of a smile in the corner of his mouth'. Hardy, seeing this, 'knelt down and gave him a good tickling'.

Hardy wrote, 'Perhaps the most disagreeable thing in a barrack room, physically, for one who is not the manner born, is the foul air he has to breathe at night. True, there are plenty of windows and ventilators and the doctors are always saying they should be kept open, but most of the occupants of a barrack-room are afraid of night air.'

Padre Hardy might have thought foul air the most abominable thing about a barrack room, but the anonymous author of *The Queen's Service*, had something stronger to say: 'Those who have not actively experienced what a barrack-room, crowded with noisy, foul-mouthed and more or less drunken men, means at night, cannot conceive what a man who is in the slightest degree sensitive feels at such times. The utter loneliness, engendered by his inability to "muck it" with his companions is unspeakable. Although a soldier is never really persecuted for his religious tendencies he is always rather despised for making a display of them. This is often his own fault. If he would only prove himself to his comrades to be as good as themselves at soldiering . . . his religious observances would be held by them to be entirely his own affair. Unfortunately the psalm-singers of a battalion are too often more renowned for their proficiency in knee-drill than in their more strictly military exercises.'*

'Let us remember,' said Hardy, 'that a large number of our private soldiers are drawn from a class that have never received any teaching on the subject of purity, beyond that conveyed in filthy jests and coarse jocularity. They join the service as mere boys, low traditions abound around them, barrack life excludes them from the purifying influences of family life, and association with pure women. Under these conditions our lads are left to blunder like blind puppies into sin.'

The results of this sin were all too striking in the last decade of the century and for a while after. The wards of Netley Hospital were full of men, often under twenty-five years of age, disfigured by venereal disease. Often they were so repulsive that their own relatives and friends refused to see them. In one year 8,190 VD infected soldiers were discharged and turned loose upon the civil population; this was about the average annual figure. In Britain the admissions into military hospitals for VD were seven times greater than in the Prussian Army, four and a half times greater than in the French, three times greater than in the Austrian and 90 per cent more than in the Italian Army. But even then admission figures for the British Army in India were two and a half times greater than for the army at home. This was a sorry picture and again it was largely due to supervisory neglect. Soldiers of other nations were as

---

* Soldiers' opinions about church parades are best expressed in a maltreatment of the Fourth Commandment. 'Labour for six days and hard labour on the seventh' – a reference to all the spit and polish required to attend church parade.

apt to chase women indiscriminately as were British soldiers, but foreign armies enforced health checks on prostitutes.* Drunkenness, too, caused much of the trouble. At least 50 per cent of the single men in a barracks went to bed drunk and as many as fifty drunk cases would be brought before the CO in a single day.† Several Army Temperance Societies had been active for some years – they even issued medals to men who had been able to stay on the wagon for various periods – but they fought a losing battle.††

Writing in the *Navy and Army Illustrated* in September 1897, Trooper E.A. Gallop of the Life Guards said that he had frequently heard that a better system of rewards and a milder discipline would bring a better class of men into the army. He refuted the suggestion. 'No change that could be made or devised would bring a better class of men into the British Army. . . .'

Writing and reading rooms were coming into army vogue, but the soldier in barracks in Britain was still bored. Even Padre Hardy noted that 'Tommy Atkins chiefly amuses himself by walking up and down the streets with the unselfish object of giving the girls a treat. To do this he dresses up smartly, arranges a little curl of hair on each side of his temples and sets his cap at what his chums in the barrack room consider the proper angle. Then he takes his walking-out stick and sallies forth.'**

Perhaps it is true, as I believe somebody has said, that Tommy Atkins is happiest when he is doing something which,

* Major Charles James in his *Military Dictionary*, 1810, listed as an item WOMEN OF THE TOWN '. . . these dangerous animals.'
† In 1883 an inquest was held on a soldier of the Durham Light Infantry who died in a Gibraltar drinking den. It was found that two days earlier the man had received a legacy of £28. The publican told the court that the soldier had handed over the £28 and said, 'Supply me with drink until the money's gone.' When he could drink no more he lay on the floor and said, 'Pour it over me. I likes the smell.' After two days of this treatment he died.
†† Padre Hardy stated that in 1900 22 per cent of soldiers were teetotallers.
** Wolseley had said, 'The better you dress a soldier, the more highly will he be thought of by the women, and consequently by himself.'

strictly speaking, is no concern of his at all. The point can be supported by what he did in Hong Kong in 1894. In May that year, with a hot summer beginning, plague broke out on the island, spread rapidly and reduced the civilian population to panic. With too few British civilians to handle the epidemic the authorities appealed for help to the First Battalion the King's Shropshire Light Infantry. The battalion was willing. Every day and much of the night the troops and their officers worked until sheer exhaustion stopped them. Continuously exposed to infection, they cleaned and disinfected houses, acted as hospital orderlies and messengers, as corpse-removers and grave-diggers. Few British soldiers have ever been in greater danger of death, but the Shropshires had only eight casualties, of whom only one, Captain G.C. Vesey, died. But 3,000 Chinese died in Hong Kong city alone and many others died elsewhere. By August the epidemic was stamped out.

The population of Hong Kong issued a medal to the men of the regiment, although officialdom in a fit of recurrent meanness decreed that it could not be worn in uniform. The Hong Kong authorities also paid for a memorial window to Captain Vesey in St Chad's Church, Shrewsbury. The devotion to these English soldiers and their cheerful acceptance of dangers was long spoken of in Hong Kong.[†]

Tommy's critics, even well-informed ones like Padre Hardy, were not doing Tommy Atkins full justice for they were not seeing him in historic perspective. Compared with earlier periods better men *were* entering the ranks and a family no longer considered that a son who had 'gone for a soldier' had also gone to the dogs. The army as a whole was not a collection of dissolute libertines, but as always a few malcontents and miscreants gave everybody a bad name.

After many years of small wars Tommy Atkins found himself, in 1899, involved in a big one with the Boers. The Boers gave

---

[†] In Quetta, India, in June 1935, many British troops worked until they dropped following the earthquake in which 40,000 people were killed. The men of the First Battalion the West Yorkshire Regiment and the First Battalion the Queen's Royal Regiment were especially prominent.

him a bloody nose. Accustomed, on the whole, to cheap and fairly quick victories in many parts of the world he was startled and puzzled when the outnumbered Boers fought back so effectively. Even when strong reinforcements, including enterprising Empire troops, were brought in, the Boers spat defiance for three years. The trouble was that Tommy Atkins fought by the book while his Boer enemy was an opportunist. Tommy had no option but to fight by the book. He had been doing it for so long that he did not know of any other method. Successful in squares, in column and in line, in proper forts and behind palisades, he had triumphed over one enemy after another. Gallantly led, Tommy had gallantly followed. But, at long last, he found that gallantry was not enough and he was profoundly shocked.

His casualties showed that Archibald Forbes's observation that 'Thomas Atkins was prone to take cover and keep cover' was hardly any longer accurate. Had the troops sought cover more frequently instead of marching into action and assaulting *en masse* strongly held rocky hills their casualties would have been more moderate. Many brave young officers were killed in these desperate assaults. Their death scotched another old story – that 'privates who made good' could easily win a commission. In the middle of the Boer War Padre Hardy wrote: 'After so many young officers have been killed there are a sad number of vacancies, but men from the ranks will not be put into many of them. In time of peace the number of commissions (from the ranks) exclusive of those of quarter-masters and riding-masters does not average more than 12 or 15 in the year and these generally go to men who have much influence and can put pressure on the authorities.'

The Boer War was a tough struggle and what largely gave England victory in the end was the army's increasing skill and mobility. One great lesson learnt was the vital importance of proper musketry instruction, marksmanship and target practice. During the war musketry had been poor and the soldiers did not make the best use of their weapons. Gunners, too, had to learn that they were no longer fighting artillery-less savages and that if they wished to live to work their weapons they must conceal them, not dress them by the right while displaying them in the open.

Tommy Atkins at last was allowed to use some of his latent resource, but not before 7,792 British soldiers were killed in action and another 13,250 had died from disease.* The very fact that twenty-six bars were issued for the Queen's South Africa Medal and two to the King's South Africa Medal – Edward VII ascended the throne during the war – is some indication of the number of actions Tommy Atkins contested.

During the war the first volunteers of the modern type fought in the ranks of the army. These were the men of the City Imperial Volunteers, who were men of good type – post office workers, shopkeepers, bank and insurance clerks, clerks of all kinds, railway workers. They wore slouch hats like Australian troops and though they did not arrive until the first and most severe fighting was over they had plenty of active service and fought well. They were, in effect, a new type of British soldier. There were other volunteers in many units and some detachments of Territorials were also sent to South Africa.

---

* According to *The Times History*. Other sources quote about 6,000 killed in action and 16,000 died of disease.

Thirteen

1900–18 (1)
The Proud Professionals

From 1900 Tommy Atkins was busy in many places. In that year he saw some hard fighting in the Boxer Rebellion; in fact, he saw more of it than did the American contingent, regardless of how Hollywood managed to make it appear in the film *Fifty-Five Days at Pekin*. In 1904 Tommy – this time represented by the Royal Fusiliers – went on campaign in Tibet. The Fusiliers hold the record for the highest altitude reached by British troops on service. And all this time other Tommies were in action on the fabled North-West Frontier, in Somaliland and in other parts of Africa.

It was clear after the Boer War that further reform was necessary and that somebody had to complete for Tommy Atkins what Cardwell had started. The task fell to R.B. Haldane, a competent, persuasive and stubborn lawyer with remarkable ability for getting along with the military masterminds. Most of his reforms concerned matters which did not directly touch the lives of the common soldier, so I cannot dwell on them here. However, one important step was to place more trust in the soldier. One noteworthy example was the removal of picquets from the streets of Aldershot – as many as 700 men were on picquet duty each night – for pubs were no longer out of bounds. Haldane believed that soldiers could be trusted – and they proved him right. Pay and housing conditions were greatly improved. Among other things a soldier could more easily, more frequently and more comfortably have a bath. In every new barracks communal dining halls were built. It was soon possible for a man to read without going half blind from poor light – and read he could, for reading-rooms, libraries and writing rooms were part of the new system. Food, though still inadequate in quality and quantity, was also better. And, from a military point of view, Haldane pushed through reforms in training. Here he met the strongest opposition, for some senior commanders, imbued with prejudice and the stifling part of tradition, were difficult to convince.

Colonel Henderson had written in 1903, in a book published in 1905, 'The idea of transforming the Militia and Volunteers into an army of marksmen, capable of coping with the picked infantry of the Continent, is a vain dream. Marksmanship in a great mass of men depends on discipline and not on partriotism, and to believe that a large mass of men will become efficient soldiers, except under compulsion, is to disregard human nature.'

Nevertheless, between 1906 and 1914 Britain built up her finest army for a long time, perhaps the finest since the New Model. In saying this I am taking into account the quality of Marlborough's and Wellington's men, but both were the tools of their respective leaders. They did not have the intrinsic self-contained quality of the army of 1914. Tommy Atkins of that year was a highly trained, disciplined, ardent and perhaps hard-bitten soldier – eminently ready for the harsh trials that were to come.

When Haldane finished his work the British Regular Army at home consisted of six infantry divisions and one cavalry division. Each division was self-contained with its staff and reserves immediately ready for service. There were fourteen Territorial divisions and fourteen mounted brigades complete with artillery, although the guns were not the latest type.

It was a small but proudly professional army, regulars *par excellence*, well trained and as tough as men can be short of being hardened by actual service, though some were Boer War or Indian service veterans. As we shall see, the army was still capable of blunders but it was also still capable of restoring hopeless situations.

When war broke out in August 1914 British mobilization plans – based on Haldane's reforms – worked with efficient rapidity and the first appearance of the British Army in the field surprised the Germans; they had not believed the British Army could intervene so quickly. British senior officers were experienced – the Boer War had ended only twelve years previously. But no German officers had seen any serious service since the war of 1870. Some French officers had had much experience of colonial fighting. But with only two machine-guns per battalion the men would have to depend for survival on their rifles. And Britain would have to depend on this small professional army until other troops could be trained, for Lord Kitchener, who had replaced Haldane as Secretary of State for War, had decided that the Territorials would not be used.*

So led by General Sir John French, Tommy Atkins went to war – with Lord Kitchener anxious about his morals. He issued a memorable order to be kept at all times in the soldier's paybook: 'Remember that the honour of the British Army depends on your conduct. . . . Keep on your guard against excesses. In this new experience you may find temptations both in wine and women. You must entirely resist both, and, while treating all women with perfect courtesy, you should avoid any intimacy.'

Faint hope!

Some of the army's actions in 1914–18 were magnificent. It is obviously impossible to mention all the regiments, to describe all the actions and all the heroism, so I have selected those which were outstanding, which show some aspect of Tommy Atkins's make-up or which were representative of the whole.

At this point it will be interesting to examine the origin of that famous expression concerning French's 'contemptible little army'. This was the most successful slogan for recruiting purposes issued during the whole of the war, for it naturally created a passionate feeling of resentment throughout Britain.

This is its history.

---

* A few picked units were serving in France late in 1914 and, of course, many other formations were later sent abroad.

An addition to B.E.F. Routine Orders of 24 September 1914, stated:

> The following is a copy of Orders issued by the German Emperor on August 19th:
> 'It is my Royal and Imperial command that you should concentrate your energies for the immediate present upon one single purpose, that is that you address all your skill and all the valour of my soldiers to exterminate first, the treacherous English, walk over General French's contemptible little army . . .'
>
> Headquarters, Aix-la-Chapelle, August 19th
>
> The results of the order were the operations commencing with Mons, and the advance of the seemingly overwhelming masses against us. The answer of the British Army on the subject of extermination has already been given.
>
> Printing Co., R.E.69

The truth of this official statement was never questioned, although one attempt was made to pretend that it was an incorrect translation.

Publication of the Kaiser's alleged statement produced immediate reaction. *The Times* Military Correspondent referred to the Kaiser's 'high state of agitation and excitability'. *The Times* leader-writer on 1 October, 1914, noted that 'In spite of the ferocious order of the Kaiser . . . today French's contemptible little army is not yet exterminated. . . .' The newspaper that same day published a poem entitled *French's Contempible Little Army.*

The following day the *Daily Express* entered the lists with: 'The Kaiser scoffed at the British Army and labelled it contemptible because it was small. He felt grossly insulted that any army that did not count its men in millions should dare to assail the might of the Hohenzollerns, and against this small British David, in a pronouncement which will certainly be historic, he directed his Goliath legions to 'concentrate their energies'.

Churchill, naturally, played on the phrase during a recruiting speech at London Opera House on 11 September and in March 1915 *Punch* published a cartoon of a battered German eagle conversing with the Kaiser. The eagle says, 'Its like this: you told me the British lion was contemptible – well – he wasn't.'

There was much more of it. I expect every newspaper in the British Isles quoted the expression and finally the original Expeditionary Force became known as the 'Old Contemptibles'.

But did the Kaiser ever use the phrase? In 1925 a German general and a British general, Sir F. Maurice, investigated the matter. For one thing, it was known that the Kaiser, indiscreet though he sometimes was, preposterous and extravagant in speech though he could be, did not issue orders on his own initiative. They were prepared for him by the Staff.

At the time the alleged order was issued the Staff did not know where the British Army was, so ordering the German Generals to concentrate their energies on exterminating it was somewhat pointless. On 20 August the day *after* the issue of the supposed order the German Chief of Staff telegrammed to von Kluck, the German field commander: DISEMBARKATION OF ENGLISH AT BOULOGNE MUST BE RECKONED WITH. THE OPINION HERE, HOWEVER, IS THAT LARGE DISEMBARKATIONS HAVE NOT YET TAKEN PLACE. Clearly, the Germans knew very little about the British Army and its extermination was hardly a matter of priority.

But perhaps the most damning evidence is this: German HQ was never at Aix-la-Chapelle. Headquarters moved from Berlin about 15 August and went to Koblenz, then to Luxembourg, and finally to Charleville on 27 September.

An exhaustive search of the German archives – which were meticulously kept – brought to light nothing even faintly resembling the order. The Kaiser himself, in exile at Doorn in Holland, was asked about it. He wrote that he had never used the expression. 'On the contrary,' he said, 'I continually emphasized the high value of the British Army, and often, indeed, in peace-time gave warning against under-estimating it.'

I can confirm this. During research for my book *Jackboot: The Story of the German Soldier* (Cassell, 1965), I frequently encountered such urgings by the Kaiser.

General Maurice had German newspaper files searched, but drew a blank. On 6 November 1925 he published an article in the *Daily News* and commented that GHQ hit on the idea of having routine orders to issue statements which it was believed would encourage and inspire the troops. 'Most of these took the form of casting ridicule on the German Army. . . . These efforts were seen to be absurd by the men in the trenches and were soon dropped.'

In 1928 a member of parliament, Arthur Ponsonby, was prepared to label the supposed order a falsehood. If it was a concoction it succeeded beyond the hopes of the British officer responsible. And in my view it was justifiable; in a basic matter like survival almost anything is justifiable – especially if it comes off. Still, it was a pity that the officer made such a careless mistake about the whereabouts of German HQ.

A week after the issue of the supposed order of the Cheshire Regiment, formerly the 22nd Foot, put up, during the Battle of Mons, its greatest fight. I have no space to describe in detail the Battle of Mons. Briefly, two Army Corps spread along the Franco-Belgian frontier prepared to hold off a greatly superior German attack. On the extreme left of the unprotected flank was the Cheshire Regiment, whose primary duty was to stop the Germans from rolling up their division, the 5th, from the left. On 29 August they were in positions in embankments, on slag heaps and in pitheads and soon they were fighting. At first they were able to keep company formation, but pressure was so great that control broke down to platoons and then to sections. At this time the Cheshires were generally considered to be the best shots in the British Army. They needed to be, for though they did not know it, that day they were fighting nearly all the German Fourth Army Corps – twenty-five battalions of infantry, six cavalry squadrons, twenty-four artillery batteries and fifty-six machine-guns. The Cheshires had only their two machine-guns, but their rifle fire was so sustained and accurate – fifteen aimed rounds a minute – that the Germans for long believed that many machine-guns faced them.

Division HQ sent three orders to Colonel D.C. Boger to withdraw his regiment, but none reached him. Boger was badly wounded, but held to his positions. Only half the reserve company, found by a Staff Officer and ordered out, reached safety intact. Elsewhere the battle went on until small groups or even individual soldiers were overrun. That evening, when roll call was held, only six officers and 129 men answered their names; the unit had gone into action with 27 officers and 1,007 men. The great sacrifice was not in vain, as is shown by the report of the divisional commander, Sir Charles Ferguson. 'It was due to the gallant action of these two battalions [the other was the First Battalion the Royal Norfolk Regiment] that the division was able to extricate itself. The fact that this very heavy enemy attack was held long enough to allow the withdrawal of the division is sufficient testimony to the gallantry and devotion of the two battalions concerned.'

It is quite astonishing how English troops can manage to be so incompetent and yet so tenacious and gallant in the one action, but the classic case of L Battery, Royal Horse Artillery proves it. Not that any previous writer has even hinted at any incompetence on the part of L Battery; to do so would verge, in some minds, on infamous conduct. But it is only by displaying crass negligence on somebody's part that I can properly emphasize gallantry. During the retreat from Mons the 1st Cavalry Brigade under General Briggs reached the village of Nery. The brigade comprised the Bays, the 5th Dragoon Guards, the 11th Hussars and L Battery, with its six guns.

The brigade had been protecting the rear of the retiring army from the German cavalry and at Nery they had a rest. Early on 1 September, while the horses were being watered and breakfasts prepared, a patrol of the 11th Hussars came in at the gallop to report German cavalry on a ridge to the east of Nery. But unknown to anybody, during the night a German cavalry division had approached close to the village and helped by a morning mist had got into position about 400 yards from L Battery's bivouac.

This should never have happened. Properly posted sentries or listening posts would have detected enemy at such a short distance. Suddenly brought under gunfire and heavy machine-gun and rifle fire, the battery's position became a shambles. Three guns were knocked out at once and two others were soon wrecked. All this is proof enough that, as so often in British military history, somebody had blundered. And again, as also so often happens, somebody was at hand to make amends.

The only men in action after the first onslaught were Captain Bradbury, three subalterns, Dorrell, the battery sergeant-major, Sergeant Nelson, Driver Osborne and Gunner Darbyshire and one gun. In the face of a rain of fire, Bradbury directed his detachment as they fired over open sights into the German positions. A subaltern was killed, and Bradbury and the other two officers severely wounded. The Bays and the 5th Dragoon Guards supported the gunners and two squadrons of dragoons tried to turn the German flank.

The lone gun continued to fire. Bradbury, who had continued in command, was now wounded again, even more seriously. Sergeant Major Dorrell, also wounded, assumed command and continued the action. At this point the 4th Cavalry Brigade and J Battery R.H.A. arrived and went into action with such spirit that the Germans pulled out, with L Battery still firing into them. The stand of their one gun had largely helped to avert a serious defeat. But the unit was so badly crippled it had to be sent home to refit. Captain Bradbury died of his wounds, so did not learn of the VC awarded him. Sergeant Major Dorrell, who later became a lieutenant-colonel, and Sergeant Nelson were also given the VC for their outstanding bravery. Driver Osborne and Gunner Darbyshire were awarded the French Medaille Militaire.

For getting themselves into a sticky mess and for spectacularly getting themselves out of it, no other soldiers can equal the English.

At one point in the retreat from Mons sappers laid a demolition charge on a bridge, but all were killed. A second party of twelve engineers was covering the first and one by one they ran through heavy enemy small-arms fire to reach and light the fuse – and one by one they fell. The twelfth man achieved the task – and died a second later as the bridge blew up. This was a typical action of 1914.

The Germans at this time already had plenty of artillery and machine-guns and they made life hell for runners, who had the dangerous job of taking messages to and from the front line – messages reporting success, calling urgently for reinforcements, more ammunition, for further orders. The runner often had little chance to run, especially when the battlefield was muddy and littered with shell craters. But as a runner Tommy Atkins showed his guts. This is the story of one runner – Drummer Harry Vincent Penn, aged seventeen, of Barford, Warwickshire, told here for the first time.

When an action was particularly violent and a message was so important that it had to be got through at all costs several runners were sent off by different routes and at intervals, in the hope that perhaps one would get through. Runners sometimes broke down and trembled and sobbed with the strain of their experiences; others became temporarily insane. Some, wounded many times, somehow survived to deliver their message – and then to fall dead. Now that radio is so much used in battle runners are less frequently needed but during World War I radio was in its infancy.

Soon after dawn on the morning of 30 October 1914 the German artillery began a furious bombardment of Zandevoorde, near Ypres in Belgium. The victims of the bombardment were the men of the British 3rd Cavalry Division, one troop of which was buried alive. The trenches became untenable and the whole division fell back. In this critical situation the Guards were brought up and they, too, were subjected to heavy bombardment. At this part of the line the only British Artillery were light field guns, so the German heavy guns were able to operate at will.

The Germans did not merely batter the trenches to pieces – they laid down a barrage of fire between the British firing line and the supporting lines so that telephone lines between the trenches and the brigade headquarters were cut again and again. So repeatedly did this happen in the case of the 2nd Grenadier Guards that messages had to be sent by runner. Drummer Penn volunteered for this duty.

To reach his destination Penn had to run a gauntlet of fire and fury. First he had to cross an open field pock-marked with craters, the number of which was growing every minute as huge German shells burst on the soft ground. Then he had to pass through a farm, whose buildings were crumbling into ruin. Crossing the road leading to Zillebeke, which was under fire, he then had to make his way for more than 50 yards along a ditch and across an open ploughed field into Zillebeke Wood. This wood was the most dangerous part of his journey because it was being raked by enemy artillery systematically searching for British command posts and gun emplacements.

But Penn had to travel even further than this. After leaving the wood he had another stretch of open ground, which brought him to Brigade HQ. Then, of course, he had to make the return journey. He made this round-trip several times during that very critical day, crawling, running, slipping, slithering, diving into shellholes, being showered with debris and with shell fragments flying all around him. Miracullously, he escaped injury.

The Germans bombarded the Guards' positions without a break until dusk, by which time there was nothing but utter destruction in many places. Then the German infantry advanced. It was met by fire from the British field guns and by rifle fire from those Guardsmen still in action and just as the attack looked like becoming dangerous it faded away. Much of the credit for holding the position was due to Harry Penn, for had communications not been maintained the defence would not have been so co-ordinated. But it was the boy's great and sustained gallantry that won him the Distinguished Conduct Medal. Yet Penn's experience had not been particularly hazardous compared with the duties of runners a year or so later, when virtually all cover and landmarks had disappeared and the trench lines were shambles.

Twice, on 31 October and again on 11 November the Germans nearly borke the line surrounding Ypres and southwards to Messines; only the astonishing discipline, musketry and fighting power of Tommy Atkins kept the line intact against overwhelming superior numbers and fire power. Sir Douglas Haig commanded in the sector and despite criticisms levelled at him later his resolution at Ypres in 1914 was worthy of his men. British troops had never fought against greater odds with such success. Liddell Hart called the stand at Ypres 'the supreme memorial to the British Regular Army'.

But it was a grim stand. On 11 November Corporal John Lucy fought in Sanctuary Wood where he saw a soldier 'his belly ripped open, supporting his back against the trench while he gazed with fascinated eyes at large coils of his own guts, which he held in both hands.' This, said Lucy, was 'almost the ghastliest sight' he saw. He was fairly fortunate if he saw nothing much ghastlier.

While the old regulars were fighting and dying Kitchener was recruiting his men for his new armies, for he alone from the outset correctly predicted the probable duration of the war. He knew that many divisions would be needed. His appeal to the nation was spectacular – 'Kitchener Wants You!' – and successful. His early volunteers were, to quote Cole and Priestley, 'the finest fighting material Britain ever put in the field'. Douglas Bell says of them, 'The fine flower of the nation, the ardent spirits, first rushed to arms and were slaughtered.'

The men of Kitchener's new army were volunteers inspired by an emotional, not a deliberate sense of patriotism. Enthusiastic though naive, fit but not tough, these men have been likened to the men of Crécy in that they were 'under the spur'* of a lofty idea. I cannot believe that so many of them were inspired by an ideal. They were reacting to the Kipling influence, to the notion that nobody insulted the British flag with impunity. Perhaps they were idealists to heroism for heroism's sake.

These men were of the Victorian breed. They could say – and they did say – as they died in action, 'God bless the old regiment,' and 'Don't let them break the line!' and 'Do your duty, lads, and never mind me,' and 'Leave me; there are others more badly wounded.' One soldier said, when badly hit, 'Goodbye old man. I'm done for. Tell poor old dad I died at the front. I began a letter to him; you finish it.'

Officers shouted 'Old England for ever! Follow me lads!' Or: 'No surrender, lads; remember the regiment!' Or: 'Bravo men! That was a gallant show.'

Comments like these sound melodramatic now, but they were genuine and sincere in 1914.

And most of the time Victorian discipline prevailed. A soldier lying close by his platoon commander under fire said after a while, 'Sir, may I retire? I have been hit three times.'

---

* Colonel de Watteville's phrase.

In 1914 and the early part of 1915 some Tommies still had a sense of fun. At one place the German and British trenches were within sixty yards of each other. The Germans had aproned their trenches with wire, to which they had hung many empty tins which jangled when the wire was touched. A Tommy one night crawled out and tied the end of a ball of string to the wire. The troops then amused themselves by periodically jangling the tins to provoke the Germans into furious fire.

A soldier wrote, 'A chap in our company has a ripping cure for neuralgia, but he isn't going to take out a patent, because it's too risky, and might kill a patient. He was lying in the trenches the other day nearly mad with pain in his face, when a German shell burst close by. He wasn't hit, but the explosion knocked him senseless for a bit. "Me neuralgia's gone!" says he, when he came around. "And so's six of your mates," says we. "O Cricky," says he. His name's Palmer, and that's why we call the German shells now "Palmer's Neuralgia Cure". I am writing this under fire. Every now and again a little message from the Kaiser comes whizzing in this direction, but no damage is being done, and we don't worry. Bang! Another message.'

Late in 1914 a correspondent of the French paper *L'Independance* wrote: 'Tommy loves to laugh; he has clear eyes and smokes almost continuously a cigarette or a pipe. He is a sportsman, who views war as a continuation of the sports he practises in peace time. No one could be more placid; he does not know what it is to be nervous. . . .'

Things would change.

Getting enough officers was a serious problem. To find the thousands needed commissions were freely granted to public-schoolboys, irrespective of whatever quality of leadership they may have possessed. As it happened, most of these boys had both courage and, with experience, competence. The growing citizen-army was an extraordinary thing and many important men, Sir Henry Wilson of the War Office among them, scoffed at these men ever becoming efficient troops. They did so, but the transformation was a slow job, and in the meantime the regulars and the few Territorials were dying in the field. The loss of officers and NCOs was especially serious; they would have been so useful in 1916 and after.

With many of Kitchener's men still in training, in April 1915 the Gallipoli Campaign commenced. This is often thought of as pretty much an Australian and New Zealand affair. The Colonials certainly did their share – perhaps more than their share in proportion to their numbers – and they captured the communiqués frequently, but many English soldiers were engaged on the passionate peninsula that was Gallipoli. On that first day of attack, 25 April, the 1st Battalion the Lancashire Fusiliers displayed almost incredible valour when they won six Victoria Crosses before breakfast.

In January 1915 the Fusiliers had returned to England from India to join the 29th Division, formation of overseas garrison units which had been kept up to full strength with trained soldiers. Their arrival in England caused some surprise for they landed still dressed in red tunics. Nothing but khaki had been worn by British soldiers at home since the outbreak of war.

After a few weeks in Warwickshire, the Fusiliers sailed for Egypt as part of the 86th Brigade. Before the Brigade went into battle the Commander, Brigadier-General Hare, in a Special Order addressed to his four battalions of Fusiliers said: 'Our Brigade is to have the honour to be the first to land and to cover the disembarkment of the rest of the Division. . . . Let us carry it through in a way worthy of the traditions of the distinguished regiments of which the Fusilier Brigade is composed; in such a way that the men of Albuhera and Minden, of Delhi and Lucknow, may hail us as their equals in valour and military achievement, and that future historians may say of us, as Napier said of the Fusilier Brigade at Albuhera: "Nothing could stop this astonishing infantry."'

The leading Fusiliers' objective was W Beach west of Cape Helles. It was 350 yards wide, with cliffs about 100 feet high at each end and in the centre a mound commanding the beach. HQ and three companies of the Lancashire Fusiliers were in position off the coast in HMS *Euryalus* and at 4 a.m. on 25 April the men transferred to the ships' boats, which were towed shoreward by steam pinnaces.

A belt of wire entanglement stretched across the beach, and the order was passed that the troops would wait behind it until gaps had been made. *Euryalus* and other warships shelled the beach to keep the Turks' heads down. A few hundred yards off-shore the pinnaces cast the tows, leaving the boats to be rowed in by naval ratings. Soon the boats came under heavy and accurate enemy machine-gun and rifle fire.

The troops jumped out of the boats and waded and splashed as far as the wire, then went to ground under the hail of bullets from the front and both flanks. For some time the assault troops were pinned down as most of their rifles were jammed by sand and sea-water. A few rifles at last were forced to work and a lucky shot killed a sniper who had caused many casualties. Sergeant A. Richards, his leg almost severed, dragged himself through the wire and encouraged others in the assault.

'C' Company, under Captain R. Willis, were first of those on W Beach to gain some sort of order and start climbing to their objective, Hill 114. 'D' Company (Major G. Adams) from HMS *Implacable*, had landed at some rocks farther left below Hill 114 and, quickly scaling the cliff, surprised and beat back the Turks harassing 'C' Company. The attack on Hill 114 proceeded. Lance-Sergeant F. Stubbs led what remained of his platoon and was mortally wounded in the last rush which established the Fusiliers at a solitary tree at the top of Hill 114. Lance-Corporal J. Grimshaw distinguished himself by his calmness while sending messages from cliff-top to beach.

The centre and the right were a bloody shambles. At the wire lay more than 300 men furiously urged on by officers some distance away. But all these 300 men were dead or wounded. More and more troops stormed ashore and eventually parties of 'A' Company (Lieutenant Haworth) and 'B' Company (Captain H. Shaw) managed to mount an assault on Hill 138, the objective on the right. They reached the top – and ran into the explosion of a shell from one of the British ships, which mangled several of them.

Soon after 7 a.m., a rough line strong enough to protect the landing-beach from small arms fire, had been established. But the brigade commander had been wounded and the brigade major killed and for a time control of the operation fell to Major Bishop, commanding the Lancashire Fusiliers.

All immediate objectives were consolidated by nightfall but the strength of the Lancashire Fusiliers was then only

11 officers and 399 other ranks; casualties had amounted to 11 officers and 350 men.

After the battle Major-General Hunter-Weston, Commanding 29th Division, asked the Lancashire Fusiliers to recommend six officers and other ranks for the Victoria Cross. The names of Captain R. Willis, Sergeant A. Richards, Private W. Keneally, Captain C. Bromley, Sergeant F. Stubbs, and Corporal J. Grimshaw were sent in but the War Office, according to custom involving 'collective acts of bravery', accepted only the first three. However, following agitation, the other three, two of whom were no longer alive, were granted the award.

The Commander-in-Chief, Sir Ian Hamilton, wrote: 'No finer feat of arms has ever been achieved by the British soldier – or any other soldier – than the storming of these beaches from open boats. . . . Gallantly led by their officers, the Fusiliers hurled themselves ashore and, fired at from right, left and centre, commenced hacking their way through the wire. A long line of men was at once mown down as by a scythe, but the remainder were not to be denied. . . .'

Vice-Admiral de Robeck, in his dispatch from Gallipoli declared: 'It is impossible to exalt too highly the service rendered by the 1st Battalion Lancashire Fusiliers; the dash and gallantry displayed was superb.' And HMS *Euryalus* signalled the Battalion: 'We are as proud as can be to have had the honour to carry your splendid regiment. We feel for you in your great losses as if you were our own ship's company, but know the magnificent gallantry of your regiment has made the name more famous than ever.'*

Towards the end of May 1915 – that is, about the time the Battle of Festubert ended – the original regular army had

---

* The Lancashire Fusiliers, as Kingsley's Regiment, were one of the six British regiments that fought at Minden in 1759. In 1782 they became the twentieth or the East Devonshire Regiment. Recruiting in Devonshire failed and before the end of the century the Regiment moved to Preston. The Lancashire Fusiliers guarded Napoleon at St Helena where twelve grenadiers of the Regiment were his pall-bearers. In World War I, seventeen Lancashire Fusiliers won the Victoria Cross – another was gained by an attached Irish Guards officer. This was the greatest number awarded to any one regiment in that war.

done its dash in France; there simply were not many of them left.[†] Between the end of Festubert and the Battle of Loos in September many of the New Army divisions arrived on the Continent and by the end of that month General French had thirty-seven divisions.

The Battle of Loos began well and ended in disaster with 60,000 casualties. From this point Tommy Atkins knew that he was in for a bloodbath; the romanticism, the glory and the sense of adventure were leached after Loos, though the real deflation did not come until after the massacres on the Somme in 1916. And at home men were already becoming harder to find to make up the wastage overseas – something like 100,000 a month.

The first plan was Lord Derby's scheme to induce men to volunteer in order of age – the younger first, and single men before married men. But only the more conscientious men enlisted. By the beginning of 1916 the Military Service Bill was passed and then, in May, the Universal Military Service Bill, which applied to all men between eighteen and forty-one, but there were many exemptions. It must be admitted that many men, for one reason or another, did not want to become soldiers. And it was not until after the German breakthrough in 1918 that the Government passed really sweeping conscription measures.

In April 1916 British soldiers suffered a serious reverse at Kut in Mesopotamia. A force under General Townshend had been bottled up here by the Turks since 3 December 1915. Several attempts to break through the Turkish blockade were made, but all failed, until, with twenty men a day dying of starvation, Townshend destroyed his guns, ammunition and stores and surrendered. About 3,000 British and 6,000 Indian troops were taken prisoner. Something like 5,000 of them were never heard of again, for the Turks were merciless. Sick and starving, driven long distances across hard country, many men simply died by the wayside. English soldiers have rarely suffered more, but the few who survived spoke highly of the dignity and courage of this doomed column.

† The last regular divison formed of battalions brought from overseas garrison posts was the 27th, and it arrived in France in September 1915.

Fourteen

1900–18 (2)
Bloodbath for the Zealous Volunteers

On 1 July 1916 Britain's new army marched – or rather, was flung – into its first great trial, the Somme offensive. The army was new but not all the men. Most of the officers and men were the early volunteers of 1914 and it is said that the army of 1916 was the finest in quality and zeal that Britain had ever put into the field.*

This may have been so, but not all soldiers were prepared to stay and see it through. On that first day of the Somme offensive Brigadier F.P. Crozier saw a 'strong rabble of tired, hungry and thirsty stragglers' approach him from the east. 'I go out to meet them,' he wrote. '"Where are you going?" I ask. One says one thing, one another. They are marched to the water reserve, given a drink and hunted back to fight. Another more formidable party cuts across to the south. They mean business. They are damned if they are going to stay, it's all up. A young sprinting subaltern heads them off. They take no notice. He fires. Down drops a British soldier at his feet. The effect is instantaneous. They turn back to the assistance of their comrades in distress.'†

* Priestley and Cole.
† *A Brass Hat in No Man's Land.*

But Tommy Atkins got a bloody nose on the Somme. After a week's artillery bombardment designed to soften up the Germans the nineteen British and five French divisions advanced – straight into sheets of machine-gun fire and a holocaust of shells. Whole battalions were swallowed up and in front of Thiepval casualties were specially heavy.* Brigadier Crozier saw 'a wall of corpses here'. Small, determined groups got into the German trenches – and were wiped out. At the end of that one day's fighting the British Army had 57,000 casualties of whom 19,000 were killed or died of wounds – the greatest number for any single day's combat in the army's history. In return, the attackers had captured a mere 2,000 prisoners, 20 guns and a couple of small pieces of ground. By 18 July 10,000 prisoners had been taken – at a total British cost of 80,000 casualties; in the middle of September casualties amounted to 100,000, many of them caused by the German machine-guns. The final figure for the entire offensive was 400,000.

Of one sector late in September 1916 Private H.V. Drinkwater wrote: 'The wood had been attacked and counter-attacked some twenty-odd times before we took it, and everywhere the ground was literally cluttered up with dead, British and German mixed together. . . .'

It may have been about this time that somebody said – I cannot trace the source – that the Germans held their trenches with machine-guns, the French with artillery and the British with men. It was the cynical truth. Tommy gave as good as he got and all the old qualities of the men who had gone before him came to the top. A soldier needed qualities in those harsh days, for the suffering was intense and prolonged in those muddy and bloody battles.

In October and November 1917 the army suffered another 300,000 casualties – this time in the Battle of Passchendaele. This battle was fought across a terrifying sea of mud, into which many men – even fit, unwounded men – disappeared.

---

* The British War Memorial at Thiepval carries the names of 73,367 missing soldiers. They were blown to pieces or were buried in the mud of the Somme. The Somme casualty figures given here are those commonly quoted. But even now there is much controversy.

The only possible way across many square miles of this shell-chewed region was by duckboards. A man blown off a board had little chance of extricating himself from the mud unaided. The difficulties of rescuing a wounded man from the battlefield were enormous and many gallant stretcher-bearers themselves became casualties.

The task of the Royal Army Medical Service in coping with the flood of casualties is beyond comprehension.*

Life in the trenches was vile. True, in the better-disciplined units trench house-keeping was taken seriously. No rubbish was allowed and latrine buckets were situated down a short sap to the rear. Tools, bombs and ammunition were all neatly stacked. Mostly an officer would have a dugout into which he could crawl. The men would sprawl on the firestep, shivering in the bitter cold, up to their knees in mud, with rain driving into their faces. In summer the heat in a trench was intense. Large rats ran over the men as they slept; everybody knew on what these rats fed. Meals were brought from somewhere behind the line – if the ration party could get through. Often it could not. After the Somme (1916) trenches were well developed complexes with dugout protection for most of the men.

Every so often the Germans would send down a barrage. A bomb falling in the confines of a trench could do great damage and the wounded would cry out or groan with pain. A shot through joints like the kneee or through the stomach often makes a man shout out with pain but most wounds are merely numbing for the time; the pain comes afterwards. There would be a frantic effort to dig out those men buried alive by the blast. By day it was virtually suicide to show the head over the parapet. At night wiring parties or patrols of one kind or another would crawl out into No Man's Land and usually they would come back smaller than when they departed. Men

* Since the Royal Army Medical Service was reorganized in 1898 it has treated more than 14,000,000 casualties and while on active service 10,000 officers and men of the Corps have lost their lives. Corps members have won 6,500 awards for gallantry, including twenty-nine VCs. Only three men have won the VC twice – two of them were RAMC officers.

became callous in these surroundings. When thawing mud in spring revealed a hand sticking out from the side of a trench somebody would hang something on it. A lot of things like that happened. It did not show disrespect for the dead; many of the living envied the dead. Somehow, sometimes, Tommy managed to sing. One of his favourites was 'Apres La Guerre'.

> Après la guerre fini,
> Oh, we'll go home to Blighty:
> But won't we be sorry to leave chère Germaine,
> Après la guerre fini.
>
> Après la guerre fini,
> English soldier parti,
> Mam'selle français beaucoup piccaninnies,
> Après la guerre fini.

This song, which has several more verses, was a great favourite. The pidgin French was typical of the way Tommy conversed with the natives. Soldiers were at their best with this song when passing through small villages, where its truth was only too apparent. In some cases the mothers were not certain whether their war babies were French, English, or even German.

Another famous one was 'Skiboo', though what follows is necessarily a censored and abbreviated version of its forty crude verses.

Two German officers crossed the Rhine, Skiboo, Skiboo,
Two German officers crossed the Rhine, Skiboo, Skiboo.
These German officers crossed the Rhine
To love the women and taste the wine.
Skiboo, Skiboo, Skiboodley boo, Skidam, dam, dam.

They came to an inn on top of a rise, Skiboo, Skiboo,
A famous French inn of stupendous size, Skiboo, Skiboo,
They saw a maiden all dimples and sighs,
The two together said 'Damn her eyes'.
Skiboo, Skiboo, Skiboodley, boo, Skidam, dam, dam.

Oh, landlord, you've a daughter fair, Skiboo, Skiboo,
Oh, landlord, you've a daughter fair, Skiboo, Skiboo,
Oh, landlord, you've a daughter fair,
With lily-white arms and golden hair.
Skiboo, Skiboo, Skiboodley boo, Skidam, dam, dam.

Nein, nein, mein Herr, she's far too young, Skiboo, Skiboo,
Nein, nein, mein Herr, she's far too young, Skiboo, Skiboo,
Mais non, mon père, I'm not so young—
I've often been kissed by the farmer's son.
Skiboo, Skiboo, Skiboodley boo, Skidam, dam, dam.

The rest of the tale I can't relate, Skiboo, Skiboo,
For tho' it's old, it's up to date, Skiboo, Skiboo.
The story of man seducing a maid
Is not for you – you're too sedate.
Skiboo, Skiboo, Skiboodley boo, Skidam, dam, dam.

So the slaughter went on throughout 1917 and into 1918, with Tommy Atkins's gallantry only equalled by the gore with which he paid for it. Towards the later stages, with casualties seriously depleting the ranks, and reinforcements – many of them conscripts – constantly arriving there was not even the backbone-supporting influence of the regimental system. Tommy Atkins has always fought better in company he knows and in the latter part of the Great War he often went into action personally knowing nobody, for men had become mere ciphers in the senseless butchery.

One great problem for commanders of British troops in the field has always been the difficulty of working and fighting them in harness with other troops, especially Continentals. Considering the English soldier's idiosyncrasies the results were fairly good, but Tommy Atkins and the French *poilu* did not get along together very well during the Great War. General Spears believes that the main stumbling blocks concerned different methods of command and different food. '. . . food, an absorbing topic in wartime, did not bring them together,' he wrote. 'They disliked each other's cuisine. When the French commissariat fed some of our men . . . complaints were endless. . . . Our people could do nothing with the vegetables from which they were expected to devise soups and savoury messes. They hated the coffee and threw away in disgust the inordinate quantities of bread served out. . . .'* In short, Tommy Atkins, like his civilian counterpart, was rigidly hidebound in his tastes.

Spears shows another aspect of the Tommy's rigidity when both French and British artillery troops were on a roadway waiting in bitter cold for it to be cleared so that they could proceed. When German shells made the road untenable the French galloped the guns and limbers through a roadside cemetery to escape from the unhealthy spot. The British artillery stayed where they were. They 'preferred the road, the cold and the shells . . . they had got it into their heads that they were going home by road, and nothing so unconventional as a drive through a graveyard would deflect them from their purpose.'

As nearly always in his history, Tommy Atkins showed no savagery in his dealings with the Germans; he had no hate. Over and over again one finds references to British soldiers being friendly with prisoners and wounded enemy. No matter how much hate the propagandists on both sides inspired among their civilians there was little of it among the troops. There are even recorded instances of Tommies who, having bayoneted or shot a German, returned after the action to give him first aid. Other men risked their lives to crawl out into No Man's Land to bring in wounded enemy who were calling for help. Once in a while active fraternization occurred – as on Christmas 1914, when at parts of the line British and German soldiers mingled freely and visited each other's trenches.

It is perhaps equally significant that the German soldier did not hate Tommy Atkins. In German literature of World War II have found many affectionate references to the British soldier. Even when Germans have been critical, they have not been hostile. They thought that at times Tommy treated war with unseemly levity, they considered he was stupid to charge machine-gun nests, but they did not find him wanting

* *Four Years on the Western Front.*

in courage or humanity.* All this is important, for the opinions of enemies are often more revealing than those of friends.

Writing of an action at Cambrai (not the great British tank attack) Lieutenant Ernest Jünger wrote, 'The English resisted valiantly. Every traverse was contested. Mills bombs [British] and stick-bombs [German] crossed and re-crossed. Behind each we found dead or still quivering bodies. . . .' Near Vraucourt Jünger later investigated a dugout which had been used by British officers. It was 'furnished with extreme comfort, even to a little open grate and a mantlepiece, on which lay pipes and tobacco, with a circle of armchairs around the fire. Merry old England!'

The Germans made one significant distinction. When they buried their own men they labelled the stone or cross *Ruht in Gott* (Rests in God); English dead merely rested – *Hier ruht ein Engländer.* No God.

The longer the war progressed the clearer it became that the old regulars and the new volunteers were pretty much the same men; both were drawing on national qualities in their hours of trial. There was not much to choose between regular and volunteer officers, either, as at least one contemporary observer noted. 'For gallant and skilful leading there was nothing to choose between the best Regular and the best Civilian, and there were many more of the latter.'†

Regular battalions are proud units, but it is significant that the Manchester Regiment, which has a long and illustrious pedigree, has often presented the work of its 16th Battalion, a wartime-only unit, as unusually outstanding. There is much justice in this, if we taken only one incident of the 16th Battalion's service.

On 21 March 1918 the expected German storm upon the Western Front broke with great violence. On this day the men of the 16th Battalion, commanded by Lieutenant-Colonel Wilfrith Elstob, DSO, MC, were in the Forward Zone, on

---

* Both British and Germans were guilty of battle-heat excesses and there is no doubt that German other-rank prisoners had a better war then British other-rank prisoners.
† W.W. Nicholson, *Behind the Lines.*

either side of Manchester Hill near St Quentin. During the preliminary bombardment Elstob encouraged the men in the posts with frequent visits.

On his frontage of 200 yards Elstob knew that he faced eight enemy battalions, and normally he could have been fairly confident of holding them, for his positions were sound. But in the heavy fog that morning the Germans were able to advance unseen and before long the battalion was fighting for its life. The Germans were close-packed and ripe for machine-gun fire, but they had weight of numbers.

Nobody knows of all the gallantry performed during this battle, for the battalion was broken up and fought in groups. HQ and D Company fought on the hill itself, with Elstob showing he was worth his rank. Finding that the Germans had entered a redoubt he put up a bombing block between them and HQ and single-handed fought off the attackers with his revolver. Then, with grenades, he held the block against six attacks. When the Germans advanced in large numbers over the top Elstob used a rifle to help stop them.

When ammunition was required Elstob made several journeys under heavy fire to bring it up. Hit for the first time, he cheered on his men with 'You're doing magnificently, boys!' About 2 p.m. he got through by phone to Brigade HQ – the cable, well buried, had survived the artillery fire – said that most of his men were killed or wounded, that the survivors were dead-beat, but that the regiment would hold the hill to the last man.

Despite two more wounds, Elstob himself went for ammunition and was thrown several yards by a bursting shell. By four o'clock the survivors were surrounded and the Germans demanded their surrender. Elstob shouted defiance and died while the Germans rushed in and swamped those who were left. And one by one the little pockets of resistence went the same way. Elstob was posthumously awarded the VC for conspicuous bravery, devotion to duty and self-sacrifice. They were nothing more than the qualities of Tommy Atkins.

I am not concerned here with giving examples of Victoria Cross deeds for their own sake; 415 British soldiers were awarded the VC between the years 1914 and 1918 and it would be invidious to select a few from among them.

However, every VC winner would agree that the case of Padre Hardy is different.*

In the roll call of VC winners the great majority were under 30 years of age; many were under 20. Probably the most outstanding exception was the Reverend Theodore Bayley Hardy, a regimental padre, officially listed as Chaplain Fourth Class. He won his VC at 55. As it happened, there was nothing fourth class about Padre Hardy. He had led a busy life, both as a schoolmaster and a minister, before he enlisted in 1916. He was headmaster of Bentham Grammar School from 1906–13. Many friends tried to dissuade him from enlisting. They pointed out that active service was not expected of a man of his age – 53 – and that, in any case, his son and daughter were already serving – his son as regimental medical officer, his daughter in the Red Cross in France.

'I'm fit,' said Mr Hardy, 'and they need chaplains at the front.'

He was fit enough. All his life he had been keen on boating, swimming, riding and walking. He liked cricket and football, too, but in these sports he was handicapped by his extreme short sight. His fitness got him accepted for service. And, as he had said, the army did need chaplains. Soldiers were dying in their thousands and men needed the comfort that only an understanding padre could bring them. All commanding officers of 1914–18 knew that an efficient padre was invaluable in building and maintaining morale.

In September 1917 Padre Hardy won his first decoration, the DSO, for conspicuous bravery and devotion to duty. He went out into the open to help bring in wounded and then discovered a man buried in mud. The man could not be dug out, so the padre remained with him under fire 'ministering to his bodily and spiritual comfort' until he died. This appalling way of dying was commonplace in the slimy trenches and shell craters. Hardy saw men die in many ways and always he helped them to do it with dignity and courage.

Less than a month later Padre Hardy's regiment, the 8th

* Not the Padre Hardy mentioned in previous chapters.

Lincolns, made an attack under heavy fire and casualties mounted rapidly. Stretcher-bearers could not cope with the wounded and Hardy went out repeatedly to help them, all the time under heavy artillery and rifle fire. For this act he won the MC.

He was constantly active, doing much more than any chaplain was expected to do. One day a patrol was sent to attack an enemy post in the ruins of a village. Padre Hardy was at company headquarters at the time and did not know about the patrol until he heard the sound of firing. It drew him like a magnet. He followed the patrol more than a quarter of a mile beyond the front line, where he found an officer of the patrol dangerously wounded. He stayed with the officer until he could get help to bring him in. He was nearly captured by an enemy patrol, which he had not noticed owing to his shortsightedness.

On another occasion a shell exploded in the middle of a post and Padre Hardy at once hurried to the spot. Despite mortar bombs and shells, he set to work alone to dig out two buried men. He saved one man; the other was already dead. All this time Hardy himself was in great danger, not only from enemy fire but because of the condition of the building, which could have fallen on him at any time.

On yet another occasion Padre Hardy showed great devotion to his duty. He accompanied his battalion on an attack into a thick wood, but the battalion was forced back to its starting trench. A check was made and two men found to be missing – Padre Hardy and a private soldier. The news that he was missing ran through the ranks. 'The Padre's got it at last,' the men said. 'Well, he's had a good run. He couldn't expect to last forever the way he goes on.'

But Hardy soon showed up at an advanced post, where he asked for help in bringing in a badly wounded man. 'Lord love us, sir,' the sergeant said. 'That wood's crawling with Jerries and lousy with pill-boxes.'

'Quite,' said the padre. 'In fact this man is less than ten yards from a pillbox. I want a volunteer to help me rescue him.'

'Let's go, sir,' the sergeant said resignedly.

And together they managed to crawl to the man and drag

him to safety. The sergeant, battle-wise and young, thought it was quite an exploit – which it was – but to Padre Hardy it was all in his day's work.

For this series of acts and several others, all showing conspicuous bravery and devotion to duty, Padre Hardy was awarded the VC.* It was not really enough, but it was the highest honour his country could bestow.

His citation said: 'Notwithstanding the enemy artillery, machine-gun and mortar fire, this very gallant chaplain was seen moving quietly among the men and tending the wounded, absolutely regardless of his personal safety.' The citation might have added that Hardy's bravery was even more remarkable because it was cold-blooded and deliberate and not merely done in the heat of the moment. He knew the risks he was taking and he had no way of defending himself, but he took the risks. On 18 October 1918, only a few weeks before the end of the war, he was officially posted 'killed in action'. Right to the minute of his death he was on duty.

The commanding officer of his regiment said later: 'He appealed to us all by his fearlessness, physical and moral, and by his simple sincerity. . . . We loved him for his self-effacing devotion to duty and we respected him for his fearless denunciation of the coarse word or picture. . . . His gallantry in action won him distinction which will make his name famous in history, and yet his retiring nature made it almost a penance to wear those ribbons which most of us would give our right arm for. What his loss has meant to us is more than I can express . . . and a great blank has appeared in our daily lives.'

Despite the CO's fine words, we *have* forgotten Padre Hardy; his name is *not* famous in history. His fate was the same as that of any other less distinguished Tommy.

Common soldiers won decorations for bravery but the only one that could be granted posthumously was – and still is – the VC. This means that many a man who showed gallantry enough to win a Distinguished Conduct Medal or a Military

---

* Two other chaplains won the VC in the Great War. Padre Edward Noel Mellish and Padre W.R.F. Addison, both in 1916.

Medal but who died in his moment of glory could not be given the medal. Even so, during the war 24,571 men were awarded the DCM once, 469 won it twice and nine men won it three times. No fewer than 115,429 men won the MM once, and 5,695 men won bars to the medal. One soldier was awarded the decoration four times.*

But honours were not awarded in bulk to a battalion and left to the colonel and his brigade commander to distribute as they thought fit. Colonel Rowland Feilding, CO of a line regiment, revealed that recommendations had to be 'couched in the flamboyant language of the Penny Dreadful and the result is that the most deserving cases got cut out by the authorities, far behind the line . . . who have no personal or first-hand knowledge of the men or the conditions upon which they pass judgment.'

Feilding told of a man recommended for the Military Medal, the most junior award. The recommendation was denied, so the CO, who was disappointed because the man concerned deserved recognition, tried again. This time he wrote the recommendation in the most extravagant language he could dream up. His efforts paid off even better than expected: the man got the VC.

Said Feilding, 'The most difficult place to win fighting distinction is the fighting line itself. . . . I have known good men eating their hearts out through want of recognition . . . a ribbon is the only prize in war for the ordinary soldier. . . . I wish that this form of reward did not exist, seeing that ribbons must be distributed by men, not by gods. If they were given by God, how many an iridescent breast would cease to sparkle – and the contrary!'

Foreign decorations were handed over to the War Office in batches at regular intervals, by all the Allies. Feilding knew of

* Apart from purely regimental awards, which were rare, the British Army was many years behind other countries in awarding decorations for bravery by common soldiers. In 1845 a Meritorious Service Medal was instituted for sergeants. The DCM was introduced in 1854 and could be won by NCOs or privates. The Military Medal was not instituted until March 1916.

perhaps half a dozen to reach the front line, after all the various headquarters and base area formations had had their pick.

This was a war in which almost every frontline soldier who managed to endure, say, three months of trench warfare deserved special recognition and many soldiers were bitterly disappointed that no distinction came their way. Not that a whole row of medals made soldiering in *this* war any the more attractive and when the war ended everything romantic or 'glorious' about being a soldier ended with it. The splendid cavalry charges, the gallant stands of battalions in square;* the triumphant holding of isolated fortresses; the thin red line; rallying to the colours; marching into battle to tap of drum; the colour, the dash and the spectacle – all these had gone. A soldier's calling had now become strictly, totally professional.

Colonel John McCrae, a distinguished Canadian doctor, who died of pneumonia at Wimereux, France, in January 1918 movingly cyrstallized in his poem, *In Flanders Fields*, the loss of so many British and Commonwealth soldiers. One stanza reads:

> We are the dead. Short days ago
> We lived, felt dawn, saw sunset flow,
> Loved and were loved, and now we lie
> In Flanders fields.

I would make an addition to the last line—

> In Flanders fields forgotten.

*In the first months of the war a battalion of Guards actually did form square to receive a charge by German cavalry.

Fifteen

1918–45 (1)
The In-Between Years

At the end of the war more than 2,000,000 men were serving abroad in the army and another 1,600,000 were at home. Many more than 800,000 had been killed or had died on service. Tommy Atkins was legion and each man had unsavoury memories, though many professed that despite what they had been through they 'wouldn't have missed it for worlds' and that the war had been the 'greatest experience of their lives'. The more articulate of them, in the hundreds of books which followed the war, spoke of the comradeship they had found. And certainly comradeship formed in active service is very real. It was also more lasting after World War I than after previous wars because the British Legion, led and inspired by Haig, fostered it.

By September 1920 demobilization was practically complete and wartime soldiers had returned to civilian life; by 1921 the regular army numbered about 296,948 but a year later was cut to 217,477. Pay was increased to attract better-educated recruits.

However, recruits were few after the war and they became fewer, for war revulsion usually takes a few years to make its full impact felt.

The great war might have ended, but between 1919 and 1939 Tommy Atkins was engaged, as always, in Britain's small wars. In 1919 there was an expedition to North Russia, a campaign in Waziristan and a third war in Afghanistan. In 1920 Tommy put down an Arab insurrection in Iraq. He was active in Ireland in 1918–21, in Egypt in 1921, Moplah* 1922 and Khartoum in 1924.

He demonstrated in force at Chanak (Turkey) in 1922 and in Shanghai in 1927 and in 1929 he helped to re-establish law and order in Palestine. Between 1930 and 1932 Tommies were once again in Burma. That latter year was a milestone, for a complete battalion, the 1st Battalion the Northamptonshire Regiment, was air-lifted from Ismailia to Baghdad. This was the first time a complete unit had been flown to action – although, in fact, there was no action. In 1934–5 a British contingent served in the Saar and, of course, throughout the 1930s Tommies were in India.

While all these police, suppressive, preventive and punitive actions were going on, the army was being modernized – mostly by the process of cautious experiment. The steps taken were mostly technical and do not concern us until 23 December 1935 when a major reorganization was announced. Writing in *The Times*, Liddell Hart called the re-constituted force a New Model Army. It was already apparent to some people that this new army would be needed before very long. Volunteers were hard to come by and in 1938 Britain decided once more on compulsory enlistment as part of a further reshaping of the fighting forces. This step, which marked the creation of a new type of soldier, resulted from the reaction against army life after 1919. The marked dislike of the army as a career and especially the aversion to the infantry is understandable, following the butchery of 1914–18. The numerous survivors were outspoken about the appalling conditions in France and Flanders.

The recruit of 1938 was a different man from the soldier of twenty-five years before. Selected for fitness and intelligence, he was better educated and therefore easier to teach, but by the same token, he was more prone to question orders. Perhaps because of his higher education he was more tense and not nearly so phlegmatic as earlier English soldiers.

* On the Malabar coast of India.

He was certainly softer. According to Wavell, the difference between the soldier as he knew him and the modern soldier was that the former was tough, while the latter had to be toughened. This was only to be expected, for standards of living had improved tremendously and generally the better a man's standards of living the worse his physical condition. The soldier, though still not particularly encouraged to use his initiative, was no longer a mere automaton, a 'tractable beast of burden'. He was more sophisticated, more complex and methods of handling him had to conform. But he was just as cynical, with his

> If it moves, salute it.
> If it doesn't move pick it up.
> If you can't pick it up, paint it.

The soldiers of 1939–45 fought in so many theatres that it would be impracticable and beyond the bounds of this study to trace Tommy Atkins through them. My aim is to show that the qualities for which Tommy became renowned still existed in the soldier of 1939–45, but that he now had other qualities in addition. This is best done through several little-known incidents and individual soldiers of the war.

Some preliminary observations are necessary.

In one way the 1939–45 soldier was certainly less stable than Tommy Atkins of Wellington's campaigns; he was more apt to become emotionally unsettled over matters at home. In Wellington's day, and for long after, a soldier accepted as a simple, unalterable fact of life that he probably would not hear from or of his family for many years. He might occasionally have become homesick, but he did not break down. Soldiers of 1939–45 expected their mail from home – as they have every right to do in a modern army – but if letters did not arrive they would be despondent, even suspicious. A preoccupied man on sentry duty is a liability. Many unit histories report occasional suicides of men distraught because they had heard of wives being unfaithful. One such case can unsettle an entire company on active service. It was a problem earlier commanders did not have to face; their men had been much more fatalistic.

Tommies of the 1939–45 war were no more saintly than their predecessors.* Drink and women remained Tommy's two anodynes and both were apt to impair his soldierly efficiency.

For the first time, too, Tommy Atkins was systematically, extensively and intensively entertained with concerts and film shows. The Salvation Army and the YMCA were on hand to minister to some of his needs. All these amenities, including the wonderful institution Toc H,† had been in their infancy in World War I. They were useful amenities, too, because they made for greater peace of mind. Odd to think of somebody being bothered about Tommy Atkins's peace of mind!

The Salvation Army and the YMCA made the life of the active service soldier much more bearable. Their main success – though an indirect one – was in showing Tommy Atkins that *somebody* was caring about him. People who think vaguely of the Sallies as pacifists are maligning men who have won three VCs and many other gallantry awards. Since the Zulu Wars soldier-Salvationists have served in the Regular Army and equally courageous professional Sallies have risked their lives in battle-area canteens.††

The soldiers of World War II were different from those of some earlier periods in another way, too. It became impossible to distinguish between the regulars and the wartime-only soldiers, at least once the new recruits had been worn-in a little, though the regular NCO or warrant officer was generally distinguishable for what he was.

It has been said that the war of 1939–45 made greater demands on soldiers than ever before. This is not true, except

---

* During World War I the War Office issued a directive on bad language. Officers tried to put it into effect, but without success.
† Talbot House in Poperinghe and Ypres, founded by Padre P.B. ('Tubby') Clayton, one of the best friends Tommy Atkins ever had. Over the door of his room was the legend, in scroll, ALL RANK ABANDON YE WHO ENTER HERE. One afternoon Tubby Clayton had to tea a general, a staff captain, a second lieutenant and a Canadian private.
†† The first canteen opened in Gibraltar in 1895 and in 1900 the first 'active service' canteen operated in South Africa.

in one sense. The demands made on a soldier's fortitude and sanity were much greater in 1914–18 – and more damage was done to his body by trench life. Great demands were made on those soldiers of other ages who served abroad for decades on end with no prospect of home leave. The soldier of 1939–45 was better fed, clothed, equipped, housed and paid. Medical treatment was more readily available and simply because of progress surgical and medical treatment was so much more effective. Despite some catastrophes, he was consistently better led at regimental level than pre-1914 and *generally* better led at divisional, corps and army level. In any case, to talk of 'greater' or 'lesser' demands on a soldier is rather pointless, since soldiering is by its nature a profession which obviously makes demands. The great difference between the war of 1939–45 and all other wars – so far as the private soldier was concerned – was that he was expected to have greater skills, to be more versatile. He had to fight over 'normal' country (such as in France), over desert, in rugged mountains, through tropical jungle, on beaches, across rivers, in snow and against a variety of weapons and means of resistance never before encountered.

How well he did this it is the purpose of the following incidents to illustrate.

They are of small-scale actions* which deserve to be better known and they took place in areas of varying terrain – North Africa, Italy, France, Burma. All except one are splendid examples of their type – and even the exception has some quality. This is one of the remarkable things about every action in which English soldiers have fought; each one, no matter how appalling its defects, how dire its result, has been redeemed to some extent by the character of Tommy Atkins.

* I have not chosen the epic of the capture of Centuripe, Sicily, in July 1943 because it was not really an English epic. Highlanders as well as Irish Fusiliers and London Irish Rifles were also involved. Nor have I been able to include some of the most illustrious of battalions, such as the Hampshire Regiments. During the war the Hampshires served on almost every front and earned fifty-seven Battle Honours, a feat that gives them top place among English regiments, in this respect.

Sixteen

1939–45 (2)
Seven Actions of World War II

EPISODE 1: THE DEFENCE OF OUTPOST SNIPE

In no action of modern times has the spirit of Tommy Atkins been so manifest as in the action at the outpost of Snipe, on 26–7 October during the Battle of Alamein in 1942. Tradition made possible an astonishing resistance, in which every quality of the English soldier asserted itself. It is disappointing that the Battle of Alamein, being so large, has obscured some of the smaller actions which made up the whole.

The overall situation which led to Snipe is outside our scope. All that matters is that Lieutenant-Colonel V.B. Turner of the Rifle Brigade was ordered to move rapidly by night through enemy-held territory, to set up a spirited pocket of resistance – 'Snipe' – to hold it until British tanks arrived the next morning, and then to maintain it in rear of the advancing tanks.

To carry out this tall order Turner had fewer than 300 men, a mixture of regulars and wartime-only soldiers – riflemen, gunners, sappers and signallers, mainly from 2nd Battalion Rifle Brigade, 7th Anti-Tank Regiment and 7th Field Squadron. Many of the riflemen were Londoners, Cockney in outlook and speech. Altogether, the Snipe garrison was a pretty typical bunch of Tommies, some very tough indeed, some of them with reputations as bad boys, others not so tough but willing to be led.

Leadership and followership would be vital in an action of the type these men were facing. Neither was lacking in the 8th Army. One private soldier of the 8th Army, Driver R.J. Crawford of the RASC said that he found a new and different relationship between officers and other ranks in the desert campaigns; that a spirit of companionship replaced the 'old discipline'. The officers, Crawford felt, seemed to realize that all the 8th Army were members of a team and officers and men pulled together. To quite an extent this was true of the whole British Army throughout the war; officers were more relaxed with their men, less conscious of their superior rank, but more professional in outlook. But clearly, if Crawford is typical of other ranks, the men still tended to revere officers. 'They were perhaps the grandest officers out there. The men worshipped them. I nearly said would have died for them. They did; and mostly died with them.' Officers and men died together at Snipe.

The going was difficult through the soft sand and much of Turner's little force advanced behind a British barrage. When they were in position the supply trucks and anti-tank guns were called up, and they, too, had a difficult trip. The doctor and ambulances were unable to get up at all, but after strenuous activity the Snipe men and materials were in position. As it happened, Turner, through no fault of his own, was not in the right position. Next day, when asked if it was right, he said, 'God knows. But here we are and here we stay.'

The place was poor for defence. Turner held a shallow oval 900 yards by 400 yards, in which the sand was so soft that trenches and weapon pits could not be dug effienctly, though Turner was able to use a German-made dug-out for his command HQ. Low rough scrub did provide some cover. Lieutenant R. Flower took out a moonlight reconnaissance patrol in Bren carriers, found a gap in a minefield, drove a mile and had a scrap in which he took fourteen prisoners, and destroyed three trucks. They saw thirty-five German tanks, so Flower engaged them with his light machine-guns. This irritated the Germans and they advanced, forcing Flower to withdraw.

It was soon apparent to Colonel Turner and everybody in Snipe that they were in the middle of a large-scale hornets' nest, and about 4 a.m., the first of these hornets – tanks –

attacked Snipe. The defenders waited until the tanks were right on them. At a range of only 30 yards Sergeant G.H. Brown, DCM, knocked out and set fire to a big Mark IV tank with his 6-pounder. Sergeant J. Swann killed a self-propelled gun at the same time. The other enemy tanks withdrew.

After daybreak, in a cold wind, the Snipe defenders saw several German panzers at distances up to 800 yards. The targets were too good to miss and the 6-pounders opened up. The Germans found that they, too, had drawn a hornets' nest – and the stings were vicious. The Snipe gunners knocked out no fewer than sixteen tanks and self-propelled guns and then machine-gunned the crews as they attempted to escape.

But the men of Snipe most have known that such spirit would invite trouble – trouble, in fact, they could have avoided, for it was not strictly part of Snipe's mission to start trouble. By attacking the German panzers Snipe had given away its position and the Germans accurately and heavily shelled it throughout the day. Some guns were knocked out, transport was lost and casualties were suffered. The lone medical orderly, Rifleman Burnhope, had no rest throughout the battle.

Turner had been told to expect a British armoured Brigade early in the morning. The tanks turned up, too – and opened fire. On Snipe. This sort of mishap occurs more frequently in war than is realized. A Snipe officer made a dangerous trip to the forward tanks to explain the position, but it was not until Snipe gunners opened up on some other German tanks that the British tanks fully understood. At a range of 1,100 yards – a long distance for accurate shooting – the Snipe gunners knocked out three more panzers.

The British tanks now moved into Snipe, but their presence was unwelcome. The Germans opened up with a great number of weapons and despite the protective smoke screen put down, within minutes seven Sherman tanks were on fire in Snipe. Once again, somebody had blundered; Snipe was obviously a death trap for tanks and they should never have concentrated there. They withdrew to a ridge in rear, but the damage had been done. For the moment Snipe was beyond help.

A Snipe gun commanded by Sergeant R. Smith was knocked out, Smith himself was blinded for the day, and his detachment all made casualties. When a Sherman was set alight a soldier from the crew, in agony from burns, tried to get out of the hatch. Two Snipe men jumped on to the blazing tank and rescued him, but he died during the day. The position of all the wounded was dangerous and uncomfortable, so Turner sent out the more serious cases in three Bren-carriers – a hazardous under-fire task in itself.

The enemy now brought up Italian infantry to wipe out Snipe. The Bren-carriers took the initiative, shot down many Italians, sent the rest running, and then put out of action two lorries towing captured British guns into action.

Turner, his Anti-Tank Commander and other officers moved around the posts, encouraging the men.

At 10 a.m. the enemy made two determined attacks on Snipe. The first was made by thirteen Italian tanks, but after the garrison's fire had hit four the Italians thought better of the sally. Other tanks, German, were moving across Snipe's southern face to attack the British armoured brigade and to counter any action from Snipe the German commander sent half his strength in a straightforward drive at the British position. Between them the Armoured Brigade and Snipe set fire to eight German tanks, hit several others and forced the rest to retreat. But the garrison suffered, too, and by noon six more Bren-carriers had been wrecked and only thirteen 6-pounders remained effective.

Turner's main difficulty was shortage of ammunition for the 6 pounders. Calmly, Captain Bird, MC and bar, and Corporal Francis ferried ammunition from one gun to another although their jeep constantly drew fire.

The garrison was showing great gallantry, but their suffering was acute. The sun was hot and the air still. The smell throughout the position was appalling, and wreckage lay everywhere.

Every time a target showed up the garrison quickly engaged it with one weapon or another – and there were plenty of targets, for Germans and Italians moved freely about on three sides of Snipe.

Crisis mounted at 1 p.m. The enemy sent in eight Italian tanks and a self-propelled field gun against a portion of the perimeter where only one British gun could bear; here, alone, was Sergeant C. Calistan, a London East-ender. Colonel Turner and Lieutenant Toms raced to help him, Turner to act as loader and Toms as No. 1. At 600 yards this oddly crewed gun opened fire. The effect staggered the Italians. Within minutes five of the tanks and the field gun were in flames. But the other tanks came on, spouting machine-gun fire. The situation was desperate – the 6-pounder had two rounds left. Lieutenant Toms sprinted to his jeep, got some further shells and drove back with them at reckless speed. His whole act was incredibly daring, for all three tanks divined his purpose and machine-gunned him all the way. His jeep was afire and ran to a stop 10 yards from the gun.

Turner and Corporal Francis, who had come up, ran to it and helped Toms drag ammunition to the gun, but at this crucial moment Turner was seriously wounded by a shell splinter in the skull. The enemy tanks were very close now, as Toms, Calistan and Corporal Barnett, another volunteer from nowhere, re-manned the gun.

Calistan, in unflurried Tommy Atkins style, fired only three rounds. And he knocked all three tanks out. This fine soldier was recommended for the VC. He didn't get it, but he went on to win the DCM, the MM and a commission before he was killed in action in Italy.

Colonel Turner made the rounds of his post once more before weakness compelled him to go to his command post, from which he ventured now and then to cheer his men. His head wound was a bad one, however, and he suffered so acutely later in the day that even his great spirit became incapable of command. Other officers were hit, too; five shared the dubious shelter of the command post.

The garrison stewed in their own sweat, stifled in the smells, had no chance to eat and many were parched with thirst. Enemy fire was so great and so sensitive to movement that crawling was the only relatively safe way of moving. Under such circumstances there could be no unified command, but each post was definitely under command. By 4 p.m. the Bren-carriers were out of ammunition.

Neither the enemy nor their own friends would leave

Snipe alone. A little after 4 p.m. another British armoured brigade brought up their Priest self-propelled guns and pounded the garrison. Certainly Snipe was in enemy country, but this second British attack showed gross misjudgement.

The Snipe defenders had no sooner recovered from this ordeal than they were subjected to their greatest trial yet. A great many enemy tanks and guns of another Panzer unit formed up near them in two rows for a major attack on the British line, but for some reason German liaison that day was no better than the British and when the tanks moved off many of them did so flank-on to some of Snipe's guns – the four remaining guns of 239th Battery, all well concealed.

At the right moment, close-range; they opened fire. Again the effect was devastating. In just two minutes the guns had knocked out twelve tanks. The outrage provoked the enemy into furious retaliation. Many of the tanks turned directly at the guns and charged down on them, firing with everything they had. A very large tank loomed towards the gun commanded by Sergeant Cullen and though its bullets were piercing the gun-shield Cullen's gun and that commanded by Sergeant Binks hit the tank together at 100 yards. But Cullen himself was hit, then a direct shell smashed Binks's gun, wiping out its crew except for Binks. Each gun scored heavily, but one by one they were knocked out. And all the while the British machine-gunners finished off enemy tank crews as they leaped from their wrecked tanks.

The damage was too great for the enemy to bear. The tank commander withdrew his survivors out of range and into cover. But there was still the second line of tanks and from this line the enemy commander detached fifteen machines and sent them in for another all-out smash at this extraordinary desert outpost. The tanks were more cleverly used this time – and Snipe had only two guns at the point of contact, commanded by Sergeant Hine, MM and Sergeant Miles. But Lt B. Holt-Wilson, with whom was Rifleman Chard, swung his gun right round to help.

The tanks came on, machine-guns firing. Bullets hit Sergeant Miles and his detachment dived into their narrow trench. Sergeant Swann, a tough, disciplined Regular, had lost his gun earlier, so now he rushed to Miles's gun and manned it single-handed – until his inspiration drew Miles's crew back to their posts. Hine and Holt-Wilson also opened fire.

At 200 yards the destruction was terrible. The four leading tanks and two others were hit and burst into flames. It was too much for the others; they hurriedly got out of range and kept up a steady machine-gun fire.

Among them the three guns now had nine rounds. 'Impossible' is an inapt word to apply to anything connected with the defence of Snipe, but it seems impossible that the garrison could have withstood another determined attack. Out of the original nineteen guns only six could still be used – and ammunition was practically gone.

But there was no further attack. The Axis armour could not face it. Around Snipe were sixty-three enemy tanks and self-propelled guns and several other vehicles, and around them were the bodies of many dead Germans. The British material wreckage amounted to seven tanks, sixteen Bren-carriers, several jeeps and ten guns.

Night fell. Within Snipe the 200 survivors waited to repel further assaults, as they evacuated their wounded in the remaining transport. They heard that relief was on the way, but the relief force also had difficulty finding the position, and before midnight the garrison was ordered to withdraw.

The battle at Snipe was as remarkable as any in World War II. It was so talked-about that a Committee of Investigation was appointed to report on the action; they found that nothing had been exaggerated.

Several officers and men were decorated, though, of course, not enough of them. Colonel Turner won the VC Among the other most outstanding awards were the Distinguished Conduct Medals awarded to Sergeant Calistan, Sergeant Swann and Rifleman Chard.

The action proved that Tommy Atkins, well led – and good leading means setting an example, giving encouragement and taking equal risks – is virtually unbeatable in an offensive-defensive position. By all the rules and precedents of war Snipe should have been overrun, especially as the enemy had generous support from the British armour. I believe that the tradition of Albuhera, Lucknow, Rorke's Drift and Le Cateau was present at Snipe; I believe, too, that few nations could produce troops able to hold out as the English infantry and artillery did at Snipe. The similarity between Snipe and Rorke's Drift – with tanks instead of Zulus as the enemy – is particularly striking.

EPISODE 2: A COMPANY SERGEANT-MAJOR OF THE GUARDS

NCOs have been mentioned many times in this book. Each one has been a Tommy Atkins, for almost without exception they were promoted from the ranks. It is very rare indeed for a man to be given non-commissioned rank on enlistment, unless in some specialist capacity. NCOs, too, have held a unique position in the British Army. For virtually the whole of the nineteenth century the NCOs were the core of a regiment; if the CO and the NCOs were efficient, the regiment was a good one. Platoon commanders leaned heavily on their sergeants, company commanders on the company sergeant-major and the CO on the regimental sergeant-major. It is only fitting that two of these 'summing-up' episodes concern company sergeant-majors.

A company or regimental sergeant-major is much more than a dominant parade ground figure; he has extraordinary authority and influence. To the men of an infantry company the CSM sits on the right hand of God – God himself being the RSM. Having been a private soldier himself the sergeant-major knows every trick of the trade, he knows the soldier psychologically, he knows how far he can stretch mentally and physically. When the OC of the company wants information or advice, he naturally consults the CSM. If a soldier has a problem he will take it to his own section commander or platoon sergeant who will, in turn, take it to the CSM – if the CSM has the reputation a CSM should have. The CSM can awe junior subalterns only just a little less than the RSM awes them. He can make life a lot easier for a new officer; conversely, he can make it much harder, merely by denying the officer his co-operation.

On 25 September 1943, a company sergeant-major of the 3rd Battalion Coldstream Guards performed an action that showed much more initiative than an NCO or warrant officer would have been capable of in earlier years. The battalion was attacking a steep wooded hill near Salerno, Italy, but before they reached the top the right company was held up by heavy Spandau and mortar fire. CSM Peter Wright went forward to investigate, found that all the officers had become casualties, so immediately took charge and crawled forward to see what could be done. He returned, collected a section of men, told them that three machine-gun posts were holding up the attack, and put the men in a position where they could give covering fire. Then, single-handed, Wright attacked each post with hand-grenades and bayonet and silenced all three.

He led the company to the crest, but when enemy fire made his position untenable he took his men to a new post by a different direction and put them in such a well-chosen position that when the Germans launched a counter-attack the Guards beat it off. Later, under extremely heavy fire of all kinds, Wright brought up extra ammunition and distributed it. This was leadership at its best and but for Wright's action the Guards could not have taken and held their objective. He won the VC for it.

EPISODE 3: CRIMEAN MENTALITY IN 1944

It is no reflection on the 2nd Battalion the Sherwood Foresters that, following the landing at Anzio in January 1944, they had a much less successful action. They had the task of cutting the railway linking Naples and Rome by taking Campoleone railway Station. Unfortunately, somebody with a Crimean mentality – 'Theirs not to reason why' – apparently set the task and the Foresters, also exhibiting a Crimean mentality – 'Theirs but to do and die' – attempted it.

To reach the railway station the Foresters had to cross a railway embankment, which made a perfect tank and infantry trap. Beyond it German tanks fired from inside houses and machine-guns from railway trucks. Time after time the Foresters tried to cross the line, but each time they became skyline targets. One small group succeeded only to drop back into the cutting to their death. An American general, Harman, said later, 'I have never seen so many dead men in one place. They lay so close I had to step with care. A mud-covered corporal – the highest ranking officer left – stood stiffly to attention and said that there were sixteen men left and they were to hold out until sundown. The Forester added, "I think, with a little good fortune, we can manage to do so."'

Several conclusions could be drawn from this episode and at least one of them would be unfalteringly critical – it could be briefly expressed with the thought that even a suicidal mission must have a chance of succeeding – but the gallantry of these men repeatedly trying to do what they had been ordered to do is typically Tommy Atkins; so, too, is the remark by the Forester corporal.

EPISODE 4: STANDING FAST ON MOUNT ORNITO

In February 1944 a Corps Commander and a Divisional General made a four-hour climb up Mount Ornito, Italy, to congratulate the 2nd Battalion Coldstream Guards on their efforts in thirteen days of terribly tough fighting. The geneals' climb was proof enough of the fierceness and success of this little-known action.

The men themselves had made that four-hour climb, in snow, rain and mist and bitter cold. In the first forty-eight hours twelve men suffered frostbite; water bottles froze solid and in the morning blankets and greatcoats were stiff.

The German attacks were fierce and sustained. One morning the Guards beat off an attack, losing one officer and one wounded and six soldiers killed and forty-three wounded. Before dawn on the ninth day the Germans attacked up hill and dug in as well as they could just 30 yards from a Coldstream company on the other side of the crest. Neither side could see the other as they threw grenades for hours. When either side sent a man to the top to observe he was killed.

The CO ordered an artillery smoke-screen to be put down on the hill top and through it the company made a bayonet charge, bringing back twenty-six prisoners. But that afternoon the resilient Germans took up a similar just-below-crest position a short distance away. They lobbed grenades at the

Coldstreams all night. During the morning seven Coldstream stretcher-bearers went out to collect wounded – but all they found were dead. One bearer, Corporal Pickford, was pinned down by machine-guns until 25-pounders put down a smoke screen for him to get away.

Next morning the Guards again charged the Germans and inflicted such severe casualties that only ten prisoners came back. But on the 11th day the Germans attacked with 500 men, to be beaten off with heavy losses. By the time they were relieved the Guards had lost thirty-three killed and 152 wounded, they had thrown 1,082 grenades and had fired more mortar bombs than in the whole of their campaign in Tunisia. But seldom has an enemy left so many dead on a small front.

It was the sort of hold-fast action in which the Guards excel. The Germans, for all the method with which they wage war, appear never to have sufficiently studied the characteristics of the soldiers opposing them. Had they done so on this occasion they might have suffered less.

EPISODE 5: THE BATTLE OF KOHIMA AND GLORY ON NUNSHIGUM RIDGE

On the war memorial at Kohima is the inscription

> When you go home
> Tell them of us and say
> For their tomorrow
> We give our today

Many members of the British public do not give a damn about what the troops at Kohima might have given, but the story is worth telling, for again it crystallizes the gallantry of Tommy Atkins in World War II.

On 8 March 1944, the Japanese launched their anticipated assault into Assam, to be met by units of the 14th Army around the Imphal Plain. But by the end of the month the Japanese surrounded this plain. To the north, the village of Kohima commanded the main route to India. Kohima had to be held. Major-General Sato, commanding the Japanese 31st Division, had been ordered to take Kohima and dig in. A stubborn, do-or-die general, Sato intended to take the little town.

Field-Marshal Slim wrote, 'I have spent some uncomfortable hours at the beginnings of battles, but few more anxious than those of the Kohima battle.' Slim decided that the Kohima battle should have preference in the matter of supplies and ammunition, but it could only be supplied by air.

By now the British troops knew the characteristics of the Japanese soldier and they had tasted his brutality. The Japs achieved something that no other enemy, apart from some of the Indian Mutiny rebels, has achieved with Tommy Atkins: They made him hate. 'Stories of the way the Japs treated prisoners had already made Tommy despise the Japs. They provoked him to hatred in February 1944 when, in their drive towards India via Arakan, Burma, they overran the main British dressing station. It was crowded with wounded and surgeons were still operating. Men helpless on their stretchers were simply slaughtered by bayonet, sword or bullet; the doctors were lined up and shot; Indian orderlies were forced to carry back the Japanese wounded – some had been attended to in the dressing station – then they, too, were murdered. Tommy Atkins became very angry about this. A spotter pilot called up a British artillery unit to ask how they were. The reply was, 'Fine, but drop us a hundred bayonets.' General Slim said that the bayonets were dropped – and used. In this jungle, caves and cliffs of Arakan a bitter ruthless fight went on for days. At the end, of the 7,000 Japs who had penetrated the British lines over 5,000 were killed; these were the ones actually found and counted. Many more died in the jungles and could not be found. Very few reached safety. The moral should be obvious for future enemy students of Tommy Atkins: fight him fairly and he is not vengeful, but treat him barbarously and he will repay in kind.

The Royal West Kent Regiment joined the Kohima garrison late on 4 April, just after the first Japanese night attack had overrun some of the British positions. On the morning of 6 April a platoon of Indian troops escorted out of the village 200 walking wounded and some 'strays' useless in battle. Soon after the Japanese closed in around the town and its 3,000 defenders, led by Colonel Richards, who were greatly outnumbered. In any case, less than a third of them were fit to fight.

The Japanese began by making frontal attacks on Kohima by day, but as the reception was too hot, they changed to night attacks. Throughout the day and even at night between the infantry attacks, Jap artillery, mortars and machine-guns kept up a relentless fire on the defenders' positions, which formed a rough square with sides 1,000 yards long.

Because the area was so small, the Jap fire sometimes gave the defenders the impression they were being sniped from the rear – always an unnerving ordeal.

British and Jap trenches were within yards of one another and as even the slightest movement brought a shot or grenade the men could not rest.

Early in the battle the Japanese scored a success – on the night of the 5 April they captured the water supply. In this dire emergency RAF planes came in at tree-top level and dropped motor-truck inner tubes filled with water. Somebody found a small spring too, but water was still so scarce that the ration was only one pint per man each day, with a little extra for the wounded.

Gradually the British area was compressed under the sheer weight of the Japanese attack and shrank to a square with sides of 500 yards. To crush the life out of the garrison the Japs rained fire into it and threw in attack after attack. The whole hill-top, continuously wreathed in smoke, was covered with tall trees, the tops of which canopied out the sky. The undergrowth was rather thin and consisted mostly of small shrubs, with tracks running in all directions. Visibility by day was 50 yards at most; by night it was zero. An enemy soldier would simply appear suddenly at the end of a Tommy's rifle. Reflexes had to be quick.

By day, too, it was hot, but the nights were cold because of the altitude – 5,000 feet.

The Japs tried many tricks. One would shout, 'Hey! Johnny, let me through, let me through, the Japs are after me. They're going to get me!' The call would be taken up elsewhere around the perimeter. 'Let me through!' But the men of the garrison were not new to jungle warfare and they made no answer.

The Japs would then try irritation rifle fire – single, well spaced shots, apparently made deliberately at specific targets. Nervous, new troops would fire back, the Japs would spot the muzzle flashes and know how to plan an attack.

At night the Japs, wearing soft shoes and with all noise-making equipment removed, sometimes attacked as silently as possible, so that all the defenders could hear was the sound of scuffling. But at other times the Japs would scream and yell and blow battle bugles. The defenders preferred a noisy attack, for then they had a sound-target if not a visual one.

Tommies in previous eras had never fought a battle like this one, but it brought out all the old attributes and skills – doggedness, stamina, discipline. Especially discipline, for at times, mainly during the night, each man was responsible for his own. No officer could control many men at once.

Conditions were very bad for the wounded and some were hit again and again as they lay in the casualty station. They were in great pain and as drugs were scarce they could only grin and bear it. But for some the pain was so acute that they could not stop themselves from whimpering. Sometimes the stretcher-bearers and burial parties had trouble sorting battered bodies of those not yet dead from the remains of those broken beyond help.

As every fighting man in this involuntary 'fortress' did more than could humanly and reasonably by expected names are out of place, except for the one man in Kohima to win the VC.* This was Lance Corporal J.P. Harman, of the Royal West Kent Regiment.

On Easter Saturday a party of Japs broke into the British lines and established themselves in bamboo huts in the defences, from which they machine-gunned the Royal West Kents. Harman climbed out of his trench and unhurriedly approached the most dangerous machine-gun. At a range of 30 yards he threw two grenades at the post, silenced it, and then ran into the hut, where he shot and bayoneted some enemy before coming out with the machine-gun. His example inspired other

---

* In the years 1939–45 the army won sixty-one Victoria Crosses, thirty-three of them posthumously.

men into an assault. In the same action Harman trapped some Japs in a bakery, where they hid in ovens; Harman dropped a grenade in with each of seven enemy soldiers. . . .

Some days later the Japanese set up a machine-gun post on a ridge overlooking D Company's position. From their commanding position the Japs could easily dominate the British position. Harman at once saw that if this post were not smashed his company would suffer heavy casualties. Ordering his Bren-gunner to give him covering fire, Harman found a position from which he could overlook the Jap post and shot dead one Jap. Then he advanced alone, again in an unhurried way, despite the Jap fire now being directed at him. Thirty yards from the machine-gun Harman fired, killing another Jap; then at bayonet-point he took the post.

He started back towards his own trenches – still moving without haste, despite warning shouts from his own men. A machine-gun burst hit him in the back before he reached safety. He refused medical attention, probably because he knew the doctor already had more wounded than he could handle. In any case, Harman knew he was dying. He said before he died, 'I got the lot – it was worth it.'

Relief came in the end at six o'clock on the morning of the 20th Colonel Richards handed over command and collected his men. Three hours later they marched out of that little arena of death, dust, destruction and din. Just 1,387 British, Indian and Gurkha soldiers had died there.

They had endured much, wrote General Slim. 'Forced into an ever contracting circle by the relentless assaults of vastly superior numbers, their casualties had been severe. . . . Sieges have been longer but few have been more intense, and in none have the defenders deserved greater honour than the garrison of Kohima.'

During the same series of actions in Burma the Japanese held the summit of Nunshigum, a knife-edge ridge 3,000 feet high, and dominating the Imphal Plain where British and Indian troops were encircled and dependent on supply by air. From Nunshigum the Japanese had perfect observation and could direct accurate artillery fire on to Imphal airstrip. Yet the airstrip had to be used or the British would be starved out.

For four days infantry tried to take the Japanese positions, an extremely difficult and dangerous task. On 13 April 1944 B Squadron of 3rd Carabiniers with their tanks and some Indian infantry were ordered in.

It was hardly ideal tank country. The slopes were steep and scrub-covered and each tank commander had to expose his head and shoulders to be able to direct his driver. On the summit it was possible for only one tank to advance at a time – and this against strong enemy positions manned by fanatically brave men. Japanese jumped on to the tanks and the commanders shot them off with revolvers; they threw grenades into enemy positions. Every one of the commanders must have known death was practically inevitable; it was also instantaneous, for all were shot through the head. Finally, the squadron sergeant-major was the only leader left. Meanwhile, the British officers of the Indian infantry had also been killed or wounded. The squadron sergeant-major and an Indian officer together planned the final assault on the bunkers still holding out and after two more hours of fighting they captured and held Nunshigum – a remarkable feat of dogged gallantry.*

EPISODE 6: THE SAGA OF STANLEY HOLLIS

Aged 27 when he joined the Territorials in May 1939. Stanley Hollis was a product of his times – he grew up during the Depression – and of his background; he was the son of a fish-shop proprietor in Middlesbrough. He served with the Green Howards in France in the early days of the war and lived through the retreat to Dunkirk and the evacuation, swimming out to a warship for a trip home. In May 1941 he was in Iraq and the following year in the Western Desert. Here, the Green Howards were surrounded and had to break out, fighting a

* The British Army is constantly forming new traditions. Today the 3rd Carabiniers (Prince of Wales Dragoon Guards) remember Nunshigum by celebrating 13 April as a Regimental day. On that day B Squadron parades without officers, under the command of its squadron sergeant-major. The regiment was the last British cavalry to leave India.

rearguard action all the way back to El Alamein. Hollis fought at the battle of Alamein and was CQMS of his company at the Mareth Line campaign. At the Battle of Wadi Akarit the CSM of B Company was killed and Hollis was given his job.

A competent CSM, in July 1943, in Sicily, Hollis took two men of his company and in a bayonet charge attacked and captured an 88 mm gun and took the crew prisoner. The following week, in an engagement at Catania Airfield, he was slightly wounded by a mortar-bomb explosion and flown back to North Africa. After a further spell in Sicily he returned to England for leave.

In 1944 CSM Hollis of D Company sailed with his battalion for the D-Day invasion of 6 June. A and D Companies of the Green Howards went ashore through pounding water, with D Company making for a gun battery at Mont Fleury. Heavy German fire smothered the landing craft and several were hit. At 7.30 Hollis's company waded ashore, negotiated a minefield and were approaching a house which happened to be the enemy battery HQ. At this point Hollis and his OC noticed that they had by-passed a concrete pillbox which could do great damage to the company and to following troops.

As they approached it, the Germans opened fire. Disregarding the fire, Hollis ran at the pillbox, firing his sub-machine-gun into the slits; he jumped on top of the post, recharged his magazine, tossed a grenade into the pillbox and fired again. He killed two Germans and captured another five.

Seeing some Germans in a nearby trench he attacked and captured them, handed them over to an escort and rejoined his company. The German defence was now recovering from the initial shock and British casualties were mounting. The observant Hollis – most CSMs are observant – saw a couple of dogs showing interest in something behind a hedge and crawling up he spotted a German field gun. At this point enemy machine-gun fire pinned down what was left of the company, so Hollis crawled to a flank with a PIAT gun and two Bren gunners, whom he posted in a house to cover him. A sniper's shot grazed Hollis's cheek then the field gun, at a distance of 30 yards, also fired at him, but hit and knocked down the house, trapping the Bren gunners.

Hollis said he would get them out. Under constant fire he went forward alone, firing a Bren gun and drawing even heavier fire on to himself in a deliberate diversion which enabled the gunners to get out of the wrecked house.

The OC ordered the advance, but again, as they approached their objective of Christot, enemy machine-gunners forced the company to ground. Hollis went into single-handed action again, charging the gun position and killing the crew.

After a day's continous action Hollis was wounded, though not too badly, and was evacuated to a casualty station, probably more exhausted than hurt. He was back in action at Falaise where in even tougher fighting than that of D-Day he was again wounded. His wounds this time were serious enough to keep him out of action for good.

Hollis's VC citation read, in part, 'Wherever fighting was heaviest, CSM Hollis appeared and in the course of a magnificent day's work he displayed the utmost gallantry . . . his courage and initiative prevented the enemy from holding up the advance at critical stages. It was largely through his heroism and resource . . . that casualties were not heavier and by his own bravery he saved the lives of many of his men.'

EPISODE 7: THE ONE-MAN VICTORY

Of all the acts of gallantry none surpasses the bravery of Private Richard Henry Burton of the Duke of Wellington's Regiment on 8 October 1944. Burton was a runner in A Company when two companies assaulted Mount Ceco, 1,950 feet, north of Rome. This strongly-held feature dominated the main axis of the Allied advance and its capture was vital. Platoons of A Company led the attack, in thick mud, and reached to within 20 yards of the crest when four enemy machine-guns on the top pinned down the leading platoon. The follow-up platoon was called forward and Private Burton rushed ahead, killing the three-man crew of one of the Spandaus with his Tommy-gun.

Two other Spandaus raked the Dukes and again the attack halted. Burton again ran forward, firing his Tommy-gun until his ammunition was exhausted. Then he picked up a Bren-gun and, firing from the hip. destroyed the two machine-gun posts. He had cleared the way and his comrades clambered on the top of the hill, to consolidate in the mud.

The Germans furiously counter-attacked, a wave of them sweeping up the hill to rush the Dukes off the crest. By now the British companies had suffered severe casualties and probably they could not have held on, but once more Burton ran forward and sprayed the Germans with Bren-gun fire until they broke and ran. However, the enemy was not yet finished and later in the day they counter-attacked. For a fourth time Private Burton went into action, this time showing intelligence as well as gallantry. He ran with his Bren to a flank and brought such heavy fire on the Germans that they broke off the battle and retreated.

It can be seen from most of these episodes, especially in the case of the VC winners, that Tommy Atkins had developed some traits – notably the ability to think for himself – not apparent in earlier years. Many people would have denied that he had these traits. But given the opportunity he displayed them. The opportunity came about for three main reasons:

1.   The entire army system had changed, partly through the work of the pioneers in army reform, partly because warfare had radically changed.

2.   The common people, the citizens of Britain, were better educated, hence Tommy Atkins could apply more intellect to his warfare.

3.   Junior leadership was better, more professional.

It goes without saying that the exigencies and emergencies of war had also given Tommy an opening for his enterprise and gallantry.

For centuries Tommy Atkins was expected to do nothing more than stand fast. Now he was expected to use some initiative as well. How well he used it can be gauged by the fact that more NCOs and men won VCs than did officers. That men far outnumbered officers is irrelevant because officers, because they lead, have many more opportunities to distinguish themselves. Their actions were duly recognized with awards such as the Distinguished Service Order and the Military Cross.

It is very clear from a study of Tommy Atkins's hundreds of actions that he is at his best in an offensive-defensive situation – Albuhera, Waterloo, Lucknow, Rorke's Drift, Ladysmith, Snipe, Kohima, to mention a few. He is not at his best in a straightforward attack nor in a retreat. Here I think I can usefully make a few comparisons. The Australian is much better than the Englishman in attack, the German is much better in retreat. This is because the Australian is more resourceful and the German more methodical. But neither is as level-headed and as steady as Tommy Atkins.

Seventeen

1945
Ubiquitous Mr Atkins

Little remains to be said about the development of Tommy Atkins since World War II ended in 1945, though much could be said about national ignorance or indifference about what English soldiers have done. They have kept the peace – or tried to do so – in the face of great provocation. They have worked mightily in times of disaster. They have endured many insults and indignities, some of which, in earlier times, would have led to punitive campaigns. And they have fought in one major war – in Korea.

The gallantry of the Gloucestershire Regiment in the Battle of the Imjin River in 1951 is well known and is an action which shows that tradition and what it means plays a big part even in modern battle. Other units have not had so much publicity, whether fighting and serving in Greece, Kenya, Palestine, Cyprus, Malaya, Borneo, Brunei, Aden, the Suez Canal operation, Kuwait, Hong Kong, British Honduras, British Guiana . . . among other places.

When somebody had to deal with the vicious Mau Mau tribesmen who did it? Tommy Atkins. When help was desperately needed after a serious hurricane in Honduras who provided it? Tommy Atkins. When rival political factions in Guiana called for protection who gave it? Tommy Atkins. Who had to sort out the post-war mess in Palestine (Israel) and suffered while doing it? Tommy Atkins. Who survived another burning troopship? Tommy Atkins.*

Somehow, through it all Tommy has remained unruffled, unperturbed and patient – at least outwardly. As late as 1953 Sir Alfred Duff Cooper noted[†] that English soldiers 'are probably the least cruel of fighting men'. But at times Tommy Atkins has been profoundly irritated. He thinks it unreasonable, for instance, that knowing that he is going to be shot, he must wait for the shot to be fired before he can shoot back. That is, if he can find an officer to give him permission to shoot.

During peacetime – and periods of peace are usually quite violent – British soldiers and their leaders are usually militarily emasculated by their politicians.

I have been unable to find any word of thanks for anything Tommy Atkins has done, but I am told that the civic authorities of Honduras did thank the troops for what they did during and after the hurricane. I suppose there must be individuals here and there who thanked individual soldiers for help received. But Tommy Atkins is accustomed to doing his duty without thanks.

Inevitably in a large organization there have been 'incidents'. There were some malcontents in Germany who disrupted the civil peace; a couple of the Blues took an unauthorized holiday in Spain; some cry-babies made a lot of noise at Pirbright Camp because, they said, conditions were too severe. The few misfits always get much more publicity than the great mass of men who are a credit to their uniform.

No greater insult could be offered Tommy Atkins than to suggest – as many have done – that the hoodlums and ne'er-do-wells of Civvy Street be put into the army. The modern Tommy Atkins is of too fine a quality to be expected to live and serve with hoodlums. One can only hope that this quality

---

[*] On 28 March 1954 the *Empire Windrush* caught fire in the Mediterranean. Apart from four members of the crew killed in the engine-room when the fire started, not one of the 1,276 soldiers and their families was lost. Discipline saved them all. The captain of the Dutch ship Hensefjell said, 'No other nation could have behaved like this.'

[†] In *Sergeant Shakespeare*. I regret to say that Sir Alfred added 'but it cannot be pretended that they are the most honest [troops]'.

will be raised still further by training and encouraging Tommy Atkins to show even more enterprise, initiative and dash.

As recently as October 1963 Captain A.S. Jeapes, MC, felt that few, if any, infantry units were fully trained, and proceeded* to outline the most enlightened approach to modern training that I have encountered. 'We are trying to produce a mature and thoroughly trained soldier *who is capable of acting on his own initiative on the battle field.* To achieve this the soldier must be treated as a mature, responsible individual. . . . The soldier must continually be given responsibility. . . .'

Captain Jeapes knows what he is talking about and would, I imagine, be as exasperated as I am about some of the advertisements supposedly calculated to attract potential officers. The one I find particularly objectionable incorporates a photograph of a number of soldiers in the middle of the jungle, all looking lost and bewildered, and saying, in effect, 'What now, sir?' If modern training is efficient private soldiers would not look lost and bewildered.

The soldier of today is no mere machine, no cipher, no yokel. It is no longer enough for him to be able to obey orders and fire his rifle. The infantryman must be a man of many parts with skill in the use of several weapons, able to read an ordnance survey map, with some knowledge of signalling and co-operation with various arms of the service. He must be trained to use his own initiative should he be left without an officer or NCO, and taught how to survive under arduous conditions. A modern army is such a complex organization that many soldiers must be specialists of various kinds, and highly skilled specialists at that, but all infantrymen should have 'specialist' skills. All this means that a much higher standard of education is necessary than ever before. Many weapons are extremely sophisticated and the soldiers who use them must be intelligent enough to absorb the technical training necessary. It remains true that the infantryman – commandos and paratroops are basically infantry – is the most

* In an article in *The British Army Review.*

important cog in the army wheel, but soldiers of armoured, artillery, engineer and signal units are almost as vital. The whole structure of an army is so complex that the infantryman could not long stay in action without the help of many other soldiers behind him. It is said that seven men behind the line are needed to keep one man in the line. This one man is the real soldier of the eight – the spiritual descendant of the men who followed Cromwell, Marlborough and Wellington.

In 1947 an unofficial history of the 2nd Battalion Coldstream Guards' part in World War II was rounded off with 'a message' from the battalion's 'old soldier' – Sergeant W. Larbey. I intend to round off my book with the same message, for it says all that needs to be said. A great many other people have had their say about Tommy Atkins; he himself can have the last word.

Sergeant Larbey wrote: 'Twenty-three years ago I joined this battalion. I joined it as people join it today, wondering what I should find and what sort of life I would have. . . . I have experienced something that I would not have missed . . . a comradeship that bound men together in life and death, a comradeship that seemed to be capable of terrific sacrifice, a comradeship in which honour played the largest part.

'There have been times when we swore, and there will be times when we will swear again . . . we have laughed and we will laugh again. We have been very happy . . . and very sad. Friends have passed from our side, new faces have come and gone, everything seems to be changing. In my time I have seen many changes, from the red and blue of a peace-time Guard to the mud and rain of a mountain sentry – from the smooth-worn stones outside "Buck" to the dusty roads of France – from the measured tread of one hundred and twenty to the minute to the mad race back to Dunkirk.

'And yet it has all been worth while. On the surface things may have changed, but the spirit of the battaltion is just the same. And I do not think it will ever change. . . .'

Acknowledgements and Bibliography

I have referred to so many sources for this book that to list all would make tedious reading, so I have mentioned only those books which were particularly helpful. But I should like to thank Mrs George Bambridge, Rudyard Kipling's daughter and the owner of his copyrights, and Messrs Methuen and Macmillan for permission to quote three verses from the poem *Tommy* taken from *Barrack-Room Ballads* by Rudyard Kipling. Books, however, provided only part of my source material. I have drawn on the large collection of soldiers' original letters in my possession; the earliest one is dated 1694. The various copies of *The Navy and Army Illustrated* between 1895 and 1902 have also been helpful as well as *The Royal United Services Institution Journal*, *The Army Quarterly*, *The British Army Review*, *Soldier Magazine*, some regimental histories, public newspapers and magazines of various periods and official citations concerning Victoria Cross winners. I have drawn on the mind and memory of old soldiers and serving soldiers and thank them for tolerating my sometimes difficult questions. I am specially grateful to Brigadier C.E. Lucas Phillips for permission to draw on his splendid account of the Battle of Alamein for my summary of the action at Snipe. Brigadier Lucas Phillips's book, *Alamein*, is the definitive account of the battle. I am indebted, too, to Mr D.C. Quilter, for permission to quote Sergeant Larbey's letter.

Once more, I thank my wife for her work on my behalf; to produce this book of approximately 100,000 words she had typed a quarter of a million words.

Wide variations exist in the spelling of place names. Throughout this book I have used the spellings generally adopted by the British Army. Wherever a medal or bar has been issued for a particular action I have used the spelling on the bar, for example, Fuentes d'Onor, Albuhera, Kabul – though these places might with equal accuracy be spelled Fuentes de Onore, Albuera, Cabul.

(Many other books are mentioned in the text.)

Ancell, Samuel, *A Circumstantial Account of the Long and Tedious Blockade and Siege of Gibraltar*, Liverpool, 1785

Anton, Quartermaster Sergeant James, *Retrospect of Military Life*, London, 1841

Bell, Douglas, *Soldiers of the King*, Hammond, Hammond, 1948

Book of the Army Pageant, London, 1910

Callwell, Chas. E., *Small Wars – Their Principles and Practice*, 3rd edn, HMSO, 1899

Carter, Thomas, *Curiosities of War*, London, 1859

Claver, Scott, *Under the Lash*, Torchstream, 1954

Cobbett, W. *The Progress of a Ploughboy to a Seat in Parliament*, Faber & Faber, 1933

Cole, D.H. and Priestley, E.C., Majors, *An Outline of British Military History*, Sifton Praed, 1936

Compton, Herbert (editor and compiler), *A King's Hussar*, Cassell, 1896

Craufurd, A.H., *General Craufurd and His Light Division*, London, 1850

Curling, Henry (Ed.), *Recollections of Rifleman Harris*, London, 1848

Denison, Colonel G.T., *History of Cavalry*, Macmillan, 2nd edn, 1913

Duff Cooper, Sir A., *Sergeant Shakespeare*, Rupert Hart-Davis, 1949

Eyre, Lt. Vincent, *Journal of an Afghanistan Prisoner*, John Murray, 1853

Farrer, J.A., *Military Manners and Customs*, Chatto & Windus, 1885

Feilding, Rowland, *War Letters to a Wife*, The Medici Society, 1929

Field, Colonel Cyril, *Old Times Under Arms*, Hodge, 1939

Fitchett, W.H., *Wellington's Men*, John Murray, 1912

Forbes, Archibald, *Barracks, Bivouacs and Battles*, Macmillan, 1894

Fortescue, Sir John, *History of the British Army*, Macmillan, 1930

'G.B.', *Narrative of a Private Soldier in one of His Majesty's Regiments of Foot*, Glasgow, 1819

Gilby, Thomas, *Britain at Arms*, Eyre & Spottiswoode, 1953

Gowing, Thomas, *A Soldier's Experience; or A Voice From the Ranks*, Privately printed, Nottingham, 1886

Hardy, Revd E.J., *The British Soldier*, T. Fisher Unwin, 1915

Hargreaves, Reginald, *This Happy Breed*, Skeffington, 1951

Hart, George S., *Great Soldiers*, Grant Richards, 1911

Hay, Ian, *The King's Service*, Methuen, 1939

Henderson, Col G.F.R., *The Science of War*, Longmans, Green, 1905

Hills, R.J.T., *Something About a Soldier*, Lovat Dickson, 1934

Horst, K.A. ter, *Cloud Over Arnhem*, Wingate, 1959

Hunt, J.L. and Pringle, A.G., *Service Slang*, Faber & Faber, 1943

Hutchison, Lt Col Graham Seton, *The British Army*, Gramol Publications, 1945

Jackson, Robert, *A View of the Formation, Discipline and Economy of Armies*, London, 1845

Johnston, S.H.F., *British Soldiers*, Collins, 1944

Kinglake, A.W., *The Invasion of the Crimea*, 4 vols., Blackwood, 1863

Kincaid, Captain J., *Random Shots of a Rifleman*, London, 1847

Laffin, John, *The Face of War*, Abelard-Schuman, 1964

Laffin, John, *Links of Leadership*, Harrap

MacMullen, J., *Camp and Barrack Room: or, The British Army As It Is*, London, 1846

Maxwell, Sir Herbert, *British Soldiers in the Field*, George Allen, 1902

Maxwell, W.H., *Peninsular Sketches*, London, 1858

Moodie, William (Ed.), *The Crown of Honour*, James Clarke, 1937

Napier, Sir C.J., *Lights and Shades of Military Life*, London, 1851

Napier, Sir William, *History of the Peninsular War*, 7 vols., London, 1851

Oman, C.W.C., *Wellington's Army 1809–1814*, Arnold, 1912

Phillips, C.E. Lucas, *Alamein*, Heinemann, 1962

Pringle, Sir John, *Observations on Diseases of the Army*, London, 1768

Quilter, D.C. (Ed.), '*No Dishonourable Name*' (2nd & 3rd Battalions, Coldstream Guards, 1939–45), William Clowes, 1947

Reide, Thomas, *Treatise on the Duty of Infantry Officers and the Present System of British Military Discipline*, London, 1795

Robertson, Field-Marshal Sir William, *From Private to Field-Marshal*, London, 1921

Ryder, Corporal, *Four Years' Service in India*, Leicester, 1853

Settle, J.H., *Anecdotes of Soldiers*, Methuen, 1905

Shipp, John, *Memoirs of the Military Career of John Shipp*, London, 1843

Slim, Field-Marshal Viscount, *Defeat Into Victory*, Cassell, 1956

Stocqueler, J.H., *The British Soldier*, Wm. S. Orr, 1857

Tucker, A.B., *Romance of the King's Army*, London, 1908

Watteville, Colonel H. de, *The British Soldier*, Dent, 1954

Wavell, Field-Marshal Earl, *The Good Soldier*, Macmillan, 1948

Wavell, Field-Marshal Earl, *Soldiers and Soldiering*, Jonathan Cape, 1953

Wile, Frederic William, *Explaining the Britishers*, Heinemann, 1918

Wolff, Leon, *In Flanders Fields*, Longmans, Green, 1959

Index

Abercrombie, General, 102
Abercromby, Sir Ralph, 71
Adams, Major D., 207
Addison, Padre W.R.F., 220n
Aden, 248
Afghan Wars
  first (1839–42), 150–1
  second (1878–80), 181–4
  third (1919), 223
Aix-la-Chapelle, 198
Aldershot, 164, 194
Alexander, Bombadier Alexander,
  125
Allahabad, 168
American War of Independence
  (1775–83), 62–3
Amputation, 95
Ancell, Samuel, on a soldier's life, 66
Anglesey, Marquis of (Lord Uxbridge),
  on the 28th Regiment, 70
Anne, Queen, 35, 37
Anton, Quartermaster
  on uniform, 61
  on the queue, 61
Antwerp, 86
Anzio, 236
'Après la Guerre' (song), quoted, 213
Arakan, 239
Army Certificate of Education, 173
Army Clothing Factory, 164
Army Medical Service see Medical
  service
Army Reserve, inception of, 176
Army Temperance Societies, 190
Articles of War, 117, 138
Ashanti Expedition (1873), 158
Ayub Khan, 181–2

Bailey, Colonel, 67
Bairnsfather, Bruce, 13
Baker rifle, 75
Barnett, Corporal, 232
Barr, Lieutenant, 182

Barracks
  introduction of, 68, 74, 143
  improvement of, 171
  arrangements for eating and
    sleeping, 180–1
  physical and mental atmosphere,
    188–9
  communal dining halls built, 194
Bastinadoing, 121n
Bathurst, Earl, 110
Battalions, linked into regiments, 178
Battles, other actions, and sieges
  Abraham, Plains of (1759), 52
  Abu Klea (1885), 1
  Agincourt (1415), 5, 17
  Ahmed Khel (1880), 181
  Alamein see Snipe, Outpost
  Albuhera (1811), 99, 100–7, 247
  Arroyo Dos Molinos (1811), 107
  Assaye (1803), 76
  Badahoz (1811–12), 9, 89, 107–9
  Barrosa (1811), 107
  Beaumont (1794), 69
  Bhurtpore (1805), 83, 84
  Blenheim (1704), 3, 41, 42, 43
  Brandywine (1777), 63
  Campoleone Railway Station
    (1944), 236–7
  Cartagena (1741), 46
  Cawnpore (1857), 164–8
  Ceco, Mount (1944), 245–6
  Centuripe (1943), 227n
  Ciudad Rodrigo (1812), 107
  Coa River (1810), 131
  Corunna (1809), 86, 129
  Crécy (1346), 5, 17, 204
  Deig (1804), 83
  Delhi (1857), 164
  Dettingen (1743), 48, 56
  Douro, passage of the (1809), 111
  Dunbar (1650), 114
  Duquesne, Fort (1755), 51
  Emsdorff (1760), 55

Famars (1793), 69
Ferozeshah (1845), 153–5
Festubert (1915), 208–9
Fontenoy (1745), 49, 56
Fuentes d'Onor (1811), 107, 111
Gibraltar (1779–83), 66, 74
Gundamuck (1841), 150–1
Havana (1762), 57
Hyderabad (1843), 152
Imjin River (1951), 248
Inkermann (1854), 162–4, 186
Isandlwana (1879), 185
Jena (1806), 111
Killiecrankie (1688), 31
Kohima (1944), 238–43, 247
Kut (1916), 209
Ladysmith (1899-1900), 247
Laing's Nek (1881), 132n
Lille (1708), 42
Lincelles (1793), 68
Loos (1915), 209
Lucknow (1857), 3, 168, 247
Maida (1806), 85
Maiwand (1880), 181–3
Majuba Hill (1881), 185
Malplaquet (1709), 44
Minden (1759), 52–5, 208n
Mons (1914), 199–201
Moodkee (1845), 154
Namur (1695), 33
Ne Plus Ultra Lines (1711), 44
Neerwinden (1693), 33
Nimuegen (1702), 35
Nunshigum (1944), 242–3
Ornito, Mount (1944), 237–8
Oudenarde (1709), 44, 45
Passchendaele (1917), 211–12
Philadelphia (1777), 64
Plassey (1757), 3
Poitiers (1356), 5, 17
Princeton (1776), 62
Quebec (1759), 52
Ramillies (1706), 44
Rorke's Drift (1879), 235, 247
San Sebastian (1813), 9, 89, 109
Schellenberg (1706), 43
Seringapatam (1799), 67
Snipe, Outpost (1942), 228–35, 247
Sobraon (1846), 156
Somme (1916), 209, 210–11
Steenkirk (1692), 33
Talavera (1809), 88n, 93
Tel el Kebir (1882), 186
Valenciennes (1793), 69
Vigo, retreat to (1809), 129

Villars (1794), 69
Villars-en-Cauchies (1794), 69
Vittoria (1813), 110
Wadi Akarit (1943), 244
Waterloo (1815), 3, 87, 111–13, 246
Ypres (1914), 203
Zutphen (1586), 17
Bayly, Lt Col, 129
Bayonets, 31
Beards, 170
Bell, Douglas, on Kitchener's army, 204
Bell, Dr, 134
Bengal European Infantry, 133
Beresford, General Sir William, 100–2, 105
Best, Revd, 125
Binks, Sergeant, 233
Bird, Captain, 231
Birkenhead (troopship), 157
Bishop, Major, 207
Black Hole of Calcutta see Calcutta
Black-hole punishment, 122
Blackader, Colonel, 37–8
Blakeney, Captain Robert, on the sack of Badajoz, 108–9
Bland, Lt Col Humphrey, on discipline, 45
Blasphemy, 38, 40, 117n, 120, 159
Blücher, Marshal, 111, 112
Boer Wars
    (1881), 132n
    (1899–1902), 169n, 191–3, 195, 196
Boers, 185, 191–2
Boger, Colonel D.C., 199
Bombay, 27
Books, banned by army authorities, 142–3
Booting punishment, 121
Borneo, 248
Botwood, Sergeant Ned, 52
Bounty, 170
Boxer Rebellion (1900), 194
Bradbury, Captain, 201
Braddock, General, 50–1, 62
Bread allowance, 68
Bremen, 134
Britannic Magazine, 76
British Army
    officers and human machines, 2
    regimental system, 5–6, 28, 50, 56, 173, 178–9
    effect of class structure on character of, 7

birth of Regular Standing Army, 26–7

formation of grenadier company within each regiment, 28

institution of a pension, 29

conditions in late 17th century, 29–34

under Marlborough, 35–44

early 18th century period, 44–7

mid-18th century conditions, 50–1

improvement in public attitude to, 56

prize money, 57

out-pensioners and deserters, 64–5

Duke of York's reforms, 73–4

Moore's reforms, 75–6

condition of the Peninsular army, 87–99

between Waterloo and the Crimean War, 141–50

administrative reforms after Crimean War, 164

moustache and beard fashions, 169–70

government provides kit, 170

improvement in married quarters, 170–1

Cardwell's reforms, 176–9

Haldane's reforms, 194–5

modernization after World War I, 224

the old and the new type of soldier, 224–7, 247, 248–51

unique position of the NCO, 235

see also Barracks; Discipline and punishment; Disease; Food; Health; Medical service; Officers; Pay; Uniform

British Army Regiments

7th see Royal Fusiliers

9th see East Norfolk

10th see Lincolnshire

12th see Suffolk

13th (later Somerset Light Infantry), 45

14th see West Yorkshire

15th Foot see East Yorkshire

17th Foot see Leicestershire

22nd see Cheshire

28th see Gloucestershire

29th see Worcestershire

31st (later Ist East Surrey), 57

32nd Foot see Cornwall Light Infantry

33rd see 1st West Riding

34th (later 1st Border), 81

38th see South Staffordshire

44th Foot see 1st Essex

48th see 1st Northamptonshire

52nd (later 2nd Oxford and Buckinghamshire Light Infantry), 88

57th see Middlesex

61st (later 2nd Gloucestershire), 90

62nd see Wiltshire

65th (later 1st York and Lancaster), 81

66th Foot see Berkshire

80th Foot (later South Staffordshire), 154, 155, 156

7th Anti-Tank, 228

Bays (Queen's Bays – 2nd Dragoon Guards, 200, 201

Berkshire (66th Foot), 182, 183

Bland's Dragoons see 3rd King's Own Hussars

Buffs see Royal East Kent

3rd Dragoon Guards, 101

5th Dragoon Guards, 200, 201

3rd Carabiniers (Prince of Wales Dragoon Guards), 243

Cheshire (22nd Foot), 81, 152, 199

Coldstream Guards, 17, 26, 235–6, 237–8, 251

Cornwall Light Infantry (32nd Foot), 168

Duke of Wellington's, 245

1st East Anglian, 53

East Devonshire (later Lancashire Fusiliers), 208n

East Norfolk (9th), 45, 154

East Surrey (31st), 102

East Yorkshire (15th Foot), 42, 63, 70

Eliott's Light Horse see 15th Light Dragoons

1st Essex (44th Foot), 50, 151

1st Gloucestershire (28th), 70, 86, 97, 248

Green Howards (19th), 50n, 77, 243–4

Grenadier Guards, 26n, 202

1st Horse Grenadiers, 120

11th Hussars, 45, 171, 200

Irish Fusiliers, 227n

3rd King's Own Hussars (Bland's Dragoons), 48

King's Own Scottish Borderers (25th), 53

King's Own Yorkshire Light Infantry (51st), 53, 107
King's Royal Rifle Corps (60th – Royal American Regiment), 65
King's Shropshire Light Infantry, 191
Kingsley's Regiment (later Lancashire Fusiliers), 208n
Lancashire Fusiliers (20th), 53, 54, 206–8
Leicestershire (17th Foot), 62–3
1st Life Guards, 26
2nd Life Guards, 26
3rd Light Dragoons, 155
15th Light Dragoons (Eliott's Light Horse), 55
20th Light Dragoons, 132
43rd Light Infantry see Oxford and Buckinghamshire Light Infantry
52nd Light Infantry see Oxford and Buckinghamshire Light Infantry
Ligonier's Horse (later 7th Dragoons), 49
Lincolnshire (10th), 45, 156, 218
London Irish Rifles, 227n
Manchester Regiment, 216–17
Middlesex (57th – Die Hards), 102, 103–4, 106, 163
Monk's Regiment of Foot Guards see Coldstream Guards
1st Northamptonshire (48th), 50, 132, 224
Okey's Regiment, 120
1st Oxford and Buckinghamshire Light Infantry (43rd), 75, 168–9
2nd Oxford and Buckinghamshire Light Infantry (52nd), 75
Oxfordshire Regiment, 123
Rifle Brigade, 75, 88n, 107, 228
60th Royal American Regiment see King's Royal Rifle Corps
Royal Artillery (Foy's and Macbean's), 53
Royal East Kent (Buffs), 8, 50n, 102, 105
Royal Fusiliers (7th), 104, 105, 194
1st Royal Hampshire (37th), 53, 227n
2nd Royal Hampshire (67th), 174–5 Royal Norfolk, 200
Royal Regiment of Artillery, 46, 53
Royal Welsh Fusiliers (now Royal Welch Fusiliers), 50, 53, 105–6
Royal West Kent, 239, 241–2

Sherwood Foresters, 236–7
1st South Staffordshire (38th), 44
South Wales Borderers, 46
Suffolk (12th), 45, 53, 54
West Norfolk, 68
West Riding (33rd), 50n, 67, 70
West Yorkshire (14th), 45, 46, 69
Wiltshire, 154
1st Worcestershire (29th), 102
British Grenadiers, The (poem), quoted, 28
British Guiana, 248
British Honduras, 248, 249
Bromley, Captain C., 208
Brown Bess musket, 53, 161
Brown, Sergeant G.H., 230
Brown, Trooper Tom, 48
Brunei, 248
Brydon (surgeon), 151
Buccellas, 97
Bully beef, 158–9
Bunbury, Sir Henry, quoted, 69
Bunny, Molyneaux, 34
Burma, 6, 115, 139, 172, 224, 227
campaign of 1824–6, 149
Burnhope, Rifleman, 230
Burrows, Major-General, 181–2
Burton, Private Richard Henry, 245–6

Ça Ira, 69
Calcutta, Black Hole of (1756), 147
Calistan, Sergeant C., 232, 234
Cambrai, 216
Camden, William, Annals, on drunkenness, 27n
Campbell, Sir Colin, 3, 168
Canteens, 226
Capital punishment see Executions
Cardigan, Lord, 160
Cardo (officer), 88
Cardwell, Edward, 176–9, 194
Carib War (1773), 114
Castlereagh, Lord, 87, 132
Cat-o'-nine-tails, 20, 119, 129, 132 see also Flogging
Catania Airfield, 244
Catherine of Braganza, 27
Cattadinia, 77
Cautions and Advices to Officers of the Army (by 'an old officer'), on beating soldiers, 56–7
Central America, 46
Ceylon, 77
Chanak, 224
Chard, Rifleman, 233, 234

Charge of the Light and Heavy
     Brigades, 2
Charles II, 26, 27, 29, 30
Charleville, 198
Chatham, Lord, 86
Chelsea Royal Hospital, 29, 56, 64
China, 172
     capture of Peking, 174
     Boxer Rebellion, 194
Churchill, Winston, 197
City Imperial Volunteers, 193
Class structure, its effect on British
     Army, 7, 12–13
Claver, Scott, 117
Clayton, Revd P.B. ('Tubby'), 226n
     quoted, 13n
Clive, Lord, 3
Cobbett, William, 132
     on the English soldier, 67–8
Colborne, Colonel, 85, 101, 102
Colchester, 164
Cole, D.H., and Priestley, E.C.
     on the purchase system, 177
     on Kitchener's army, 204
Cole, General, 105
Colliss, Gunner James, 183–4
Commissions, sale of see Purchase
     system
Commissray department, 91
     see also Food
Company sergeant major, 235
Compton, Herbert, 125n
Compulsory enlistment, 224
Contades, Marshal, 53, 54
'Contemptible little army', 196–9
Cooper, Seven Campaigns, on disease,
     95
Coote, Sir Eyre, 124
Cornwallis, Lord, 62, 63
Corruption, 30–1, 91
     see also Purchase system
Costello, Adventures of a Soldier,
     89, 92
Craig, Major-General, on the state of
     the army in the 1790s, 69–70
Craufurd, General Robert ('Black
     Bob'), 85, 129–31
Crawford, Driver R.J., 229
Creevey, Thomas, 111
Crimean War (1854–5), 158, 171
     inefficiency, shortages and general
     conditions, 159–62
     the men, 162
Cromwell, Oliver, 17, 19, 20, 26,
     251

Crozier, Brigadier F.P., on the Somme,
     210, 211
Cullen, Sergeant, 233
Cumberland, Duke of, 49, 50
Curragh, instructional camp at, 164
Cyprus, 248

D-Day, 244
Daily Express, on the Kaiser's order,
     197
Daily News, 199
Dalrymple, Lt Col, on military
     punishment, 120
Darbyshire, Gunner, 201
Darien, Isthmus of, 47
Davies, Godfrey, 88
De Robeck, Vice-Admiral, on the
     Lancashire Fusiliers, 208
De Watteville, Colonel H., 85, 141,
     204n
Debauchery, 84
Decorations for bravery, 220–2
     see also Distinguished Conduct
          Medal; Distinguished Service
          Order; Military Cross; Military
          Medal; Victoria Cross
Delafosse, Lieutenant, 166
Derby, Lord, 209
Dervishes, 1
Deserters, 65
     punishment for desertion, 139
Dickens, Charles, 142
     on John Shaw, 112–13
     on the English soldier, 164
Dinapore, 134
Discipline and punishment, 10–12
     in Marlborough's army, 37–41
     early Hanoverian period, 45
     18th century, 56–7, 64, 71
     Wellington on flogging, 87, 136–7
     in Wellington's time, 89–90
     forms of punishment, 116–39
     flogging, 124–39
     new punishment for desertion, 139
Disease, 6, 46–7, 57–9, 81, 84, 95, 147,
     171, 193
Distinguished Conduct Medal, 221
Distinguished Service Order, 247
Donaldson, Joseph, The Eventful
     Life of a Soldier, on hardships,
     89–90
Dorrell, Sergeant-Major (later Lt Col),
     201
Dost Mohammed, 150, 151
Dougald, William, 94

Drinkwater, Private H.V., 211
'Drum Major's charge', 132
Drunkenness, 27, 38, 84, 142, 159, 190, 226
Dry-room pnishment, 122
Duff Cooper, Sir A, , on the English soldier, 248
Dutch Independence, War of (1572–1648), 8
Dyas, Ensign Joseph, 107

East India Company, 84, 114, 124, 141
East Indies, 124
Education of soldiers
opposed by Wellington, 112, 143
issue of official certificates of education (1854), 158
Army Certificate of Education (1860), 174–5
Edward III, 5
Edward VII, 193
Egerton, Colonel, 163
Egyptian campaigns
(1801), 71
(1882–5), 179
(1921), 224
Elba, 111
Eliott, Colonel George, 55
Ellis, Colonel Welbore, 69
Elphinstone, General, 150–1
Elstob, Lt Col Wilfrith, 216–17
Elvas, 95
Emerson, R.W., on the English, 8
Enfield, Army Clothing and Small Arms factories at, 164
Entertainment
in the Peninsular War, 96
in World War II, 226
Essex, Earl of, lawes and Ordinances of Warre, 117
Eton, rebellion at, 146n
Euryalus, HMS, 206, 208
Evans, Samuel, 86
Executions, 118–19, 123–4, 152–3
Eyre, General, 160

'Faggot' or 'Warrant-men' system, 31
Falaise, 245
Farquhar, George, The Recruiting Officer, 36–7
Fawcett, Captain, 104
Feilding, Colonel Rowland, on recommendations for bravery, 221

Ferdinand of Brunswick, Prince, 53, 54, 55
Ferguson, General Sir Charles, on Mons, 200
Ferozepore, 154, 155
Fifty-Five Days at Pekin (film), 194
Fitchett, W.H., 85
Fitzgibbon, Hospital Apprentice Andrew, 174
Flanders, 68, 71, 224
Fleury, Mont, 244
Flogging, 20, 87, 117, 119–20, 124–39
Flower, Lieutenant R., 229
Floyd, Captain John (later General Sir John Floyd), 55–6
Flud, Robert, on drunkenness, 27n
Food
introduction of bread allowance, 68
in the Peninsular, 91
introduction of breakfast messes, 144
on troopships, 147
bully beef introduced, 158–9
in the Crimea, 159–60
in 1870s, 180–1
English soldiers' dislike of French food (World War I), 214–15
Forbes, Archibald, on the English soldier, 184–6, 192
Foreign service, as punishment for court-martial offences, 44
Fortescue, Sir John, 65
on the quality of the Regular Army, 3
on origins of modern English soldier, 8
on the Buffs, 8
on Minden, 52, 53
on Sir John Moore, 75
on bad conditions, 141, 143
on the troops in Burma, 149
Foul language, 38, 40, 159
see also Blasphemy
Foy, Captain, 53, 54
Francis, Corporal, 231, 232
Fraternization, 215
French Army, 124, 137–8, 189
French, General Sir John, 196, 209
French's Contemptible Army (poem), 197

Galbraith, Lt Col, 182
Gallipoli Campaign (1915), 206–8
Gallop, Trooper E.A., quoted, 190

Gantelope (running the gauntlet), 120, 120–1
Gascons, 5
'G.B.', *Narrative of a Private Soldier*, quoted, 74–5, 95
George I, 44
George II, 45, 48
George III, 68, 133
Gerard, Lord, 26
German Legion, 5
Ghazi tribesmen, 181–3
Ghazni (Ghuznee, Ghusni), 181
Gibraltar, 226n
Gilling (private), 133
Good Hope, Cape of, 81
Gordon riots, 68
Gough, Sir Hugh, 154–6
Gowing, Sergeant Thomas, on Sebastopol, 161–2
Grant, General Sir Hope, 174
Greece, 248
Gregory, Private Anthony, 125
Grenadier company, formed within each regiment, 28
Grimshaw, Lance-Corporal J., 207, 208
Grose, Charles
    on out-pensioners, 64–5
    on ensign's duty, 102n
    on military punishments, 118, 119, 121, 124
Guards, Brigade of, raise £9,000, 171
Gurkha Rifles, 174
Guthrie, James (surgeon), 96
Gwynne, Nell, 29

Hackett, General John, 175n
Haig, Sir Douglas, 203, 223
Hair styles, 60–1, 169–70
Haldane, R.B., 194, 195, 196
Hamilton, Dr, on flogging, 125, 132
Hamilton, Sir Ian, on Gallipoli, 208
'Hard and Tights', 61
Hardinge, Colonel (later Sir Henry), 105, 154–5
Hardy, Revd E.J., 177–8
    on the English soldier, 188–91
    on commissions, 192
Hardy, Revd Theodore Bayley, 218–20
Hare, Brigadier-General, 206
Harman, General, 236–7
Harman, Lance Corporal J.P., 241–2
Harris, Rifleman, *Recollections*
    on Corunna, 85–6
    on plundering, 88

on relations between men and officers, 91
Harrow School, rebellion at, 146n
Hatred
    none towards Germans, 215
    of Japanese, 239
Haworth, Lieutenant, 207
Hay, Ian, on inferiority complex of soldiers, 13
Health, 6, 41, 50, 57–9, 171
    see also Disease; Medical service
Heber, Reginald (Bishop of Calcutta), on the rum ration in India, 148
Henderson, Colonel G.F.R., 6, 7
    on marksmanship, 195
Henry V, 5, 27n
Henty, G.A., 1
'Here's to the Last Who Dies' (poem), quoted, 14–16
Hill, Lord ('Daddy'), 122, 138
Hine, Sergeant, 233, 234
Hodson, William, on the 80th at Ferozeshah, 155
Hoghton, General, 102, 103, 104
Hollis, CSM Stanley, 243–5
Holloway, Henry, 107n
Holt-Wilson, Lt B., 233–4
Home Defence, 178
Home leave, almost unknown in Wellington's time, 92
Hong Kong, 191, 248
Honywood, Lieutenant, 182
Hookhum Singh, 156
Horse Artillery *see* Royal Horse Artillery
Howans, Daniel, 130
Hugo, Victor, 113
Hull, Robert, 21n
Humour, sense of, 13, 205
Hunter-Weston, Major-General, 208
Hyder Ali, 67
Hythe, School of Musketry at, 164

Imperial Guard, at Waterloo, 112
Implacable, HMS, 207
L'Indépendance, on the English soldier, 205
India, 84, 115, 141, 172, 224
    Tippoo Sahib, 67
    Wellington's march to Poona, 76
    Deig and Bhurtpore, 83–4
    Burma campaign (1824–6), 149
    Gundamuck (1841), 150–1
    Scinde (or Sind) War (1843), 152

first Sikh War (1845–6), 153–6
the Mutiny, 164–9, 174
India General Service Medal, 115
Ingles, Henry (headmaster of Rugby), 147
Inglis, Lt Col, 103–4
Ireland, 65, 119, 224
Italy, 227
    Campoleone Railway Station, 236–7
    Mount Ornito, 237–8

Jackson, Ensign, 104
Jackson, Robert, on the English soldier of Wellington's time, 77–81
Jacobite Rebellion (1715), 45
Jamaica, 47
James II, 30, 32
James, Lieutenant G., his recruiting poster, 97–8
James, Major Charles, *Military Dictionary*, 190n
Japanese, English soldiers' attitude to, 239
Jeapes, Captain A.S., on initiative, 250
Jenkins' Ear, War of, 46
Johnson, Dr, on the English soldier, 6
Jordan, Thomas, quoted, 9n
Journal of a Soldier (anon), 89
Jünger, Lieutenant Ernst, on the English soldier, 216

Kabul, 181
    Roberts' march from Kabul to Kandahar, 184
Kaiser, the (Emperor Wilhelm II), alleged remark on the 'contemptible little army', 197–9
Kandahar, 181, 182, 183
Kelly, Major, 113
Keneally, Private W., 208
Kennedy, Robert (Commissary General), 91
Kenya, 248
Khaki, introduction of, 169
Khalsa, the, 153
Khartoum, 224
Khyber Pass, 115, 151
Kilmainham, Royal Hospital at, 29
Kincaid, Captain John, *Random Shots of a Rifleman*
    on Wellington, 110
    on flogging, 130

Kinglake, A.W., 141
    on Inkermann, 163
King's Bounty, 29
King's South Africa Medal, 193
Kingsley, Brigadier, 53
Kipling, Rudyard, champions the English soldiers, 3, 9, 184, 186–7, 204
Kitchener, Lord, 196
    on morals, 196
    on recruiting, 204
Kluck, General von, 198
Koblenz, 198
Korean War (1950–3), 248
Kumaon Battalion, 174
Kuwait, 248

Lal Singh, 153–4
Lancer regiments, introduction of, 101
Larbey, Sergeant W., on comradeship, 251
Latham, Lieutenant, 104
Lawrence, Sergeant, 135
Liddell Hart, Captain B.H., 203, 224
Long, Colonel, 135
Long Service and Good Conduct Medal, 115
Long-service soldier, replacement of, 176
Looting and plundering, 37–9, 70, 88, 175
    see also Sacking of towns
Low, Charles Rathbone, on Inkermann, 163
Lucy, Corporal John, 203–4
Luxembourg, 198
Lynn, Escott, 1

Macaulay, Lord, 26, 112
Macbean, Captain, 53, 54
McCrae, Colonel John, *In Flanders Fields* (poem), quoted, 222
McGrigor, Sir James (Inspector General of Hospitals), 96
Mackay, General, 31
MacMullen, Sergeant J., *Camp and Barrack Room*
    on why men entered the army, 150
    on a military execution, 152–3
Malaya, 248
Manchester Hill (near St Quentin), 217
Maori wars (1843–69), 149, 176
Marlborough, Duke of, 3, 5, 35, 37, 38, 45, 46, 195, 251

his rules and regulations, 40–1
organizes medical service, 41
on bravery of his soldiers, 43
the *Ne Plus Ultra* Lines, 44
Married quarters, 143–4
improvement of, 170–1
Marshall, Dr Henry (Deputy
Inspector General of Army
Hospitals), 119n
Mau Mau tribesmen, 248
Maunding Soldier, The (ballad),
quoted, 33–4
Maurice, General Sir F., 198, 199
Mawhood, Lt Col Charles, 62
Medals, 114–15, 193
number of DCMs and MMs awarded
1914–18, 221
Medical service
Marlborough's, 41
Wellington's, 95–6
improved after Crimean War, 164
at Passchendaele, 212
in World War II, 227
Medley, Captain, *An Early Campaign
in India*, on the introduction of
khaki, 169
Mellish, Padre Edward Noel, 220n
Mercer, General, 62
Messines, 203
Metropolitan Police Force, 145
Miles, Sergeant, 233, 234
Military Cross, 247
Military General Service Medal, 106n,
114
Military Medal, 221
Military Service Bill (1916), 209
Monk, Lord, 26
Moore, Captain J., 165–7
Moore, Sir John, 77, 125
ability, 73
training reforms, 75–6, 85
at Corunna, 85–6
Moplah, 224
Moustaches, 169–70
Musketry, poor quality of in Boer
War, 192
Mutiny Act (1702), 35

Nana Sahib, 165, 167, 168
Napier, Sir Charles, 85–6
on Sobraon, 156
Napier, Sir William, 206
on the sack of San Sebastian,
109
on the Peninsular War, 111

on military punishments, 127, 128,
134
on the English soldier, 140–1
Napoleon, 111–12, 113, 208n
Navy and Army Illustrated, The, 14,
190
on the English soldier, 4–5, 113
NCOs
rarely mentioned in despatches, 2
their unique position in British
Army, 235
awards for, 246
Nelson, Sergeant, 201
Nery, 200
Netherlands campaign (1793-5),
68–70
Netley Hospital, 189
New Model Army, 17–18, 25, 27, 195
formation of, 19
composition, 19
the Soldier's Catechism, 20–5
disbanded, 26
New Zealand, 149, 172, 176
Nightingale, Florence, 160, 171
North Africa, 227
see also Battles, Snipe, Outpost
North Russia, expedition to (1919), 223
North-West Frontier, 194
see also Afghan Wars

Officers
disproportionate number of awards
to, 12
more officer POWs escape than
other ranks, 12
emergence of a better type (mid-
18th century), 56
Rifleman Harris on their kindness,
91
of the 1860s, 172
public regard for, 174
made responsible for training of
their commands, 179
in later 19th century, 187
First World War shortage of, 205
relationship with other ranks in N.
Africa, 229
O'Hara, Major, 107
Old Contemptibles, 198
Osborne, Driver, 201
Out-pensioners, 64–5
Oxford, Earl of, 26

Palestine, 224, 248
Paris, occupation of (1814), 111

Parker, Captain Robert, on Marlborough's march to the Danube, 41
Parkin, Surgeon, 136
Parsons, Private Robert Browning, on conditions in the Crimea, 160
Patterson, Captain John, on the British soldier, 141
Pay
    stoppages of, 50, 143
    in 18th century, 61–2, 63, 71
    in Wellington's time, 91
    reforms of the 1860-70s, 178
    increase of after World War I, 223
Pay sergeant, 143
Pearson, Sergeant Andrew, 90
Peking, 174, 175
Pembroke, Earl of, 55
Peninsular War, 9, 85–6, 158n
    condition of the army, 87–99
    Albuhera, 100–7
    Badahoz, 107–9
    sack of San Sebastian, 109
    the British achievement, 110–11
Penn, Drummer Harry Vincent, 202–3
Penny, *Traditions of Perth*, on punishment, quoted, 64
Pensacola, 57
Pension
    in Charles II's time, 29
    in 18th century, 64
Picketing (form of punishment), 119, 120
Pickford, Corporal, 238
Picquets, removal of, 194
Pirbright Camp, 249
Pitt, William, the younger, 68, 74
Plug bayonet, 31
Plundering *see* Looting and plundering
Police duties, soldiers relieved of, 145
Ponsonby, Arthur, 199
Poona, 76
Portugese, 5, 101
Primrose, General, 181
Pringle, Sir John, *Observations on Diseases of the Army*, quoted, 57–8
Prize Money, 57
Professionalism, beginnings of, 176
Prostitutes, 190
Provost-Marshal, duties of, 117–18
Prussia, 126n
Prussian Army, 157n, 189
Punch, 4, 160, 173, 174, 198

Punishment *see* Discipline and punishment
Purchase system, abolition of, 176–7

Queen's Service, The (anon), on the barrack room, 188–9
Queen's South Africa Medal, 193
Queue, 60–1

Raglan, Lord, 162
Ramsey, Captain Norman, 111
Rank *see* Purchase system
Rations *see* Food
Recruiting
    17th century, 29–30
    in Queen Anne's reign, 35–7
    Act of 1779, 65
    in Wellington's time, 97–8
    Kitchener's, 204
Red tape, 96, 160
Regimental sergeant major, 235
Regimental system, 5–6, 28, 50, 56, 101, 173, 178–9
Reide, Thomas, *Military Discipline*, quoted, 71
Religion, soldiers' attitude to, 189
Richards, Colonel, 240, 242
Richards, Sergeant A., 207, 208
Robbery, 38
Roberts, Sir Frederick, 184
Robertson, Field-Marshal Sir William, on his early army experiences, 179–80
Robinson, Corporal Thomas, 106
Roses, Wars of the, 17
Royal Commission of 1835–6, 135–8
Royal Horse Artillery, 111, 155, 181, 182, 183, 200, 201
Royall, Lt Col, 90
Rugby school, rebellion at, 146–7
Runners, 201–3
Running the gauntlet *see* Gantelope
Russell, Colonel John, 26
Ryder, Corporal, on a day's march in India, 153

Saar, the, 224
Sacking of towns, 38–9, 89
    Badahoz, 108–9
    San Sebastian, 109
Sackville, Lord George, 51, 54, 55
Salvation Army, 226
Sanctuary Wood, 203
Sarah Sands (troopship), 157
Sato, Major-General, 238–9

Saxe, Marshal, 49
School rebellions, quelled by soldiers, 146–7
Scinde (or Sind) War (1843), 152
'Scum of the earth', 35, 87, 109–10
Scutari, 160
Self-denying Ordinance, 19
Seringapatem Medal, 114
Seven Years War (1756-63), 57
Shakespeare, 17, 34
Shanghai, 224
Shaw, Captain H., 207
Shaw, Corporal John, 112–13
Sheerness, School of Gunnery at, 164
Shelton, Colonel, 151
Sherwood, Mrs, on conditions aboard a troopship, 147–8
Shipp, John, on his experiences in the army, 77–81, 122, 125–6, 148
Short Service Act (1870), 176
Sidney, Sir Philip, 17
Sikh War, first (1845–6), 153–6
Singing, 213–14
'Skiboo' (song), quoted, 213–14
Skiddy, Dan, 93
Slim, Field-Marshal Lord, Field-Marshal Lord, 6
on Kohima, 239, 242
Small Arms Factory, 164
Smith, Sergeant R., 230
Smollett, Tobias, 46
Socket bayonet, 31
'Soldier's Alphabet, The', quoted, 76–7
Soldier's Catechism, quoted, 20–5
Somaliland, 194
Soult, Marshal, 100–1, 103, 105
on Albuhera, 106
Soutar, Captain, 151–2
Southey, Robert, Espriella's Letters, on English martial law, 126
Soyer, Alexis, 160
Spaniards, 101
their behaviour at Albuhera, 101–2
Spanish Succession, War of the (1702–14), 45
Spears, General, on Tommy Atkins and the poilu, 214–15
Stanley, Captain, 163
Steel ramrod, 45
Sterne, Laurence, Tristram Shandy, 33
Stevenson, Private Thomas, 49

Stewart, General, 101, 106
Stewart, Sir Donald, 181
Stocks, punishment in the, 122
Stocqueler, J.H.
on Marlborough's men, 39
on Harry Wilson, 94
on the men in the Crimea, 162
Story (chaplain), 32
Strachan, Sir Richard, 86
Strappado, 121
Straubenzee, Major, 62
'Stripes', 20
see also Flogging
Stubbs, Lance-Sergeant F., 207, 208
Suez Canal operation (1956), 248
Surgeons, become regimental officers, 26–7
Sutlers, 38, 118
Swann, Sergeant J., 230, 233–4

Tactics, in Marlborough's time, 43
Taku Forts, 174–5
Tangier, 27
Teesdale, Sergeant, 134
Tej Singh, 155
Temple, Sir William, on the English character, 39
Territorials, 193, 195, 196, 205
Thackeray, W.M., pillories the soldier, 142, 145
Thiepval, 211
Thirty Years War (1618–48), 39
Thomas, Ensign, 102
Thomson, Lieutenant, 167
Tibet, 194
Times, The, 224
on the Kaiser's order, 197
Tippoo Sahib, 67
Toc H, 226
Toms, Lieutenant, 232
Tomsk Regiment, 163
Tooley scandal, 30
Townshend, General, 209
Trained bands, 16
Transport, the first regular system of, 74
Trench life, in World War I, 11, 212–13
Trevelyan, G.M., on public attitude to the soldier, 44
Troopships, 147–8
the Birkenhead and Sarah Sands, 157
Turenne, Vicomte de, 35
Turks, 207, 209

Turner, Lt Col V.B., 228–32, 234
Turner, Sir James, *Pallas Armata*, on
  military punishment, 118
Typhus, 95

Umbeyla (Ambeyla), expedition to
  (1863), 176
Uniform
  New Model Army, 19–20
  under George II, 45
  mid-18th century elaborations,
    60–1
  earlier 19th century, 142
  criticized by Colonel Luard (1852),
    159
  introduction of khaki, 169
Universal Military Service Bill (1916),
  209
Uxbridge, Lord, 113
  see also Anglesey, Marquis of

Varna, 61n
Veitch, Lieutenant, 104
Venereal disease
  prevalence, 59, 189
  punishment for, 123
Vernon, Admiral, 46
Vesey, Captain G.C., 191
Victoria Cross, 2
  the youngest recipient, 174–5
  forfeitures of, 184n
  awarded to Lancashire Fusiliers
    after Gallipoli, 208
  number awarded to soldiers 1914–
    18, 217
  awarded to padres, 220n
  number awarded to soldiers 1939–
    45, 241n
  more won by NCOs and men than
    officers in World War II, 246
Victoria Lodging House, London, 171
Victoria, Queen, 149, 169
Virginia Regiment, 62
Volunteers
  modern type of, 193
  quality of, in early period World
    War I, 204
  shortage of, in 1930s, 224

Waggoners, Corps of, 74
Walcheren Expedition (1809), 86
Waldegrave's Brigade, 54
Waller, Sir William, quoted, 19
Walpole, Sir Robert, 46
Walsh, Ensign, 104

War Office, 171
  Cardwell's reorganization of, 177
'Warrant-men' system, 31
Washington, George, 62
Water problem, 92
Waterloo Medal, 114
Wavell, Field-Marshal Earl, 4, 10,
  224–5
Waziristan, 223
Weapons
  improvement of, after
    Killiecrankie, 31
  introduction of steel ramrod, 45
  Brown Bess musket, 53, 161
  Baker rifle, 75
Wellington, Duke of, 3, 4n, 5, 35, 50n,
  70, 77, 86, 141, 147, 158n, 159,
  195, 225, 251
  in India, 76
  on punishment for 'the scum of the
    earth', 87
  unpopular with the common
    soldier, 89
  and the medical system, 96
  and red tape, 96
  Badajoz, 108, 109
  on English soldier's inability to
    march, 110
  and the Pont de Iéna, 111
  on the English infantryman, 112
  opposed to education of soldiers,
    112, 143
  severity in punishment, 132, 133,
    136–7
  on Ferozeshah, 155
  on the *Birkenhead*, 157n
Wentworth, General, 46
West Indies, 44, 46, 72, 81, 134
Wheeler, Major-General Sir Hugh,
  165, 166, 167
William III, 30, 31, 32, 33, 119, 159
William IV, 169
Willis, Captain R., 207, 208
Wilson, Harry, 94
Wilson, Sir Henry, 177, 205
Wilson, Sir Robert, 132
Winchester College, rebellions in, 146
Wives, soldiers', 92–3, 143–4, 171
Wolfe, James, 48, 51–2
Wolseley, Sir Garnet, 187
  Soldier's Pocket Book, 173
  on plundering, 175
  his order on *Squadron Battery and
    Company Training*, 179
  on dress, 190n

Wooden-horse punishment, 120, 121
Woodville, Caton, 186
World War I, 11, 226
    mobilization plans, 195–6
    'French's contemptible little army',
      196–9
    Mons, 199–201
    runners, 201–2
    Drummer Penn, 202–3
    Ypres, 203
    quality of early volunteers, 204
    shortage of officers, 205
    the Fusiliers at Gallipoli, 206–8
    Loos, 209
    Kut, 209
    the Somme, 210–11
    Passchendaele, 211–12
    soldiers' songs, 213–14
    relations between English and
      French soldiers, 214
    attitude to Germans, 215–16
    Colonel Elstob, 216–17
    Padre Hardy, 218–20
    decorations for bravery, 221–2
    comradeship, 223
World War II, 6, 159n
    new amenities for soldiers, 226–7

type of soldier in, 224–7, 246
defence of Outpost Snipe, 228–35
CSM Peter Wright at Salerno, 236
Campoleone Railway Station,
    236–7
Mount Ornito, 237–8
Kohima, 238–43
Nunshigum, 242–3
CSM Stanley Hollis, 243–5
Private Burton at Mount Ceco,
    245–6
Wounded, fate of in Wellington's
    time, 93–6
Wright, CSM Peter, 236

Yellow fever ('Yellow Jack'), 46, 57, 71
YMCA, 226
York, Duke of (later James II), 26
York, Duke of (son of George III), 90
    in the Netherlands, 68–9
    his reforms, 73–4
    and punishment, 132
    and army education, 158n

Zandevoorde, 202
Zillebeke Wood, 203
Zulus, 235